They
Love
to Tell
THE
STORY

To Dr. Terry J. Dibble,

who taught me

that answers to questions are like Linus' blanket,

that life is like trying to juggle invisible balls without being able to touch them,

that finding something new in a work of literature is a glorious and humorous event,

that sometimes you have to grade on potential,

and that baby birds eventually have to leave the nest and fly on their own.

Contents

*A*cknowledgments

Acknowledgment pages are much like Oscar speeches, only without the orchestra to keep people in check. Writers get to thank a whole host of people who have been important to them, but whom the reader probably has no connection to whatsoever. And, like Oscar speeches, people who write acknowledgment sections are terrified that they will omit someone who should definitely have been included, or they'll simply not give them enough credit for their support. With both of those concerns firmly in mind, I'll try to keep mine short enough to finish before the music begins, but expansive enough to cover everyone who should be mentioned; if I fail on either of those counts, I'll ask forgiveness in advance.

Several sections of this work have appeared in other places, either in print or at conferences. Thus, I'd like to thank Melanie Ethridge and *PLL: Papers on Language and Literature* for publishing my article on Mary Magdalene; James Schick and *The Midwest Quarterly* for publishing my article on John the Baptist; and Gordon College and the participants of the Christ in Contemporary Cultures conference, where I presented a portion of the chapter on Jesus' humanity and his relationships with women.

Similarly, I need to thank Dr. Laura Dabundo for her editorial suggestions on early drafts of the book, as well as Jennifer Clifton, Shirley Parker-Cordell, Danielle Flynn, and Michelle Hinson for their work. Special thanks goes to Holly Miller of the Kennesaw State University Press for all she has done to help this book see publication.

I'd like to thank three libraries where I did research, though people connected to two of those libraries have no idea that I did so (and, in one case, don't even know who I am). I worked as the librarian at Charles Wright Academy in Tacoma, Washington, during the year when I wrote the first draft of this book, and, as such, I certainly made use of our databases and a few books. I assure the administration that I did not shirk my duties to do any of this research, but I certainly did do some of it while on the clock. At the same time, I spent many Sunday afternoons at the University of Puget Sound's library making use of its collection. As far as I can remember, I did not speak to a single person on those days, but I am certainly thankful that the librarians put together as useful a collection as they did.

The one library that knowingly helped me did so in many ways. The staff at the Squires Library at Lee University has assisted me in countless ways since I was hired, and this project certainly drew on their resources more than any other. I visited the interlibrary loan department several times a week, and they became frequent e-mailers. The religion databases and resources put together by the librarians there provided my book with the depth it needed after that first draft.

Along the same lines, my colleagues and friends in the Language and Literature Department have been steadfast in their encouragement of my research. The funding from the university has enabled me to publish and present portions of this manuscript. However, it is the near constant support I receive from Dr. Jean Eledge, our department chair, and the faculty that enables me to continue writing and re-writing, both on this project and on many others. My students have also been wonderfully supportive, and they have pushed me to become a better teacher and scholar.

Then there are those who support my work from a distance with encouragement during the lean times and congratulations when work goes well. My family always encouraged my educational pursuits and let me know of their pride in my accomplishments. Mark Benson and Kate Reed are friends who may be distant geographically, but who remain close through their support.

I also have to thank those professors who have encouraged me along the way and who have become my models for teaching, research, and love of students. Dr. Terry Dibble, to whom this book is dedicated, changed my major to English, but, more than that, he changed the way I see the world, the epitome of great teaching. Three professors from East Tennessee State University—Dr. R. Chesla Sharp, Dr. Styron Harris, and Dr. Jack Branscomb—helped make the two years I was there two of my best years. They taught me about literature, to be certain, but, in truth, they taught me how to behave in the profession and how to truly influence students. I would be hard-pressed to find four professors who are more different from one another, but they all changed at least one life through their influence, and I would guess many more beyond mine.

There are three people who stand beside me in more ways than I could ever convey, either in word or deed. DJ Dycus and Steve Simmerman have seen my writing from the outset, beginning nearly two decades ago in graduate school, and have read, criticized, and strengthened much of what I have written since then. More than that practical help, though, they have celebrated my successes as if they were their own, the true definition of friendship. My wife Courtney was the first person I told of this project—"the book I've always wanted to write," as I told her—and her encouragement has been unwavering. When the inevitable rejections came, she listened to me debate whether or not I wanted to continue working on this project, allowing me the time I needed to process that rejection, then encouraging me to pick it up again. While my ego would like to believe I could have written this book without her, everything else in my being tells me how wrong I would be to think so.

$\mathcal{T}$elling the Story, $\mathcal{A}$gain

Christians refer to the gospels as the Greatest Story Ever Told, and an argument can certainly be made for that moniker.[1] The main character is a young man with ignoble beginnings who arrives out of nowhere to bring hope to an occupied people. His following grows to such an extent that the authorities become threatened, and they seek a way to kill him. One of his followers goes to the authorities in secret and betrays the one he had chosen to follow. After the main character is put to death, there are rumors of his resurrection and promise to come again.

This story has all of the elements of a great narrative: intrigue, conflict, drama. It is, to use an oft-repeated phrase, a page-turner. Why, then, would writers come back to this story time and time again in order to try to improve upon it? First of all, there is the story itself. The authors can rely on an already given plotline that is clearly a great story; there is no need for them to create a story from their imaginations when they can draw on one that many people are at least reasonably familiar with already.

However, the main reason writers continue to come back to the story of Jesus is not because of what the gospels tell us, but what they do not. The main character is a young man without a past; readers see a birth story, one incident when he was twelve, and then he is roughly thirty years old. His father completely disappears after the incident in the temple when Jesus is twelve, and his relationships with his mother and brothers seem strained at best. His followers have no background, either, save for an occasional mention of employment or, in Peter's case, a mother-in-law. And, oh yes, he just might be God, as well.

---

[1]Reynolds Price not only argues that the gospel of Mark is "the most influential of human books" (38), but he says that he assigns his students to write a gospel because "the career of a particular Palestinian Jew of the first century and the effects of that life on world history have proved so magnetic in their mystery as to demand ceaseless watch and question by human beings, whose minds have ranged from the caliber of Augustine, Aquinas, Luther, and Calvin through numerous lunatics, sadists, masochists, plain readers, and selfless ministers to the sufferings of others" (234–35).

Not only are readers not given basic information about the main character, they are given none of the motivations of the secondary characters. It seems that "the Gospels provide novelists with relatively few clear-cut characters. Most of the disciples are leveled down to a faceless chorus from which only Peter and Judas emerge in any sharp detail. As a result, we find in these novels primarily those few figures who are clearly defined by their function in the New Testament" (Ziolkowski 278). No one knows why Peter willingly left his fishing trade to follow Jesus or why Matthew gave up his job as a tax collector, and no one even knows what Thaddeus does, more or less why he left it. Of course, the greatest mystery when it comes to motivation is why Judas betrayed Jesus. Was it simple greed? Was Judas a nationalist who was disappointed when Jesus didn't live up to his idea of the Messiah? Or was Judas forcing Jesus' hand by turning him in? Or protecting him from authorities in Jerusalem whom Judas thought he knew better than Jesus? Or did Jesus want Judas to turn him in so that he could be crucified for the world's sins?

Another problem is Jesus' claimed dual nature. How can someone be both God and man at the same time? What kinds of temptations did he suffer, and how did he deal with them? How did he react when he first realized that he was the Son of God? Did he ever think of giving it all up and having a nice, normal life?

All of these questions are left unanswered in not one narrative about Jesus' life, but four different narratives. They present different parables, different miracles, even different teachings, but none of them tell readers what the characters are thinking, what motivates them. Instead, they tell the same basic story of hope and betrayal and hope again, yet it is a story that moves people to change their lives, even without the motivations and thoughts of the characters.

Authors have different ways of trying to retell this story, though, and rather than trying to focus on the multiple ways, I will focus on one. In *Fictional Transfigurations of Jesus*, Theodore Ziolkowski outlines five types of gospel novels: (1) fictionalizing biography; (2) *Jesus redivivus*; (3) the *imitatio Christi*; (4) "pseudonyms" of Christ; and (5) fictional transfigurations. The *Jesus redivivus* consists of "stories set in modern times, in which—miraculously—the historical Jesus appears" (17) while the *imitatio Christi* is a group of "novels in which the hero makes up his mind to live consistently as Jesus would have lived had he been born into our world" (23). Thus, Sheldon's *In His Steps* would be an example of an *imitatio Christi* while Rilke's *Visions of Christ* or Sinclair's *They Call Me Carpenter* would be an example of *Jesus redivivus*. The "pseudonyms" of Christ are "restricted to those works in which, all questions of meaning aside, the events as set down immutably in the Gospels prefigure the action of the plot" (26). Ziolkowski believes that this category "has often been expanded to include so many different works that, as a literary category, it has become virtually meaningless" and that "no character who lies down or dies with his arms outstretched—like the heroes of Hemingway's *The Old Man and the Sea* and Kafka's *The Trial*—is safe from the critical cross" (28). Thus, it is not a terribly useful category any longer, but it can still be clearly distinguished from the fictionalizing biographies that I am concerned with. The fictional transfigurations that make up the subject of Ziolkowski's book are "fictional narrative[s] in which the characters and the action, irrespective of meaning or theme, are prefigured to a noticeable extent by figures and events popularly associated with the life of Jesus, as it is known from the Gospels" (6). Thus, his work deals with Kazantzakis' *The Greek Passion*, but not *The Last Temptation of Christ*. Instead, works like *The Last Temptation of Christ* and the other four I deal with in this book are "fictionalizing biographies," in Ziolkowski's scheme of classification. In a fictionalizing biography, the author attempts to re-create Jesus in his historical setting based on the events of the gospel, but is in no way slavishly dependent upon the gospel stories.

In each chapter, I try to examine the different characters and the way that the five authors have presented them. In the first chapter, I talk about the religious background of the authors and what may have motivated them to retell the story of Jesus. Then, in the second chapter, I examine their views of the gospel accounts, the stories they hope to tell anew. From then on, each character is examined with a biblical and historical background of the characters. These backgrounds are not intended to be comprehensive, as book upon book has been written about many of these characters; instead they are merely intended to show where the authors might have gathered some of their ideas for their incarnations of the characters.

The novels are compelling largely due to the changes they make to that original story. The interest in these novels would be significantly lower if not for the interest in the story of Jesus in the first place; thus, it is the changes I try to focus on, with the gospels serving as foils to highlight what takes place in the novels.

Other authors will tell and tell again the story of Jesus, going back to that rich story for inspiration. The insistence with which they do so only works to confirm its place as the Greatest Story Ever Told.

CHAPTER 1

*W*hy They Attempt to Tell the *S*tories

RELIGIOUS BACKGROUNDS AND MOTIVATIONS

The five authors come from a variety of traditions, though none are traditional Christians. This distinction can largely be explained by the fact that traditional Christians tend to simply expand on the gospel accounts rather than making significant changes to them; they see no need to change the gospel story, as it has already been told truthfully in the Bible.[1] It takes a certain renegade spirit to want to try to tell it again (and, perhaps, better), and it takes a certain amount of hubris. Most of them do, however, have some sort of religious background, with Saramago being the notable exception. Their differing religious backgrounds help influence their interpretations of Jesus and the events surrounding his life, providing widely divergent views.

Anthony Burgess, like many Irish writers, was raised Roman Catholic, and, again, like many Irish writers, later left the church, but not its influence. Like many Irish boys, Burgess went to a Catholic elementary school where there was "the inevitable presence of the one terror-inspiring nun who figured prominently both in school lore and nightmare . . ." (Stinson 2). However, Burgess did not feel any particular ill will toward his parents, the school, or any teachers at the school for his time there.

He gave up practicing his faith when he was sixteen years old: "He began reading philosophy and studying metaphysics on his own, and about

---

[1]There have been numerous retellings from the traditional Christian viewpoint. While a study of those works would be interesting and enlightening, it is not my purpose to do so in this book. Interestingly, even Reynolds Price, who is a Christian but who also drew from some apocryphal gospels and other historical sources, comes out with a fairly traditional interpretation in his "An Honest Account of a Memorable Life," his approach to a gospel in *Three Gospels*.

the age of sixteen, he decided he was through with Catholicism. But it was a renunciation that gave him little joy; although intellectually he was convinced he could be a freethinker, emotionally he was very much aware of Hell and damnation" (Aggeler 5). Burgess, though, does not like to say that he renounced his faith: "I say that I lost my faith, but really I was no more than a lapsed Catholic. . . . For Catholicism is, in a paradox, a bigger thing than the faith. It is a kind of nationality one is stuck with forever. Or, rather, a supranationality that makes one despise small patriotisms. . . . Again, the Catholic Church, since it preaches a philosophy as well as a theology, leaves the renegade with certain convictions that he does not have to square with religious belief" (*Little Wilson* 148).

Thus, his Catholic background still heavily influenced his work, though he died in 1993 formally broken with the church. It is odd, though, what beliefs do still influence him. Geoffrey Aggeler writes, "With regard to religion, Burgess still maintains a 'renegade Catholic' stance that is oddly conservative in some respects. He despises liberal Catholicism, which seems to have become another religion in the process of gaining acceptance in the modern world. The ecumenical movement repels him, as do the liturgical changes and the use of the vernacular" (27). Concerning the new Mass, Burgess wrote, "The vernacular Mass was a disgrace. I had met priests in America who no longer knew what they believed in. It was considered virtuous for a cardinal to have forgotten his penny catechism and say that love and love alone counted. The cult of a fat personality had driven out the old intellectual rigour of the faith" (*You've Had Your Time* 349).

Despite all his attempts to completely break from the church, though, he found that harder to do as he grew older: "In old age I look back on various attempts to cancel my apostasy and become reconciled to the church again. This is because I have found no metaphysical substitute for it. . . . I know of no other organisation that can both explain evil and, theoretically at least, brandish arms against it. The Church has let its children down too often to be regarded as a good mother, but it is the only mother we have" (*LW* 149). And, thus, "like Joyce and Dedalus, Burgess was still supersaturated with a Catholicism he allowed to lapse long ago" (Stinson 2).

2

Burgess wrote the screenplay to *Jesus of Nazareth*, which was directed by Franco Zeffirelli. *Man of Nazareth* is supposedly the novelized version, more or less, of that screenplay. However, there is evidence to suggest that Burgess was working on both projects at the same time, so it is unclear which one influenced the other. Stinson writes, "The book jacket of the novel *Man of Nazareth* (1979) states that it is the novel on which the television series, *Jesus of Nazareth*, was based. Some Burgess remarks, however, seem to indicate that the creation of the novel and the miniseries were nearly simultaneous— that he was writing the novel during intervals when he was not being pressed for script revision" (137–38).

Burgess, in one of his autobiographies, *You've Had Your Time*, implied that he had indeed been writing the screenplay and the novel at the same time, as he finished the novel just after the series concluded filming: "The work of writing the novel, provisionally entitled *Christ the Tiger*, ended in Ansedonia, among bodies honeyed by the sun by the sea and black hair smelling of woodsmoke. Surrounded by animal calls of the pagans, I resuscitated the dead Christ." Burgess went on in this passage to show that he made changes from his ideas for the screenplay because Zeffirelli rejected them: "Zeffirelli was not quite orthodox in wishing to end the series with a great *Pietà*. . . . He had to be reminded, gently, that the Resurrection was the whole point of the death. . . . I could see his point; artistically speaking, the Resurrection is something of an anticlimax" (307). He also had to adjust the screenplay for theologians who were brought in to consult, which he did not have to do for the novel: "Gennarino Gennarini [an Italian theologian] and his colleagues never read the novel out of which the script was squeezed or hacked. They would not have been pleased by my presenting Christ as a married man" (306).

To prepare for the writing of *Jesus of Nazareth*, Burgess felt that he had to do a great deal of research. He not only read and reread the gospels, he read them in Greek,[2] but he felt he had to go beyond even that approach: "The gospels were not enough. I had to read Josephus's *History of the Jews* and

---

[2]Oddly enough, Price went the other way: after spending years translating the gospels in an attempt to understand them better, he decided to try to write one of his own (28).

manuals on the technique of crucifixion. The traditional image of Christ carrying the whole cross, dear to the fundamentalists of the American South, apparently flouted historical fact. He would have carried merely the crosspiece, which would then be affixed to a permanent upright at the place of execution" (*YH* 304).

What ultimately motivates Burgess to tell this story again is what motivates many authors; the story is a compelling story, but it is poorly told: "The more I read Matthew, Mark and Luke the more I became dissatisfied with their telling of the sacred story. They remain fine propagandists but mediocre novelists. 'The devil entered Judas,' says John. How hopelessly inadequate" (*YH* 304).

In an interesting contrast Marianne Fredriksson wrote *According to Mary Magdalene* exactly because we can never know what truly happened, and she wants to highlight that fact. She was inspired by a quote from Simone Weil in *The Person and the Sacred*: "A correct understanding of Christianity has become almost an impossibility for us owing to the profound secrecy surrounding the early history of time" (ix). Thus, rather than trying to lay out characters who know exactly what happened, she focuses on the contrast between what her Mary Magdalene saw and what Peter and Paul are teaching. Thus, she draws on and directly quotes both the *Gospel of Mary* and many biblical books, such as Paul's letters to the Corinthians, I Peter, and the gospel of John.

Christopher Moore, author of *Lamb: The Gospel According to Biff, Christ's Childhood Pal*, tends to agree with Fredriksson: "I researched *Lamb*, I really did, but there is no doubt I could have spent decades researching and still managed to be inaccurate" (438). He knows that there are multiple views, even among scholars who have devoted their lives to studying Jesus' life and culture. He points out that "some historians postulate that Yeshua of Nazareth would have been little more than an ignorant hillbilly, while others say that because of the proximity of Sepphoris and Joppa, he could have been exposed to Greek and Roman culture from an early age. I chose the latter because it makes for a more interesting story" (439). Despite Moore's assertion that no amount of research would enable him to be completely accurate, he went so far as to tour Israel in an effort to find out as much as he could in a reasonable amount of time.

Unlike the three authors previously mentioned, Nikos Kazantzakis was definitely religious. In fact, his purpose in writing *The Last Temptation of Christ* was so that "every free man who reads this book, so filled as it is with love, will more than ever before, love Christ" (4). However, he did not follow traditional Christianity at all. Middleton and Bien write, "Although Kazantzakis attempts in his oeuvre to make sense of divine and human becoming, we probably should not think of him as Christian—certainly not as Christian in a narrow sense. . . . Another way of saying that he was a profoundly religious person is to describe him as a true witness, by which we mean someone who acts in a fashion that makes no sense at all if God does not exist" (7–8).

This break from traditional Christianity came early in his life: "Even as a youngster, Kazantzakis was agitated by spiritual turmoil. He enjoyed kicking over the traces, disrupting schoolroom activities, and probing teachers with uncomfortable questions" (Middleton and Bien 2). He later traveled extensively, searching for new ideas; one of his ways of doing this was to spend time at monasteries where he would have long discussions with the monks (Middleton and Bien 4).

He was searching not just for answers to his religious questions, but for a new faith altogether. In her biography of Kazantzakis, Helen Kazantzakis, his daughter, writes, "To found a religion, to found a religion at all costs, this was the obsession haunting Kazantzakis over a long span of years, driving to the farthest extreme his innate tendencies toward asceticism and renunciation sanctified by laughter. After harsh struggles, he came to realize and know that the 'new myth' had escaped him" (61). He revealed one of the aspects of this religion in a letter to his friend, E. Samios: "The third and highest stage [of enlightenment in my religion] is: 'We are fighting neither for ourselves nor for man. All of us, voluntarily or involuntarily, consciously or unconsciously—plants, animals, human beings and ideas—are struggling for the salvation of God'" (H. Kazantzakis 27). While this may be evidence of a deep spirituality, it is not traditional Christianity.

This struggle with God seems to be a theme in all of Kazantzakis' works. In a letter to Börje Knös, he argues that it may be his only theme: "The major and almost the only theme of all my work is the struggle of man with 'God': the unyielding, inextinguishable struggle of the naked worm called 'man' against the terrifying power and darkness of the forces within him and around him" (qtd. in H. Kazantzakis 507). Middleton and Bien agree with his assessment when they write, "The more one considers Kazantzakis's life, especially his formative years, the more one comes to appreciate his work as an extended diatribe against spiritual mediocrity" (5). His daughter wrote that Kazantzakis "was not an angel, but a profoundly religious nature, seeking God with determination, demanding that He be a just and liberating God" (23). Kazantzakis struggled with his idea of God, seeking to understand Him and convey that understanding, or at least the struggle, through his writing. While he certainly agreed with aspects of traditional Christianity, he also rebelled against much of it, as well.

Norman Mailer has often been criticized for not focusing on "Jewish issues" in his writing. In fact, he has often been seen as being too critical of Jews altogether. His approach to his Jewish background is complicated, as might be expected with Mailer. In an interview in 1988, he says that his being Jewish is important to him, but that he won't capitalize on it: "Two formative currents of personality came together to make my nature. . . . One of them is being Jewish. I'm not a Holocaust hustler, I'm not asking for pity, but every Jew alive feels his relationship to the world is somehow more tenuous than other people's, and so to affirm his existence is somehow more important" (Begieling 317). However, some critics have seen him as rejecting, or at least ignoring, Jews in his writing: "Yet though he was born into a very Jewish community, and appeared sensitive to his Jewish origins while at Harvard, his work (with the exception of *The Naked and the Dead*, which exposes the anti-Semitic bigotry aimed at characters such as Roth and Goldstein) shows few explicit signs of a self-conscious Jewish sensibility at work. In an interview in 1963, he admitted that his 'knowledge of Jewish culture is exceptionally spotty' . . ." (Glenday 5).

Even this is not clear, though, as there is a Jewish tradition of individualism that Mailer may be drawing upon:

> For Alfred Kazin, Mailer belongs rather to another Jewish tradition, that of radical individualism: "Jewishness Mailer disliked because it limited and intellectualized. . . . With his contempt for the knowledge-as-control, his desire to leave all those centuries of Jewish tradition (and of Jewish losers) behind him, Mailer represented the unresting effort and overreaching of the individual Jewish writer who seeks to be nothing but an individual (and if possible a hero). Mailer, then, perpetuates a line of Jewish individualism of which his rabbi grandfather would have approved, for he was the unofficial rabbi who 'never wanted a congregation because he said the rabbis were schnorrers and he wouldn't live that way.'" (Glenday 5)

Regardless, the struggle between good and evil, God and the Devil shows up in Mailer's writing on a consistent basis. He views both sides as necessary, however. He writes,

> The minority is not God or the Devil, Black or white, woman or man. Rather it is that element in each which has somehow been repressed or stifled by conformity to system—including systematic dialectical opposition—or by fear of some power, like death, which is altogether larger than the ostensible, necessarily more manageable opponent apparently assigned by history. The minority element in males or Blacks or God is the result of their inward sense of inferiority which the outward or visible opposition from women or whites or the Devil did not of itself necessarily create. (qtd. in Poirier 112)

Though both good and evil, God and the Devil are necessary, men and women can still sway the battle: "The war between God and the Devil figures in nearly everything Mailer has written, and in his theology a man's efforts can apparently help one side or the other" (Poirier 114). Regardless, balance will always be maintained: "without the Devil there could be no God in Mailer's universe, only entropy. He is quite unable to imagine anything except in oppositions, unable even to imagine one side of the opposition without proposing that it has yet another opposition within itself" (Poirier 114). When *Black Book* magazine challenged authors to write a short story in only six words, in fact, Mailer's dealt with the opposition and balance of God and the Devil: "Satan—Jehovah—fifteen rounds. A draw."

What is most interesting about Mailer's interest in the story of Jesus, though, is why he decided to write *The Gospel According to the Son* at all. His motives smack of pure arrogance. First, like Burgess, he believed that he could tell the story better than the gospel writers:

> What happened is that I was not that familiar with the New Testament. And I read it a couple of years ago. And I was struck with the gap between the great and beautiful lines in the New Testament and the spaces between, which were written by committee. And I thought, there have to be at least a hundred writers in the world who can do a better job with the same story than the committees that wrote the synoptic Gospels. And I thought I'm one of those hundred writers, and I want to try it. ("The Gospel According to Mailer")

Second, he believes that he can identify with Jesus:

> And I thought this one [*The Gospel According to the Son*] was fine because I have a slight understanding of what it's like to be half a man and half something else, something larger. Believe it if you will, but I mean this modestly. Every man has a different kind of life, and mine had a peculiar turn. It changed completely at twenty-five when *The Naked and the Dead* came out. Obviously, a celebrity is a long, long, long, long way from the celestial, but nonetheless it does mean that you have two personalities you live with all the time. (qtd. in Wood)

This type of arrogance should not surprise readers familiar with Mailer. However, a comparison of oneself to the Son of God seems a bit much, even for Norman Mailer.

Nino Ricci, like Anthony Burgess, was raised Roman Catholic. In fact, he was a devout child, though he gave up his faith at a rather early age:

> I was quite devout at the age of 6 or 8, then certain things stopped making sense. In Grade 8, when I was of age to receive confirmation, which is the first time you are asked to make a decision about your faith, I found myself approaching that rite of passage with no overwhelming commitment. You do it at school, with your whole class, so I did it, but later I stopped going to confession. Faith, it seemed to me, shouldn't be a tepid thing. In high school, I even joined an evangelical, fundamentalist group to see if it would feel more real. It didn't. (Stoffman J15)

He did attempt to return to some sort of faith, though, as he got older. In an interview, he commented,

> In my 20's, . . . I went through a strong intellectual rejection of Christianity. I came to realize, however, that somewhere between formal Christianity and my complete dismissal there had to be a middle way. And while I didn't believe the Gospels, I did believe that there was a kernel of truth in them, that there was probably a charismatic Jewish leader of some kind in the first century named Yeshua who left behind a body of teachings and that, over time, stories grew up about him—some of which had some basis in reality, many of which were myths. (Starnino G1)

It was this religious conflict that led Ricci to write *Testament* as a way of working out his feelings about Jesus. He tells Paul Gessell, "When I went to write this book I didn't know what I felt about Christian teaching. I went through a strong Christian faith as a child and shed it over my years of adolescence until I was a young adult and was more or less an atheist or at least an agnostic" (F1). Though he was "raised Roman Catholic, enthralled as a child by the merciful miracle-worker Jesus, as an adult he lost Christianity, but he could not shake Christ" (Wald-Hopkins EE-01). He did not end up becoming a Christian, as doing so would mean that he would have to recognize Jesus as divine, which Ricci does not, but writing the book did give him "a whole new respect for Jesus and his teachings." In fact, he says that he became a "Jesus follower" by the end (Gessell F1).

Ricci also wanted to write the book because he believes it is a story worth hearing again and again.[3] In an interview, he states, "We are at a moment of spiritual crisis. Jesus had something to say that's valid in our times, a philosophy and a religion that's at the heart of Western culture" (Stoffman J15). Comments like this one have caused critics to view Ricci as a "Catholic novelist in the tradition of Graham Greene, tormented by a sense of guilt and sin. Religion formed his imagination" (Stoffman), regardless of whether or not Ricci views himself that way.

Jose Saramago does not say much about religion because he does not believe much about religion. He is a staunch atheist and Communist—Richard Preto-Rodas reminds us that Saramago "has never concealed his Marxist ideology" (697)—views that have earned him outsider status in Portugal, a largely Roman Catholic country (Nash 17). In fact, when he published *The Gospel According to Jesus Christ*, his name was stricken from the list of nominations for the European Literature Prize because the novel offended Portuguese Catholics (Nash 17).

It seems, though, that many of his works have commented on Christianity, even if indirectly: "Christianity/Christian themes are present in almost all Saramago's novels but not necessarily as the narrative's center. For example, in *Lavantado do Chão*, the birth of a new, revolutionary generation represented by the character of Maria Adelaide is described through Christian symbolism and in *Memorial do Convento*, the hypocrisy of the false religiosity and the deeds of the Inquisition are under scrutiny" (Kaufman 449). As to why he wanted to write *The Gospel According to Jesus*

---

[3]Reynolds Price argues that the gospel of Mark "has proved the most influential of human books" (38).

Christ, Saramago simply comments that he wanted to "fill the blank spaces between the various episodes of Jesus's life" (McKendrick 31). In doing so, not surprisingly, he created a Jesus that offended many.

These five authors clearly bring their religious backgrounds to their novels in telling the gospel story. In doing so, they provide fresh perspectives on the characters and events of those stories, though they clearly stray from the gospel accounts in relation to their backgrounds.

CHAPTER 2

To Tell the Truth,
No Matter the Facts

THE GOSPEL ACCOUNTS

People primarily look at the gospels in one of three ways. There are those who view the Bible as the literal words of God, without error or fault. The Southern Baptist Convention's statement of faith on the Scriptures, for example, says, "The Holy Bible was written by men divinely inspired and is God's revelation of Himself to man. It is a perfect treasure of divine instruction. It has God for its author, salvation for its end, and truth, without any mixture of error, for its matter. Therefore, all Scripture is totally true and trustworthy" (Southern Baptist Convention).

The other extreme would be those who view the Bible as nothing more than a collection of legends with no connection to historical truth whatsoever. The American Atheists organization states that "The Bible story of Jesus is a contradictory and confusing account. The Bible shows that this Jesus fellow spoke and taught many absurd and foolish things, and often believed he was having a conversation with devils" and "Jesus is a myth just like all the other saviors and gods of old" (*American Atheists*).

In-between these extremes lie a variety of beliefs, ranging from those who believe that the Bible is inspired by God, yet written by men,[1] and, as such, is largely true, but is colored by those men's impressions, to those who believe that the Bible has some bit of truth in it, but that truth is almost completely inaccessible due to problems with historical distance, absence of manuscripts, and the biases of the authors of the biblical books.

The five authors whose novels are under scrutiny here all question the

---

[1]There are a few scholars, such as Harold Bloom in *The Book of J*, who believe that women wrote part of the Bible, but most scholars assume it was written entirely by men.

validity of the gospel accounts up to a certain point. Burgess is the most consistent in his acceptance of the gospels, while Mailer questions some aspects, but still remains, for the most part, faithful to the record. Saramago is at the other extreme, questioning most of what is in the gospels, with Ricci and Kazantzakis staking out a middle ground.

Burgess believed that most of the gospels are fairly reliable, but he also believed that the book of John poses problems: "There are four versions of the life of Christ, and the most popular is the least reliable. This is the highly romantic novella written by St. John, too long after the historical events, with a wedding at Cana and the resurrection of Lazarus, of which Matthew, Mark and Luke say nothing. These three evangelists are so like each other that they can be studied as a single book called the Synoptic Gospels" (*YH* 304). While his position is the most consistent with the gospel accounts, his narrator does call into question legends that go beyond the gospel accounts. When John the Baptist is born, the narrator says,

> I think it must be made clear at this point that, despite the legends put about after his death, this child was not a giant. We have all heard the stories of the severed head preserved in a huge wine-jar, how this head was the size of a bull's and so on, and of the heaviness (this tale was put about by a Gaul) that required two or three men to lift it, but none can say where the head is. The child was a big child who grew into a man of a stature uncommon among the Israelites, who are a small people, but he was no Goliath nor, to keep within the bounds of the faithful, even a Samson. (*Man of Nazareth* 28)

The same types of legends abound concerning the birth of Jesus, and the narrator dismisses those as well. These are drawn from the more suspect noncanonical gospels, which provides Burgess with the opportunity to attack them when he is discussing Jesus' childhood. The *Infancy Gospel of Thomas*, among others, has stories of the child Jesus performing miracles, such as creating birds from clay and striking another child dead. In *Man of Nazareth*, Jesus "did not make birds out of mud and bid them fly off. He seemed sometimes to listen to voices that were not there, but this meant merely that he was unusually sharp-eared—a matter of hearing voices afar before others heard them" (64). His childhood is normal in that he fights with the other children, and he breaks dietary laws, much as a child would, but he also is able to read early and naturally. This fact does not set Jesus apart from any other precocious child, and it fits in well with the gospel account of Jesus' speaking to the leaders of the Temple when he was twelve.

Early in the book, it appears that Burgess is going to take the approach most writers take when dealing with this subject matter. Most writers show the miracles as exaggerations and not having truly taken place. When Jesus is still living in Nazareth, before he has begun his ministry, he supposedly heals a blind man, though the man was not truly blind:

> But there had been a notable occasion when an old man shrieked that he had been struck blind—a time of sorrow for him, his wife recently and suddenly dead and his son, according to a letter from a cousin in Jerusalem, taken to such evil ways that he had been thrown into prison—and Jesus, using the spittle of his mouth, stroking hands, gentle words and yet an authoritative manner, had persuaded him that he was not truly blind, only stricken to his soul by calamity, and he had seen again, shouting praise to God and spreading, to the embarrassment of Jesus, words about a young worker of miracles. (83)

People also believe Jesus' presence prevented robbers from doing them any harm, and his healing miracles are often attributed to curative techniques he learned while the family lived in Egypt to avoid Herod.

Jesus also does not actually turn water into wine at the wedding at Cana (Jesus' wedding in Burgess' work). Instead, it is a game he plays where he jokes with them that he has turned the water into wine, but only those who are righteous will taste the difference. Thus, people come forward and drink from the jars and proclaim it to be the best wine they have ever tasted, when everyone there knows it is not wine. However, Burgess does not state or even imply in this passage that Jesus could not have turned the water into wine; thus, he avoids limiting Jesus' divinity as so many other writers do.

Later in his work, though, Burgess' Jesus is clearly able to perform miracles, and there is no question as to whether or not the gospel accounts are historically correct. Burgess' novel simply restates the miracles and does not call them into question at all. Jesus casts out a demon in a synagogue; he raises Jairus' daughter and Lazarus from the dead; and he rises from the dead on the third day, all just as indicated in the gospel accounts (though with some narrative exposition, of course). From the time Jesus begins his ministry, Burgess' novel sounds much more like a combination of the three synoptic gospels fleshed out than a new gospel account. Given Burgess' traditional Roman Catholicism, this approach is in keeping with what he would want to do with this story.

Ricci, however, presents the other extreme and shows that Jesus possesses no supernatural powers, as far as healing is concerned; rather, Jesus is educated in Alexandria to know how to cure many ailments. However, the people who witness these events do not know of Jesus' education, nor would they understand the methods Jesus uses to cure. Soon after Judas meets Jesus, a young girl is brought to him to heal. From the description of her affliction, most of the people of Jesus' time would have assumed that she is possessed by a demon. She even lunges at Jesus, which requires both Jacob and John, two disciples, to pull her off of him. Jesus, however, realizes the girl is pregnant and that her father is the father of her child. He has his disciples feed her, and he cleans her up a bit. What heals her is Jesus' treating her as if she were human rather than how her family has been treating her. The reader can see, though, how this event might be misinterpreted to argue that Jesus has healing powers. In fact, the disciples tell Judas fantastic stories when he joins them, and he comments to himself, "Later, of course, I would hear them recount in these same exaggerated tones the story of Yeshua's treatment of the young girl in Tyre" (33).

This exaggeration of Jesus' actions is a theme Ricci returns to time and time again throughout the work, especially in major miracles that Jesus supposedly performs. Jesus is called to help Elazar (Lazarus) after he is struck on the head during a riot. Simon of Gergesa, the narrator of this section, clearly believes that Elazar is already dead, as do the others around him. Simon even comments that an ember from the fire sparked out and landed on Elazar's leg, but he did not flinch from the pain.

Jesus, however, continues to work on him, in an effort to cure him. It is getting dark, so Simon admits that he's not even sure of what he's seeing, but he believes that Jesus

> put his fingers right down inside the man's skull, right through the bone like that, and after he'd felt around in there for a bit, something gushed out from the fellow's head into Jesus's hands, dark and alive. Rachel [Elazar's sister] was standing close by and she sucked in her breath, surely thinking it was some devil that had come out of him. And I thought the same, because when Jesus tossed the thing into the fire it sizzled and squealed there like something dying. (401)

Elazar lives, of course, thanks to Jesus' action, and he then says to Jesus, "You must be the son of god himself, if you brought me back from the dead" (402). Even though everyone, including Jesus, laughs at Elazar's comment, it is evident that this story would later morph into the familiar resurrection-of-Lazarus story.

Ricci admits in an author's note that he read books by "the Jesus Seminar and of other contemporary scholars who have tried to arrive at an understanding of the historical Jesus" (457). What is interesting, though, is that Ricci does not allow Jesus any supernatural power, though even the Jesus Seminar does concede some miracles. However, this admission reveals that Ricci is trying to present a Jesus of history rather than a Jesus of the gospels, whom he believes is based on exaggerations of what may actually have happened.

However, even in Ricci's illustrating the exaggeration of the gospels, he includes evidence of Jesus' supernatural love. When Jesus puts a splint on Jerubal's leg on the way to the cross, Mary the mother is looking on, and Simon comments, "But now she saw him with Jerubal, not just the skill he had but the dignity" (442). It is that dignity that Jesus conveys in helping others that attracts people to him, which may be supernatural in its own right. Ricci would probably not argue that this portrayal of Jesus makes him in any way divine, merely a man who goes beyond what most of the men of his day can do, but Jesus' love for everyone he meets can cause most people to at least view him as a saint.

Ricci also points out other exaggerations people create; however, unlike Burgess, he does so as a way to call into question the gospel accounts, including the basic tenets of Christianity. He focuses on the theme of the exaggeration of the stories of Jesus when it comes to the resurrection, and he uses the occasion to illustrate how all of the stories of Jesus grow out of proportion to what he does:

> It was probably the shock of Jesus's death that started twisting them, and that they had to strain to make sense of the thing, and that in time, with someone like Jesus, things got distorted. Now for every little thing he did when he was alive some story gets put in its place, and if he'd lanced somebody's boil it turned out he'd saved a whole town, and if there were fifty in a place who'd followed him, now it was five hundred. Then there was the story that went around that the morning after Jesus was killed, Mary and Salome went to the grave and his body was gone. . . . But eventually it got told that he'd risen from the dead and walked out of the place, and there were people enough to come along then to say they'd met him on the road afterwards looking as fit as you or me. (452)

Even though Simon of Gergesa seems to allow that he may be wrong—"For all I know, it might have happened that way—wasn't I there myself when Jesus brought Elazar back, who'd been dead as stone" (453)—it is evident that he doesn't truly believe it. Ricci, in fact, won't even allow Jesus to be killed for a good reason; he has Jesus arrested accidentally. An argument starts in the temple, and Andrew begins to howl, and the Roman soldiers move in and arrest everyone involved. Jesus is then sentenced to die because of his association with Judas, who is a member of a rebel group, not because he has done anything wrong or is a threat to the Romans or Jewish leaders. This scene also illustrates how Judas is turned into the one who betrays Jesus, as none of the group liked him all along. By providing enough of the traditional gospel story to show how the story may have originated, Ricci illustrates that there is a core truth underneath the gospel accounts. However, he reminds the reader on a regular basis that the gospels are heavily influenced by the agenda of their authors and throws into question the final presentation of the gospels, specifically as they relate to the divinity of Jesus.

Kazantzakis addresses this idea much more clearly. He adds Matthew to the disciples to introduce the theme of the reliability of the gospels, as Matthew begins writing his gospel soon after he decides to follow Jesus. What is interesting is Matthew's reasoning behind his writing a gospel at all. At first, his reasoning is what one might expect, to spread the gospel so that others might hear of Jesus: "God had placed him next to this holy man in order that he might faithfully record the words he said and the miracles he performed, so that they would not perish and that future generations might learn about them and choose, in their turn, the road of salvation" (*The Last Temptation of Christ* 326). However, when Jesus is being tried by Pilate, Matthew is not concerned about Jesus' well-being; instead, he is worried about the events that he is unable to record in his gospel: "Matthew was sitting on hot coals. He wanted to learn what happened at Caiaphas's palace, what at Pilate's, what the teacher said, what the people shouted, so that he could record it all in his book" (440). He could be interested in the events merely because he wants to get every bit of information for his gospel, seeking only to make it accurate; however, his arrival at Mary and Martha's house during Jesus' last temptation reveals Matthew's main motivation for writing the gospel: "Think of the magnificence with which I began to write your life and times. I too would have become immortal, along with you" (487).

Regardless of his motivation, though, Matthew is not even reliable in recording the facts of Jesus' life, partly because of his humanity and partly because of God's agenda. Peter has a dream that Jesus walks on the water to meet him and the other disciples in the middle of a storm, an event that actually takes place in the gospels. Matthew is the only person awake, so Peter tells him of his dream. Matthew takes the dream, and he begins "to turn over deeply in his mind how he could set it down the next day on paper. It would be extremely difficult because he was not entirely sure it was a dream, nor was he entirely sure it was the truth. It was both. The miracle happened, but not on this earth, not on this sea" (343). Matthew's presentation seems completely disingenuous here, but Kazantzakis seems to present him as honestly trying to present what he sees as the truth. He does not have Matthew admitting to himself that it was a dream; instead, Matthew seems confused about whether or not the event actually happened.[2] Thus, it is the fact that Matthew is a human, with all of his limitations, who is writing the gospel that causes it not to accurately represent historical truth, not the fact that Matthew was maliciously trying to mislead his future readers for his own purpose.

Matthew also sees Jesus' actions as fulfilling prophecy, as Matthew was well-educated in the Hebrew scriptures, so he makes certain to fit Jesus' actions to those prophecies. When Jesus rides a donkey into Jerusalem, Matthew sees this action as fulfilling a prophecy from Zechariah, and he decides to determine why Jesus is riding in on a donkey: "Rabbi . . . it appears you're tired and can't go to Jerusalem on foot" (405). When Jesus replies that he is not tired, that he merely had a sudden desire to ride instead of walk, Matthew sees this decision as evidence of Jesus' messiahship. Again, Matthew does not make up events to try to make Jesus fit prophecy; since he is steeped in the Jewish scriptures, he simply sees the events of Jesus' life in terms of prophecy, and he ignores the ones that might call it into question.

However, Matthew does not even have control over what he writes when he is able to convey the facts of Jesus' life accurately. When Matthew is struggling over how to begin his gospel, an angel comes to him to tell him what to write. He forces Matthew to write that Jesus is not the son of Joseph, but that he is born of a virgin; that he is born in Bethlehem, not Nazareth;

---

[2]Marianne Fredriksson, in *According to Mary Magdalene*, complements this idea by having her Mary Magdalene question her own memories: "At home in Antioch, Mary Magdalene was making a supreme effort to recall those difficult images. What is true? What is fiction? Where does the boundary run? How much can anyone remember without falling apart?" (25).

that he is born in a stable, not a house. Matthew resists this information, though: "But Matthew grew angry. He turned toward the invisible wings at his right and growled softly, so that the sleeping disciples would not hear him: "It's not true. I don't want to write, and I won't." The angel responds, "How can you understand what truth is, you handful of dust? Truth has seven levels. On the highest is enthroned the truth of God, which bears not the slightest resemblance to the truth of men. It is this truth, Matthew Evangelist, that I intone in your ear" (349).

This idea of a higher truth that goes beyond factual, historical truth is reiterated in Jesus' last temptation, when he is living with Martha and Mary. Paul, formerly known as Saul, encounters Jesus who is now in the guise of a new Lazarus. He begins to tell Jesus about the gospel that he is spreading, about Jesus of Nazareth, who died and rose from the dead on the third day. Jesus corrects him and says that he is Jesus, and he neither died nor rose from the dead. Paul, however, responds that the factual truth does not matter when it comes to providing salvation to the world: "In the rottenness, the injustice and poverty of this world, the Crucified and Resurrected Jesus has been the one precious consolation for the honest man, the wronged man. True or false—what do I care! It's enough if the world is saved! . . . What is 'truth'? What is 'falsehood'? Whatever gives wings to men, whatever produces great works and great souls and lifts us a man's height above the earth—that is true. Whatever clips off man's wings—that is false" (477).

Kazantzakis is trying to argue that the historicity of Jesus' existence does not matter nearly as much as the truth that Jesus preached. Regardless of whether or not Jesus is born in Nazareth or Bethlehem, he preaches a gospel of love that has the possibility of changing people's lives, like that of Paul. Thus, the fact that Jesus may not have literally walked on the water, that it might have happened in Peter's dream, ultimately does not matter if it helps people move more closely to God. There is a higher truth than historical truth, and it is that truth that Kazantzakis wants the reader to accept.

Mailer also points out the unreliability of the familiar gospel accounts. Because he chooses to tell the story from Christ's point of view, not from the past as if Christ is experiencing the events of his life as they unfold, but from a contemporary point of view, Mailer can also point out how the gospels have later been interpreted.[3] This approach enables his Christ to set the record straight on his life, not just in the facts, but also in the interpretation of those facts.

To begin, Mailer has his Jesus question the reliability of the gospels. Thus, in the second paragraph, Mailer's Jesus comments, "While I would not say that Mark's gospel is false, it has much exaggeration. And I would offer less for Matthew, and for Luke and John, who gave me words I never uttered and described me as gentle when I was pale with rage. Their words were written many years after I was gone and only repeat what old men told them. Very old men. Such tales are to be leaned upon no more than a bush that tears free from its roots and blows about in the wind" (*The Gospel According to the Son* 1–2). In case the reader has forgotten the purpose of this story, Mailer has his Jesus return to it at the close of the novel as well when he is discussing his resurrection: "In the lifetime of those who came after me, pious scrolls were written by those who had known me. Gospels were set down by those who had not. (And they were more pious!) These later scribes—now they were called Christians—had heard of my journeys. They added much" (242).

This questioning of the gospel accounts sets up the idea that the reader has been misled by the gospel accounts, and, thus, Mailer's Christ has to present his own story so that the truth may finally be known. Therefore, Mailer has his Christ set out this distinction at the outset of the novel to make sure the reader understands that the purpose of Christ's telling his story is, first and foremost, to clear up any misconceptions that might have accrued over the ages: "So I will give my own account. . . . Yet I would hope to remain closer to the truth. . . . It is also true that whether four gospels had been favored or forty, no number would suffice. For where the truth is

---

[3]Christopher Moore takes the same approach in *Lamb*, as he uses Biff, Christ's childhood pal, to tell Joshua's (Jesus') story. Biff has to sneak a copy of the Bible, as an angel is guarding him while he writes his gospel, and he sees the flaws in the four canonical gospels: "What I'm saying is that these guys, Matthew, Mark, Luke, and John, they got some of it right, the big stuff, but they missed a lot (like thirty years, for instance)" (317). And, in fact, Moore's book focuses on the missing thirty years much more than the three years of Jesus' ministry, where Moore tends to follow the major events of the gospel accounts fairly accurately.

with us in one place, it is buried in another. What is for me to tell remains neither a simple story nor without surprise, but it is true, at least to all that I recall" (2).

Jesus' insistence on truth here is of importance later in the novel. It is not enough for him to point out that the gospels were written by men with agendas: "Mark, Matthew, Luke, and John were seeking to enlarge their fold. And the same is true of other gospels written by other men. Some of these scribes would speak only to Jews who were ready to follow me after my death, and some preached only to gentiles [sic] who hated Jews but had faith in me. Since each looked to give strength to his own church, how could he not fail to mix what was true into all that was not?" (2). Mailer's Jesus even singles Luke out specifically when Jesus says that Luke "was not a Jew. So his account is rank with exaggeration; he hated Jews" (64). Mailer, though, goes beyond this assertion and has his Jesus state that to exaggerate the truth is an action that can only come from Satan, thus implying that the writers of the gospels have given in to this temptation, while he will not.

Concerning the gospel writers on this point, Mailer writes, "Yet my disciples added fables to their accounts. When a man sees a wonder, Satan will enter his tale and multiply the wonder" (243). When Jesus feeds the 500 (in Mailer's work), he refers to the gospel writers' exaggeration directly and says quite clearly that "Exaggeration is the language of the devil, and no man is free of Satan, not even the Son of God (and certainly not Matthew, Mark, Luke, or John). So I knew that many of my followers would increase the numbers of this feat" (121).

Jesus' assertion, then, that his tale is as true as his recollection will allow it to be is set off as a foil to the gospel writers' accounts. This approach heightens Jesus' comments that he is "the way, the *truth*, and the life" (John 14:6, emphasis added) and that his hearers shall "know the truth and the truth will set [them] free" (John 8:32). Also, when Jesus is brought before Pilate, Jesus tells him that he can "bear witness to the truth" (226), which causes Pilate famously to respond, "What is truth?" (226). Mailer uses this idea of truth during Jesus' trial to raise the idea of perception again when Jesus thinks of the Jews who are accusing him, "If pious Jews knew nothing else, they knew what was truth. And on this morning their truth was that I should be condemned by the Romans" (226). Thus, the Jews have their truth, as do Matthew and the other gospel writers, but only Jesus, in this telling of his story, has the truth of what happened in his life.

Mailer clearly differs from Kazantzakis, then, as Mailer argues that historical truth is the most important truth. Mailer's Jesus does not grant that the gospel writers are trying to convey truth in their accounts, merely that they get many facts wrong. His Jesus is not writing his account in order to further the cause of spiritual truth, but to clear up what happened, historically speaking. Kazantzakis' work presents a view of truth that is more mystical, one that understands that an event need not have happened to convey a spiritual truth that gospel readers (or readers of Kazantzakis' novel) need to hear.

Ricci expands upon this idea of truth through the narrative structure that he uses for his novel. From the very structure of his book, with four separate narrators of the same events, Ricci calls into question the reliability of any story, but, more directly, the reliability of the gospels. In an interview, Ricci comments, "I got that premise [multiple narrators], in part, from the canonical Gospels, how each of them assumes a very particular point of view. The gospel writers, however, had an agenda; they needed to propagandize this figure as a means of spreading his word. Not that they were trying to deceive people. They were simply using a standard literary technique of the day" (Starnino G1). It is interesting that Ricci argues that the gospel writers have an agenda while he seems to imply that he does not. Of course, if one extends his argument logically, it is clear that he has an agenda of his own, one facet of which is the questioning of the nature of a universal truth. By having Judas give his interpretation of events, then having Mary Magdalene relate many of the same events but with a much different interpretation, Ricci wants to remind the reader of the lenses through which we interpret the events we experience and witness.[4]

---

[4]In *According to Mary Magdalene*, Marianne Fredriksson takes a similar approach. She includes direct quotes from the gospel of John, I Peter, and Paul's letters to the Corinthians, but also includes direct quotes from the gnostic *Gospel of Mary*. She wants to remind the reader that there are always multiple views of events.

Saramago's novel The Gospel According to Jesus Christ does not deal with many of the events of the Biblical gospels; thus, he does not address the issue of the reliability of those gospels very often. However, he does provide a few hints as to what he thinks about their portrayals of Jesus. When Jesus is thirteen and wandering around Jerusalem, for example, Saramago writes,

> There are certain moments in life that should be arrested and protected from time, and not simply be transmitted in a gospel or a painting or, as in this modern age, a photograph, film, or video. How much more interesting it would be if the person who lived those moments could remain forever visible to his descendants, so that those of us alive today could go to Jerusalem and see with our own eyes young Jesus, son of Joseph, all wrapped up in his little threadbare mantle, beholding the houses of Jerusalem and giving thanks to the Lord who mercifully restored his soul. . . . Alas, he has moved, the instant is gone, time has carried us into the realm of memory, it was like this, no, it was not, and everything becomes what we choose to invent. (165)

Given Saramago's acceptance of relativism, the reader should not be surprised by such an attitude. To Saramago, the world is indeed something we invent, and this approach goes beyond memory. In the first chapter of the book, Saramago describes a painting of the crucifixion, going around and discussing each of the major characters. When he gets to the thieves on the cross, he says that Jesus "only a moment ago praised the Good Thief and despised the Bad Thief, failing to understand that there is no difference between them, or, if there is a difference, it lies in something else, for good and evil do not exist in themselves, each being merely the absence of each other" (6).

Oddly enough, though, Saramago does make one comment early in the work that implies that his work is more factual than those of other writers. When Joseph goes to the elders to tell them of the beggar and the glowing soil, the elders send three envoys to determine what has actually happened.

Saramago mentions them by name—Abiathar, Dothan, and Zacchaeus—and says that these "... names [are] recorded here to forestall any suspicion of historical inaccuracy in the minds of those who have acquired their version of the story from other sources, a version perhaps more in accordance with tradition but not necessarily more factual" (22). Helena Kaufman argues that Saramago ranks his "gospel" with canonical gospels: "Adopting Luke's words to introduce his own narrative suggests that Saramago would like it to be considered on the same level with the Gospels, as one more version of the well-known story." She adds, though, that "this does not necessarily imply that the author wants us to see the Gospels as pure fiction. To the contrary, by making his narrative in many aspects faithful to the Gospels' version and by filling it with historical details as well as freely drawing upon the supernatural, Saramago stresses any narrative's characterization as subjective, representational, mediated, and, therefore, fictitious in the sense of not being equated with reality" (453). Ilan Stavans agrees when he quotes Saramago as saying that this novel "was never meant to dismiss what others have written about Jesus or to contradict their accounts" (676). By adding another account, Saramago simply wants to remind the reader of the multifaceted aspect of truth and, for Saramago, the impossibility of ever arriving at one truth.

Dan Brown, in *The Da Vinci Code*, seems to agree with Saramago's skepticism concerning the reliability of the gospels. When Teabring is explaining Da Vinci's views of the Bible to Sophie, he tells her, "The Bible is a product of *man*, my dear. Not of God. The Bible did not fall magically from the clouds. Man created it as a historical record of tumultuous times, and it has evolved through countless translations, additions, and revisions. History has never had a definitive version of the book" (231). However, much like Kazantzakis, Langdon later argues that, while the Bible is very much a fabrication, it still is useful and necessary: "Sophie, *every* faith in the world is based on fabrication. That is the definition of *faith*—acceptance of that which we imagine to be true, that which we cannot prove. Every religion describes God through metaphor, allegory, and exaggeration, from the early Egyptians through modern Sunday school" (341). He makes it clear, though, that the stories are true only as metaphors: "Should we wave a flag and tell the Buddhists that we have proof the Buddha did not come from a lotus blossom? Or that Jesus was not born of a *literal* virgin birth? Those who truly understand their faiths understand the stories are metaphorical" (342). Thus, for Brown, the gospels are reliable in that they tell part of the story, and they are effective metaphors that help "millions of people cope and be better people" (342), but it is also clear that none of them could even possibly relate what actually did occur. Thus, the ideas that Mary Magdalene and Jesus were married, that Mary had his child in France after his crucifixion, and that located at the feet of Mary's bones is actually the Holy Grail are just as likely to be true as what any reader can find in Matthew, Mark, Luke, or John. Both Saramago and Brown use their novels to undercut the truth of the gospels and set up the idea that all truth is equally valid.

Margaret George, in *Mary Called Magdalene*, shows how seemingly reliable eyewitness testimony progresses to the circulation of stories that are clearly untrue during one lifetime. In a nod to the gnostic *Gospel of Thomas*, Thomas tells Mary that he is "writing down some of the things Jesus has said. You know, here and there. I'm afraid I'll forget them otherwise. I've already forgotten so many."[5] And when she tells Thomas that she never heard Jesus say anything Thomas has written down, Thomas responds, "He says different things to each of us. . . . It depends on whether you were standing near at the time. You could compile your own list, I'm sure" (461). Thus, even though this is an eyewitness account of Jesus' sayings, Mary doesn't accept it as true. After Jesus' death and resurrection, Mary realizes that she should have been writing down Jesus' teachings herself, as she knows that "we will make mistakes, we will forget" (555), though she does not write anything down until she is just past ninety. And in her story we find the lack of reliability that is already creeping into stories about her: "How did he know my story? How accurate was it? But after I died, how could I go

---

[5]Since the *Gospel of Thomas* is merely a collection of Jesus' sayings with no narrative backbone, George has her Mary say to Thomas, "You ought to explain when and why he said these things. . . . It's hard to understand otherwise." Thomas merely responds, "It's only for me. . . . I won't forget" (461). Of course, the reader knows that it ultimately was not just for Thomas and that we do not have the benefit of his knowledge when we read them today.

about correcting all the false stories? Even now, it would be an impossible task. The false stories about Jesus, about Peter, about James, about John, about Jesus's mother, about me. . . . No, already it was not humanly possible" (596, author's ellipses). Even though George hews more closely to the gospel accounts than does any other contemporary author, save for Reynolds Price, whose work is more of a translation of the gospels than a re-telling, she is also quick to call their reliability into question.

Though all the authors acknowledge some sort of supernatural element in their re-tellings, even if, as with Ricci, it is merely through the way Jesus is able to love those with whom he comes in contact, they also all question the reliability of the gospel accounts. Rather than allowing for the idea of spiritual truth that goes beyond that of historical truth, most of the authors question the gospels' historicity and work to expose the agendas of the authors of the gospels. As they are all writing in an age where relativism has become commonplace, it is not surprising that they present reality as being shaped by individual perceptions, not as a universal truth that God conveys to people through the Bible. Though not quite representing the entire range of modern belief, they do capture a range from the more accepting of the gospels to the nearly complete denial of them.

CHAPTER 3

.*A* Mother's Love and Expectation for Her *C*hild

THE RELATIONSHIP BETWEEN MARY AND JESUS

There is little about Mary in the gospels beyond her role as the mother of the Son of God. As Theodore Ziolkowski reminds us, "the figure of the Virgin Mary is singularly colorless in the Gospels and offers little material for the writer. . . . It was not until medieval times that the emerging Marian cults gradually endowed the Virgin Mother with the characteristics subsequently popularized in art and legend" (282). The two subjects that are mentioned in the gospels—Mary's marriage and pregnancy and the relationship between Mary and Jesus—thus become topics for the authors who retell the gospel stories. If one struggles with the idea of the Son of God, then one also struggles with how a woman could possibly be a mother of that Son of God. Almost all of the authors, Mailer being a visible exception, show a Mary who does struggle with her role in Jesus' life, as might be expected. These five writers are consistent in their presentations of Mary. Apart from Ricci, who clearly states that Mary was raped, and Saramago, who ignores the subject altogether, the authors show her as a virgin. They also show her as knowledgeable about what Jesus can accomplish, that he is set apart somehow, yet almost all of them, save for Burgess, also show her as trying to prevent him from leading anything other than a normal life. Ricci and Saramago, too, use Mary to consider women's roles in the Jewish culture of Jesus' time.

It is not surprising that most authors who portray Mary choose to focus on her virginity and the divine conception of Jesus. From the Bible, the main emphasis placed on the character of Mary is that she is the mother of Jesus and that, more notably, she gives birth to Jesus without having had sex. Thus, her being chosen as the mother of the Messiah shows that she has, as the angel tells Mary, "found favor with God" (Luke 1:30). In fact, there is almost nothing more about Mary's relationship with Jesus when he is a child.

The writings of the early church expand on this idea of the virgin birth. According to the *Book of James* (or *Protevangelium*), Mary was dedicated to the temple as a virgin when she was a child. She married Joseph, who was an old man at the time, because of a sign from God. However, they never consummated their marriage, and the supposed brothers and sisters of Jesus are from Joseph's marriage (Cunneen 69–71, 74).

The orthodox concept of Mary, though, developed near the end of the fourth century and into the fifth century, leading to the declaration at the Council of Ephesus of Mary as *Theotokos* (God-bearer), moving the focus away from Mary as a person and toward her role as Jesus' mother.[1] This idea became the main way that Mary was perceived (Cunneen 101).

According to the *Book of James*, again, Mary was supposedly born to rich parents, Joachim and Anna, who had prayed for a child for years. When she was born to them, they dedicated her to God. She was one of seven virgins who was working on a new curtain for the temple when she was chosen to marry Joseph. Because she was pregnant before they were actually married, she and Joseph were forced to undergo the water test for pregnancy found in Numbers 5:16, which they passed (Blair 293).

Despite Burgess' Catholicism, Mary is not very visible in his novel. Her portrayal is quite traditional, and Burgess clearly emphasizes her virginity. In fact, Burgess presents Mary as a young woman who wants to keep her virginity forever, never marrying. Thus, Joseph, with his inability to have sex, seems to be the perfect husband for her. Even though she is not even fifteen years old, she seems to understand the decision she is making concerning

---

[1]This is not to say that she is not seen as holy in her own right, just that the focus is on her role as the bearer of Jesus. There are other legends of her as set apart from other women. For example, according to the *Liber Transitus* (*Assumption of the Virgin*), Mary died in Jerusalem, where the apostles were miraculously assembled. A Jewish priest attempted to overturn the bier on which she lay, but he was unable to do so and was not able to let go of it until he confessed faith in Jesus. After her death, Jesus raised her from the dead and took her to heaven. A papal bull issued November 1, 1950, stated that she was taken up into heaven after her death, and that belief continues to hold sway (Blair 293).

her abstention from sexual activity. The most important sacrifice, as her mother tells Joseph, is that she will be "shut off from the hopes that go with the carnal life, the hope of Jewish women, I mean" (19). Her mother does not merely mean that she will not be able to produce children, but that she will not have the hope of producing the Messiah. Since Burgess does not question Jesus' role as the Messiah or Mary's virginity, her mother's comment becomes obviously ironic, as if Burgess is trying to draw even more attention to Jesus' miraculous birth.

In fact, all of the women in Burgess' book, the traditional Jewish women anyway, seem to be obsessed with the possibility that their child could be the Messiah. The men, too, of this time seem obsessed with the idea of the Messiah. In a morning study, Mary and Joseph's rabbi, Gomer, insists that the correct interpretation of the passage from Isaiah concerning the woman who will give birth to the Messiah is that she is a virgin, not merely a young woman, as the Hebrew might also be translated to mean. Burgess here clearly lays out his presentation of Mary as a virgin, in the face of scholars who have begun to interpret the passage to mean that a young woman, not necessarily a virgin, will produce the Messiah. By having Gomer insist so clearly that the woman must be a virgin, Burgess, as he does with Mary's mother's comment, draws even more attention to the miraculous birth of Jesus. Given his Roman Catholic background, his position is not surprising at all.

Ricci's portrayal of Mary is dramatically different from Burgess', as well as from the other authors' portrayals. Mary is usually presented as a young, poor, innocent girl, but Ricci puts her in different social class. Her father is a clerk in Herod's court; thus, one might assume that she will make a good marriage. Her father is not presented as a good Jew because he's willing to consider a marriage for her outside of the Jewish faith, which is not surprising given his work for Herod. He seems more concerned with advancing the family fortune.

Thus, Joseph presents Mary with a few men whom she might marry, but she passes on them. One, however, is a Roman legate. Mary's father leaves the two of them alone, and the legate forces himself on Mary with threats of violence, and she becomes pregnant. Some scholars believe that Mary was not a virgin when she was married and that Jesus is the result of a rape. E.P. Blair, for example, points out that the concepts of Mary's virginity and the virgin birth do not appear in any of the sermons in Acts or in Paul's letters, raising the question of whether or not the idea is added later (290). And, given Ricci's research into the writings of the Jesus Seminar, most of the participants of which do not believe in a virgin birth, this change in the gospel story removes yet another supernatural event from Jesus' life. Ricci's changes in Mary's status from a virgin in a different social class create a situation in which no one will marry her, so her father turns to Joseph, a forty-five-year-old widower who has already put one wife away for barrenness. Since Mary has already proven herself to be fertile, she is an appealing wife for Joseph, but he still makes Mary's father pay an exorbitant dowry: "Nonetheless, to make up for the dishonour of me and the expense of being saddled with a child not his own, he asked much above the usual dowry, all in coin, and offered no bride price. It cost my father all his small fortune to satisfy him, in which however I took some bitter consolation, for he had ruined my life in the hope of advancing his own ambitions" (228). Mary clearly recognizes that her father is to blame for what has happened, but she also does not condemn the Roman legate; in fact, she seldom mentions him again and then only when talking about what resulted because her father left her alone with him.

Kazantzakis hews more closely to the traditional interpretation by at least having Mary be a virgin when she gives birth to Jesus. In fact, the events surrounding Jesus' birth are even more supernatural than the other events in the gospels. Thus, Mary should be the character in Kazantzakis' novel who has the most reason to believe that Jesus is, if not divine, at the least called by God for some great purpose. She remembers the odd events that occurred around his birth, which Judas recalls hearing when he first begins to wonder about Jesus' purpose:

> Jostling in his mind were the signs and prodigies which had
> surrounded this youth from his birth, and even before: how,

when the marriage candidates were assembled, the staff of Joseph—among so many others—was the only one to blossom. Because of this the rabbi awarded him Mary, exquisite Mary, who was consecrated to God. And then how a thunderbolt struck and paralyzed the bridegroom on his marriage day, before he could touch his bride. And how later, it was said, the bride smelled a white lily and conceived a son in her womb. And how the night before his birth she dreamed that the heavens opened, angels descended, lined up like birds on the humble roof of her house, built nests and began to sing; and some guarded her threshold, some entered her room, lighted a fire and heated water to bathe the expected infant, and some boiled broth for the confined woman to drink. . . . (22)

Mary also remembers how she and Joseph went to Elijah's summit the day of their wedding in order to petition the prophet, so that she and Joseph might have a son: "They wanted to beg the fiery prophet to mediate with God so that they might have a son, whom they would then dedicate to the prophet's grace" (60). While on the mountain, a thunderstorm comes, and Joseph is struck by lightning and paralyzed, but Mary hears God speak to her from behind the thunderstorm. She is unable to recall what God said to her until the rabbi comes to visit, and, even then, all she can remember hearing is God saying, "Hail, Mary!" (62). Kazantzakis' reference to the ave Maria here is also echoed in his account of Mary's origin, thus further strengthening the idea that she is a virgin and is to be revered for her role in Jesus' birth.

When Peter sees Mary at the crucifixion of a zealot, he remembers her family, whom he lived near when growing up. He believed that "the angels went regularly in and out of their simple cottage, and one night the neighbors saw God Himself stride across their threshold dressed as a beggar. They knew it was God, because the house shook as though invaded by an earthquake, and nine months later the miracle happened: Anne, an old woman in her sixties, gave birth to Mary" (43). Thus, this story opens up the possibility that Mary is herself the offspring of God, and at least shows the reader that Mary is someone specially chosen by God.

As in Kazantzakis' novel, Burgess presents a Mary who has knowledge beyond that of the other characters. Burgess' Mary is assured that she will be the mother of the Messiah.[2] In fact, Joseph points out in the study with the rabbi that the Messiah must be born in Bethlehem, as David was. Mary, however, argues that the Messiah will be of Bethlehem, not necessarily born in Bethlehem, and, as Joseph is descended from the House of David, then Jesus will be of Bethlehem.[3]

Since Burgess' Mary knows what Jesus is destined for, she never stands in his way. There is no passage in *Man of Nazareth* where Mary considers him insane or tries to stop him from leaving, as there are in the gospels and in other novels. Instead, she sees his impending death even before he is born: "Mary sat and saw in the fire pictures that gave her no pleasure. She saw one picture that made her catch her breath with fear; there was a pain in her midriff, as if a sword had struck" (42). This passage should remind the reader of the prophecy made by Simeon in Luke that a sword will pierce Mary (Luke 2:35). Roman Catholics through the ages have depicted Mary's suffering in the image of the pietà, which heightens Mary's role as the God-bearer. Thus, it is not surprising that Burgess would choose to focus his story on this idea.

One of the ways Mary encourages Jesus to realize his true calling is to discourage him from getting married, which she thinks will distract him. Given her ideas of virginity and marriage, we can understand her thinking. Thus, she questions his marriage and has another presentiment that it will end badly:

> Jesus's mother thought much of the meaning of this [Jesus' wife's two miscarriages] but kept her own counsel, wondering

---

[2]Christopher Moore, in Lamb, takes this idea further by having his Mary quote prophecies that Jesus is fulfilling, even as a child. For example, when a cobra follows him home, she quotes the book of Isaiah that says "the suckling child shall play on the hole of the asp" (22).

[3]Interestingly, Reynolds Price has his Jesus born in Nazareth, not Bethlehem, though he tends to stay closer to the gospel stories than almost any contemporary writer who tackles Jesus' life.

> no doubt about the propriety of the destined Messiah's
> begetting sons and daughters like other men. Indeed, the
> very propriety of his marriage remained in doubt with her,
> and she had strange presentiments about the future of it.
> One morning, at cock-crow, she had a vivid dream in which
> Sara [Jesus' wife] melted like wax before her very eyes, while
> cooking the evening meal in the kitchen. (89)

Of course, Sara does die, trampled to death by Syrian soldiers, and Mary's dream proves to be prophetic. This shows a Mary who not only knows more than other characters in the novel but also who knows more than Jesus himself. Even though Jesus argues that he must know all parts of being human, Mary sees the suffering that will come from that experience, not just suffering on Jesus' part, but on Sara's part, as well.

Through such events Burgess is at least implying the inevitable divinity of Mary, if not laying it out completely.[4] She is able to sense what will happen, at least where it concerns Jesus and his ministry. Thus, whenever she visits a place where he is or encounters a disciple, she wants to know how he is currently doing. When Jesus sends the disciples out to preach on their own, John visits Nazareth where Mary meets him after he has finished teaching. After finding out that he is doing well physically, she reminds John that Jesus is "much hated. [She] fear[s] for him" (197), though she still plans to meet him in Jerusalem for the Passover. She is much more actively involved in Jesus' ministry than is shown or suggested in the gospels where her only encounters with Jesus during his ministry are times when she tries to stop him from teaching.

Unlike Burgess, Mailer's Mary's appearances are in keeping with what readers familiar with the gospel stories expect, though Mailer makes minor changes and expands a bit, as well. Mary and Jesus' brothers try to stop

---

[4]In *Lamb*, Christopher Moore satirizes our culture's obsession with the divine Mary when he has her face appear on the wall of a temple in India. When Biff tells Joshua (Jesus) about this event, Joshua merely responds, "Yeah, she does that. . . . She used to do it all the time when we were kids. She sent James and me running all over the place washing down walls before people saw. Sometimes her face would appear in a pattern of water drops in the dust, or the peelings from grapes would fall just so in a pattern after being taken out of the wine press. Usually it was walls" (298–99).

him from preaching. The gospel accounts have them saying that Jesus is crazy, though Mailer does not let them go that far at this point. He does, however, indicate Mary's having said that Jesus is "wrong to perform cures on the Sabbath and so must be full of devils" (92). This event echoes Mary's first appearance in Jesus' adulthood, after Jesus has come down from the mountain, but before he begins his ministry. Jesus wants to become a wandering minister, but Mary wants him to stay in Qumran and become a good Essene. She is portrayed as someone who believes that authority should be followed, not rebelled against, which is why Jesus does not tell her about his temptation on the mountain: "Yet she was also a mother. She knew me very well. So she could now surmise that it had not only been my Father who was with me on the mountain but the Other. If the Devil owned the powers of darkness, then I was weak enough, as she would see it, to have been tainted. Therefore I must be guided by a community of the most devout" (60). Like Burgess, then, Mailer gives his Mary the ability to know things about Jesus, but he does not give her supernatural knowledge; instead, her knowledge comes simply from being a mother. Mailer's Mary is not divine, but a good, human mother.

Saramago also stays close to the gospel accounts and thus presents Mary as believing Jesus to be insane[5]; Saramago's Mary does not believe Jesus when he comes to tell her that he has seen God. And even when Jesus tells her of this event, she still does not relate to him what happened when she was pregnant, despite the fact that she knows Jesus has been working with Pastor (the beggar) for the past four years. Instead, she believes that Jesus is in Satan's power. In the end, though, Pastor appears to Mary and tells her that Jesus is the Son of God. She sends James and Joseph to look for Jesus without telling them what she has learned, but he refuses to come home because they did not believe him. She has supernatural knowledge in Saramago's work, but it is only through revelation; otherwise, she does not truly know who her son is, even with the odd events surrounding his birth.

---

[5]It is interesting that an atheist, such as Saramago, and a confessed Christian, such as the Protestant Reynolds Price, both show Mary as believing that Jesus is insane. Not surprisingly, though, they both differ radically from Roman Catholic Burgess.

Though Kazantzakis presents his Mary with compelling evidence that Jesus is the Son of God (or at least called by God in some manner), she still wants him to have a normal life, as she conveys to the rabbi when he begins to imply that Jesus might be the Messiah: "Have pity on me, Father! A prophet? No, no! And if God has it so written, let him rub it out! I want my son a man like everyone else, nothing more, nothing less. Like everyone else. . . . Let him build troughs, cradles, plows and household utensils as his father used to do . . ." (64). In fact, she has long wanted the rabbi to cast out the demons that she believes make Jesus act the way he does: "How many times had she prostrated herself before her brother-in-law the old rabbi, who was versed in exorcizing devils. The afflicted came to him from the ends of the earth and he cured them. Just the other day she had fallen at his feet and complained: 'You heal strangers but you do not want to heal my son'" (29). This event echoes the gospel portrayal of Mary's believing that Jesus is insane, though it takes the idea even further by creating a Mary who believes her son is possessed by the devil. Leavitt describes Kazantzakis' Mary as "a prototypical Jewish (read Greek) mother: domineering, possessive, embittered by her son's refusal to lead the life she outlined for him" (Leavitt 65), but he misses part of the point here. Yes, she does want Jesus to live the life she has in mind for him, but she also attributes his unwillingness to do so to the devil, not to the rebellion typical of a son. This portrayal is a far cry from Burgess' Mary who makes sure Jesus does not get off the course he needs to pursue to be the Messiah, yet both Marys want to guide Jesus' life.

It's obvious that Kazantzakis' Mary loves Jesus and wants him to return home rather than traipse over the countryside preaching to the poor, but he always shuns her when she comes to find him, which only makes her bemoan her situation even more. When Salome tells her that Jesus is "in safety now; he's under God's roof," Mary replies, "A mother's pain is heavy, Salome. . . . God sent me but one boy, and he a blemished one" (167). Later, after Salome has seen angels behind Jesus as he taught, though Mary has not, Salome tries to tell Mary of what she has seen: "While he spoke, didn't you see blue wings, thousands of blue wings behind him? I swear to you, Mary, there were whole armies of angels" (189). But Mary has no interest in angels' wings: "What good are angels to me, Salome? I want children and grandchildren to be following him, children and grandchildren, not angels!" (190). Kazantzakis does not make clear whether or not Mary does not see the wings because she does not want her son to be the Messiah or that God has kept her from seeing, for whatever reason.

Thus, despite the ample evidence Mary had from Jesus' birth, she still wants Jesus to be normal, more than anything else, still wants him not to be who everyone else seems to think he is. In doing so, she often appears callous and self-centered, in that she is more concerned for the things of this world than heavenly issues, as Jesus might say. The only time Mary seems to focus on anyone other than herself is when the crowd is chasing Mary Magdalene in order to stone her. Mary Magdalene hides in Zebedee's house, and Mary and Salome try to comfort her. Mary Magdalene is crying because she does not want to die; she simply loves being alive, and Mary tells her, "Do not be afraid, Mary. . . . God protects you; you won't die." And when Mary Magdalene asks her how she knows this, Mary simply responds, "God gives us time, Magdalene, time to repent" (171). It is true that Mary was originally repulsed by Mary Magdalene's previous life and that this repulsion probably motivates her statement that Magdalene needs time to repent, but she moves outside of herself, beyond her repulsion, and tries to comfort Mary Magdalene in the only way she knows how.

Ricci's Mary also tries to prevent Jesus from the life he chooses; thus, almost every time Mary encounters Jesus when he is teaching, Jesus shuns her. Stoffman points out, "Ricci's Jesus . . . is a great teacher, fearless in argument, a man of compassion, an inspired healer, bonesetter, diagnostician, a wise friend, but a cold and distant son to his fearful and conventional mother" (J15). In the gospel accounts, Mary is anxious about Jesus when he is grown, but he seems to take little notice of her, even to the point of rudeness. Other than John's report that Jesus made sure Mary was taken care of after his death, the encounters Mary has with the adult Jesus are all negative. Mary and Jesus' brothers seek him because they think that he has gone crazy, but Jesus will not even meet them. Instead, when they send someone to tell him of their presence, Jesus responds by teaching the crowd: "Who are my mother and my brothers? . . . Here are my mother and my brothers! Whoever does God's will is my brother and sister and mother" (Mark 3:33–35). Ricci follows the gospel accounts in this instance and creates a tenuous relationship between Mary and Jesus. When Mary goes to Kefar Nahum to try to speak with Jesus, he will not come out of the house; instead, he sends Mary Magdalene, a young girl in Ricci's book, to deliver the message: "It seemed a tremendous mistake now to have come, only to trouble myself with humiliation, to be sent a girl to turn me away so that I might understand the fullness of his contempt" (291). Jesus does not send Mary Magdalene as a sign of contempt, but it is clear that he does not focus on his relationship with his mother. Whether this is because he is more focused on his teaching, because he simply does not understand how to relate to her, or because he is a typical child who is rebelling against his family is unclear. In light of Ricci's human Jesus, the second and third reasons make much more sense than the first.

There is one moment in the gospels, though, when Mary and Jesus' relationship is loving, especially from Jesus' side. The gospel of John shows Mary at the cross at Jesus' crucifixion, and Jesus asks John to take care of her (John 19:26–27). Drawing on John's account, the authors show Jesus, near the end of his life, treating Mary much more kindly. Burgess, for example, has her meet him in Jerusalem, but only briefly before he is taken prisoner. Instead, she accidentally rooms with Mary Magdalene and Salome, and they become friends. In fact, it is because of Salome's connections that Mary is able to be near the cross as Jesus is crucified. She also arrives at the tomb, along with Mary Magdalene, before the disciples, and it is she alone who hears Jesus' voice in the tomb telling the disciples to go to Galilee to meet him. The switch from Mary Magdalene hearing Jesus after his resurrection confirms Mary's high standing in Burgess' novel. If Mary Magdalene was the original apostle in the gospels and in early church tradition because she was the first to take the message to the disciples, in Burgess' novel, Mary the mother has taken that role away. Thus, not only does she give birth to Jesus, but now she is the one to hear the message of his resurrection, as well.

Mailer's Mary's last appearance is when Jesus is on the way to the cross. He sees her in a crowd, and he realizes at that moment that her love was "a gift from the Lord, and so, in her awe of me, she had contended with all I did" (233), and his understanding of this concept leads him back to her: "I belonged to my mother again" (233). Thus, he picks out a disciple (Timothy in Mailer's account, though John in the gospels) to protect her now that he is going to die. This protection explicitly contrasts with how Jesus has treated her earlier, when she and his brothers came to stop him from preaching. Someone calls out to Jesus, "Behold, your mother and your brothers look for you," to which Jesus responds, "These are my brothers! Those who are with me. For he who does the will of God is my brother and my mother" (92). Even then, Jesus wants to take those words back, as he hears they've made his mother cry. But he believes that her fear of Romans and her lack of pride in dealing with wealthy Jews have only served to fuel his anger. Thus, by trying to stop Jesus from doing what he is called to do, she leads him down the path where he can best fulfill his duty to God.

For Ricci, at the last meeting, Jesus treats his mother with respect, almost as if he knows what is going to happen to him, though Ricci does not give the reader any indication that he does. When he sees her, he introduces her and his brothers to his disciples; then Mary comments, "Then he embraced his brothers and took my hand in both of his and brought it to his lips, which in all his life he had not done" (307). Mary eventually meets Mary Magdalene, and they comfort each other after Jesus' arrest: "So grateful was I to find a stranger who shared sympathy with me that I forgot all resentment towards her and embraced her, also falling to tears. For a moment we stood there unable to speak for emotion" (312). They go together to the crucifixion, and Mary the mother comforts Mary Magdalene there: "I noticed now that the mother had an arm around Mary, the two joined under the mother's cloak as if they'd been brought to the same level, helpless like children who'd been left behind. It didn't seem to matter any more how differently they'd seen Jesus—it had come to the same thing, in the end, that neither had got what they'd wanted from him, and now they'd lost him" (448). Mary the mother does not see Jesus after his supposed resurrection, nor does she see the empty tomb. Her last glimpse of Jesus is on the cross, watching him suffer, unable to turn away. Though Ricci's portrayal of Mary is otherwise quite different from Burgess', they both show Mary's suffering, which is one of the main attributes of her character in the gospels.

In addition to drawing from the gospels and the legends surrounding Mary, both Saramago and Ricci go beyond these ideas and use Mary to comment on women's roles in their society. When Saramago first introduces her, in fact, he writes, "Unlike Joseph her husband, Mary is neither upright nor pious, but she is not to blame for this, the blame lies with the language she speaks if not with the men who invented it, because that language has no feminine form for the words upright and pious" (16). Saramago uses other women to convey this point as well; on the road to Jerusalem the men pray, but the women "merely mumbled the words, for it is pointless raising your voice if no one is likely to listen, even though they ask for nothing and are grateful for everything" (35). Because Judaism at the time did not allow women religious education or practice, the women rightly conclude that it does them no good to attempt to participate. Mary becomes the main representation of this idea throughout the novel.

The connection between the Jewish religion and Mary's status in society is reinforced when Jesus is born. Jesus, though still a child, is allowed to learn about religious matters, while Mary cannot even ask him what he has learned. She shows her cleverness, though, by learning what she can from what Jesus tells Joseph about what he learned in class that day. Saramago also takes pains to point out that Mary is not able to enter the Temple, having to stop at the Court of the Women, while Joseph goes forward to offer the sacrifice. Instead of being able to participate in this event, Mary "will not stir until Joseph returns, she simply steps aside so as not to obstruct the passage, and waits, holding her son in her arms" (73). Helena Kaufman points out that Saramago's narrator, "far from accepting it, . . . stresses the inferior position women were assigned in Jewish society and religion" and "recognizes that the difference by which the feminine can be described results from the socio-political structure" (456). Saramago does not use his novel, then, merely to criticize Christianity's portrayal of God, the devil, and Jesus; instead, he also uses it to examine the roles of women, mainly in ancient Israel, but certainly with echoes for today.

Mary's background, with her lack of rights, helps explain some of her actions later in the novel, especially what she does not share with Joseph. From the outset, when Mary encounters the beggar at the door who knows she is pregnant, though she has told no one, she does not tell Joseph that she believes he is an angel. Because the beggar leaves a bowl with soil, which seems to glow, with them, Joseph suspects that the beggar might have been an angel or a devil, but Mary does not tell him that the beggar knew she was pregnant. Mary, in fact, never tells him about the beggar, even though she sees him several more times before Joseph's death. Mary's interactions with Jesus also center around what she tells him, though this relationship also involves what he tells her. Mary does not tell Jesus of the beggar's appearance when she was pregnant, nor does she tell him about the circumstances surrounding his birth in Bethlehem. It is only when he begins having his nightmare that she is forced to tell him everything. As Mary has been denied access and knowledge in the early part of the work due to her status as a woman in this culture, she also denies knowledge to the men around her. Knowledge becomes her only power in this society, and she uses it wisely to attempt to get what little power she can get.

In Ricci's work, Mary is not happy being married to Joseph, but there is nothing she can do, as a woman, in her culture. She endures Joseph, especially in the area of sex, which she compares to her rape by the Roman; there is no emotion or love. However, after Joseph dies, she realizes just how good he was to her:

> It surprised me then the grief that went through me, for I had not imagined I loved him. Indeed, perhaps I had not, except that I had been with him some fifteen years, and had borne his children, and he had spared me, as I saw now, a life surely far worse than the one he had given me. Never once had he raised his hand against me or asked of me anything it was unreasonable for a man to ask of his wife, and the fairness of

mind I had detested in him as a bride had in the end stood me
well in all my years with him. (272)

Ricci does not accept the culture that he portrays here, but he also
does not represent it falsely. He does not create a Joseph who allows Mary
to learn or have a voice in the decisions of the family, but he does create
one who is as kind to Mary as a man could have been in ancient Israel.
Mary's recognition of this reinforces those limits without necessarily
accepting them.

When Joseph moves Mary and Jesus to Alexandria where no one knows
Jesus is not his son, Mary, without Joseph's knowledge, explores the city
and learns Greek, showing how different the Egyptian culture is from the
Jewish culture. As Mary says, "But in this [learning Greek] I was no different
from the other women of Alexandria, be they Greek or Jew, for they did
not believe there, as in Judea, that a woman was only a chattel but that she
might make her own life" (237). This idea that she can learn on her own, just
as a man can in Israel, serves as a foil to the culture they have left and to
which they will return. Though she ultimately turns her back on learning,
she at least experiences a culture that shows her that women can be more
nearly equal to men, and when she does shift her focus to her family, she
later regrets giving up on learning. It is only near the end of Jesus' life that
she realizes what she has given up, and it is Jesus who helps her to this
realization, though not directly:

> And the restlessness I had felt as a young woman in Alexandria
> began to return to me, for I saw how my mind had been open
> then but had grown complacent, and how I thought only of
> my position now, just as Yeshua [Jesus] had once accused me,
> when before I had cared more for truth. Indeed it seemed that
> since Yeshua had gone from me I had put from my mind all
> thoughts except those of the marriage of my daughters and
> sons, and that the doorway he had opened for me had been
> closed. (285)

Even Judas can tell a difference between Mary and the other Nazarene women: "She was the first woman I'd seen in the town in whom there was any sign of an intrinsic beauty, though it was clear from her look, which had something of the Arab to it, and from her bearing, which was that of a city woman, that she did not belong to the place, and that indeed she would gladly have kicked the dust of it from her heels" (76). It is not just the education she receives that changes her, but the recognition that she might have a different status in a different society, the appreciation of her knowledge, which makes her different from the other women.

Though Mary does not have much power as a woman, all the authors allow her a knowledge that provides her with power. In some cases, she hides this knowledge as a means of gaining power over the men around her. The knowledge also scares her; thus, she seeks to prevent Jesus from becoming whatever it is that God has in store for him. Only Burgess presents a Mary who uses her knowledge to support Jesus in his role. The others hew more closely to the gospel stories, showing her struggles with Jesus' role, making her a more human mother.

CHAPTER 4

The Unknown Father

JOSEPH

With the character of joseph, authors seem to have a blank slate with which to work. There are few appearances of Joseph in the Bible, none after Jesus reaches the age of twelve. There is almost nothing known of Joseph beyond the fact that he was the father (adopted father or foster father or however one decides to term his role) of Jesus. He was betrothed to Mary, yet he found out that she was pregnant, and he decided to end their relationship. Other than those facts, though, the gospel authors tell us nothing about Joseph. In fact, after the birth narrative (and the trip to Jerusalem in Luke), Joseph is completely absent, noticeably so when Mary and her sons come to try to take Jesus home. If Joseph were still alive, it would be his job to perform such actions, not his wife's or sons'. Because of his lack of appearances, it is largely believed that Joseph must have died before Jesus began his ministry (Blair 979). There is one work, the *History of Joseph the Carpenter*, which describes Joseph's death in detail, but it is not considered to be historically reliable, especially as Joseph dies at the age of 111, despite his not being mentioned in the gospels after Jesus turns twelve (Blair 980). The early church does not help in this matter, either. Joseph Lienhard states quite clearly, "Anyone who speaks about St. Joseph in the early church should begin with a warning to his hearers: don't expect too much. For the first millennium of Christianity, St. Joseph was all but ignored in preaching, liturgical celebrations, martyrologies, and theological writing." He goes on to point out that, to his knowledge, no one in the early church ever preached a homily on Joseph. There were no feasts of St. Joseph until one was celebrated in Egypt in the seventh century, and there were none in the rest of the church until 1000 ce at the earliest. There were no theological writings about Joseph until the late fourteenth century when writings about Joseph began to appear more frequently (3).

Thus, authors have to explain his absence one way or another. Largely due to this absence of information, there has been much speculation as to what happened to Joseph and what kind of man he was before he married Mary. All of them have Joseph dying earlier or being physically incapacitated, so as to remove him from the adult Jesus' ministry.

Almost all of the authors under consideration here begin with what would be expected in their portrayals of Joseph. In Saramago's work, Joseph is a carpenter, barely in his 20s, who is honest and pious. He works hard, though he does not have a great deal of money, and he seems like a typical Jewish male of that time.

Similarly, in *Man of Nazareth* Joseph is a carpenter who has two apprentices, James and John. The mention of these two names at first might make the reader think of Jesus' disciples with these names; however, in light of Burgess' Roman Catholic background, it seems he is trying to show how some people, namely Protestants, might think that Joseph had other children by Mary, as James and John are two of the names of the sons of Mary and Joseph listed in the Protestant Bible.

The Gospel According to the Son, too, has Joseph working as a carpenter, and he takes Mary to Bethlehem for Jesus' birth, but in Mailer's book, Joseph does this (not because of the census) because he is descended from King David, and King David was born in Bethlehem. Thus, as Joseph has been born in Bethlehem, he believes Jesus should be born in Bethlehem, too. For Mailer, who is Jewish, it is easy to see his reasoning. He understands the importance of the Davidic line for the Messiah, which would be much more important than Jesus' fulfilling a minor prophecy of birth in Bethlehem (Matthew 2:6). This focus on Jesus' ancestry is apparent in both Matthew and Luke, as Matthew shows how Joseph's lineage can be traced back to Abraham, and Luke traces it all the way back to Adam. Though the genealogies differ, in both cases Joseph traces his ancestors through the line of David, important for one who is going to serve as the father of the Messiah, for the Messiah is to come from the line of David.

Testament, however, changes Joseph's occupation from that of a carpenter, as in the gospels, to being a stonemason; however, Joseph is still on the economic level he would have been in the gospel accounts. This change is not surprising since Ricci draws much of his information and inspiration from "the Jesus Seminar and . . . other contemporary scholars who have tried to arrive at an understanding of the historical Jesus" (457). The Greek word that is translated as "carpenter" in the Gospel accounts is actually *tekton*, which can be translated as "craftsman" (Filas 57). Thus, Ricci is trying to be as historically accurate as possible.[1]

This seeming minor change of vocation actually has a major impact on the work. Like Ricci's usage of ancient spellings for the characters' names, it reminds the reader that translations have changed the Gospel accounts, leading to major changes. Through Ricci's calling into question the translation of a word as simple as "carpenter," he forces the reader to question the translation of more important passages.

Another change that *Testament* makes, at least for most modern readers, is to indicate that Joseph, about forty-five, is nearly three times Mary's age when they marry. He has been previously married, but he has put the first woman away because she failed to produce an heir, the main purpose of a woman in Jewish society at that time. Joseph knows that Mary can produce an heir because she has already become pregnant with Jesus. In fact, Mary's pregnancy is the only reason she marries Joseph, as he is beneath her social status. He lives with his brothers before she comes to be with him, and he threatens to put her away if she fails to produce an heir.

Though this change seems to make Joseph a much less likeable character, Ricci is again reminding the reader of the social and cultural mores of the time. We have tried to turn Mary and Joseph into a modern couple who were in love with each other, a modern-day Romeo and Juliet, especially by an emphasis on Joseph's willingness to put Mary away quietly; however, a man in the Jewish culture of that time both wanted and needed an heir more than he needed a spouse he loved.

Man of Nazareth, on the other hand, has Joseph completely unable to have children because of an accident he had when he was younger. When

---

[1] In "An Honest Account of a Memorable Life, "Reynolds Price also changes the vocation of Joseph to that of a builder. As Price has spent years studying Greek, the similarity is not surprising.

Mary's mother talks with him about the possibility of marriage, he responds, "You know well enough that I can be the husband of nobody. That I was injured in this very shop when it was my father's, God rest him, and injured where it is most shameful for a man to be injured. Meaning that I cannot do a man's part, if I may say this to a lady" (19). Mary's mother does not believe this story; she thinks it is an excuse that Joseph has used not to marry, though he is middle-aged. Joseph, however, returns to the story later in the work, and it is evident that he and Mary never have any other children, though it remains unclear as to whether or not they ever had sex, and the brief description of Joseph's injury makes that seem unlikely.

The idea that Joseph and Mary do not have any children is in line with Burgess' Roman Catholic background, which defines Mary as a perpetual virgin. This tradition began at least as early as *The Book of James* (probably written prior to the second century), which presents the idea that Mary remained a virgin throughout their marriage. Because, according to *The Book of James*, Joseph was a widower with children from his previous marriage, the brothers and sisters of Jesus mentioned in the gospels are actually his half-brothers and sisters (Cunneen 74). This is further strengthened by Burgess' book giving its Joseph two apprentices, James and John, who either are or who might be mistaken for Jesus' half-brothers.

While Burgess works hard to illustrate how this mistake might be made, he does not deal with the other siblings of Jesus mentioned in the Bible.[2] He also neglects to point out how Mary's virginal conception of Jesus affects Joseph's circumstances concerning having an heir. If a Jewish man could not have children, but then was given the opportunity to have an heir, one would assume that he would be ecstatic. It is true that Jesus loved and respected Joseph, which implies that Joseph treated him as his true son, but that is more told than shown in the novel. What might have been a rich idea for Burgess to develop is glossed over as he seeks merely to fulfill an ideological requirement he has.

Mailer's approach is much more similar to that of Ricci concerning children and the sexual life of Mary and Joseph. His book shows Joseph as a

---

[2]Matthew 13:55–56 and Mark 6:3, for example, name his brothers and mention that he has sisters.

widower when he meets Mary; thus, he is many years older than she is. This arrangement was not uncommon at the time, and Mailer does not indicate that Joseph has any children from the previous marriage; therefore, he likely would have wanted to carry on his family by having children with Mary. Again, as we have seen already, the necessity of a Jewish male for an heir motivates the portrayal of Joseph. Because of his focus on obtaining an heir, Joseph is obviously upset when Mary becomes pregnant before their marriage. He first blames himself for not protecting her, but then he blames her.

Here, *The Gospel According to the Son* draws on two legends about Joseph. Both the *Book of James* (Protoevangelium) and the *History of Joseph the Carpenter* (fourth century) show Joseph to be a widower with children from a previous marriage, and both show him marrying a twelve-year-old Mary (Blair 980). Mailer's Joseph is an older widower, but his Joseph is one who wants children. This modifies Joseph's character in two ways: First, it allows Mailer's book to make Joseph more human by having him become angry when he first hears of Mary's pregnancy. However, he quickly recovers himself and decides to put her away quietly, which is more in line with the gospel accounts.

Second, it explains the debate over Jesus' brothers and sisters. Since Jesus is not Joseph's true heir, he feels the need to create heirs of his own. If Mailer's Joseph had been an older widower with children, he would have felt no compulsion to carry on his family line. And, in fact, he may have been too old to do so, had Mailer not made this minor change.

Mailer's Jewishness stands in stark contrast to Burgess' Roman Catholic background here. Burgess' book is so concerned about keeping Mary's perpetual virginity intact that it ignores the possible reaction that Joseph probably has to news of Mary's pregnancy. Yes, he would be upset that she cheated on him, but when the angel tells him that Jesus is from God, he should have a much stronger reaction than he does. Mailer, on the other hand, knows the importance of Joseph's producing a true heir, so he removes the children from the Joseph legend.

What makes Mary's pregnancy more troublesome for both Joseph and Mary, though, is that Mailer's book presents them as members of the Essene community.[3] Since sexual sins were viewed much more severely by the Essene community than by ordinary Jews, Joseph rightly deduces that Mary could be stoned to death if he told the Essene priests about her pregnancy out of wedlock. This change heightens Joseph's righteousness in his willingness to put Mary away quietly. Rather than simply being held to Jewish law, by having them as members of the Essene community, Mailer's book raises the stakes of consequences for Mary. Thus, instead of being shunned by her family and community, she would probably be killed. And this change makes Joseph's actions seem even better by comparison.

Joseph's reaction to the news that Mary is pregnant is one of the defining characteristics about him in the biblical accounts. He has been betrothed to Mary, yet he finds out that she is pregnant, and he decides to end their relationship. He plans to do so quietly, though, because he "was a righteous man and did not want to expose her to public disgrace" (Matt. 1:19). However, an angel appears to him and convinces him to marry her anyway and raise the child as his own. It is his reaction to Mary's news that is important here. Joseph has every right to bring her before the religious leaders of the day and have the betrothal annulled, leading to Mary's being ostracized by the community. But, because he is a "righteous man," he plans to put her away quietly, as Mailer's portrayal of Joseph shows.

Burgess' book may have Joseph related to the Essenes, as well. His injury seems to have made him consider joining a group of either Gnostics or Essenes in his younger days, though it is unclear which. The group is described merely as "a very cleanly sect [sic] of people who believed only in the spirit, condemning the body and the things of the body as evil, eating and drinking with groans and dunging [sic] in horror" (32). His loose affiliation with this group leads people to believe that his account of his injury has been invented and that it is his association with this group that has kept him pure.

---

[3]Oddly enough, the only other author I found that clearly has Joseph as an Essene is Christopher Moore in *Lamb*. Since his book is not the most serious account of Jesus' life, it seems strange that both he and Mailer would reach the same conclusion regarding Joseph's background.

Thus, when Joseph finds out about Mary's pregnancy, he is convinced that she has cheated on him. One of the few times Burgess' book strays from the gospel accounts is when it shows Joseph reacting angrily to Mary's confession, with no indication that he plans to put her away quietly, though the book also does not show his saying that he will bring her before the law. Instead, Mary simply tells him to go home and that they will talk about it the next day, knowing that God will speak with him that night, and an angel does appear to ease Joseph's mind. Throughout the entire debate, it is clear that Mary is portrayed as the person in control of the situation, a fitting depiction given Burgess' background.

The Last Temptation of Christ goes beyond this resolution and also creates a physical problem for Joseph to explain the silence in the gospels. For Kazantzakis' book, though, the physical problem may have a supernatural cause. On Mary and Joseph's wedding day, Joseph is struck by lightning and paralyzed, though obviously not to the extent that it prevented their having children (Jesus has brothers, which dispels the idea of Mary's perpetual virginity). It is interesting that Kazantzakis' book does not use this event to prevent Mary and Joseph from having children, unlike the accident that Burgess' book ascribes to Joseph. Joseph's injury in Kazantzakis' novel does not preclude at least one aspect of a normal, married life, while Burgess' novel clearly uses an injury to show that Joseph and Mary's marriage is not sexually normal.

Before this event, though, Joseph seems blessed by God: "When the marriage candidates were assembled, the staff of Joseph—among so many others—was the only one to blossom" (23). Kazantzakis, like Burgess and Mailer, seems to be drawing on an event from *The Book of James* (*Protoevanglium*). There, Mary is dedicated at the temple when she is a child, and, when she is twelve, the priest decides it is time for her to marry. He gathers a group of widowers together, and "a dove leaves the staff of Joseph and flies onto his head"; thus, he must be the man. Joseph tries to argue with the priest, pointing out that he is old and already has sons, but the priest assures him it should be this way (Cunneen 69–71). Although in Kazantzakis' retelling the event changes from a dove's leaving Joseph's staff to his staff's blossoming, the underlying idea is the same. Out of a pool of marriage candidates, Joseph is the one miraculously chosen to be Mary's husband.

It is easy to see both the blossoming of the staff and the lightning strike as evidence that Joseph will be involved with something wonderful, but the lightning strike and paralysis seem nothing more than an effective way to remove Joseph from the remainder of Jesus' life. In fact, he is seldom mentioned when Jesus still lives at home, and, even then, it is only negatively, as Mary seems to have gotten tired of taking care of him. And his removal from the novel seems to make Mary less likeable. Kazantzakis' novel may simply be trying to humanize Mary, tiring of taking care of an invalid for so many years; however, the work provides ample evidence for her humanity elsewhere.

After Jesus' birth, Ricci's book shows Joseph taking the family to Alexandria because the people of Bethlehem (where Joseph lived and where Jesus was born) know Jesus is not Joseph's child. In Alexandria, not only do the people not know, they do not care. After Mary has Yaqob (James), Jesus' brother, Joseph is satisfied with her; however, he favors all the male children Mary has after Jesus. This attitude is not surprising since male heirs are important to carry on the family name and Jesus, in Ricci's novel, is simply a bastard child, not the result of a virgin birth. Joseph, in fact, is happy when Jesus leaves home when he is ten. An infant girl who is never named dies with no mark on her, and the family thinks that Jesus is the cause: "Yehoceph [Joseph] said, There is a curse on us, and we all understood him to mean Yeshua [Jesus], though he would not say it" (250).

Both Burgess' and Mailer's novels portray Joseph much more positively than does Ricci's. In Burgess' novel, it is clear Jesus respects Joseph as a true father, though Jesus knows he is not. When Joseph dies of old age, Jesus tells him, "You have had a son's love, and you will always have it, for, since love is an aspect of our heavenly father and cannot die, so the loved and lover must also live forever" (84). Jesus then takes up carpentry, as he was taught by his father, to keep his earthly father's business going.

Burgess portrays the relationship between Joseph and Jesus as ideal, in fact, and it lays the groundwork for Jesus' talking about God as father positively.

However, it makes them into mere types of a father-son relationship rather than a more realistic one. While it is believable that Joseph has accepted Jesus as his true son (or simply the Son of God, which would further influence a positive relationship), it seems unlikely that there would be no tension. Thus, even though Burgess' novel doesn't clearly portray Jesus as a perfect child, the implication abides through his relationship with Joseph.

Mailer's book actually shows Joseph helping to prod Jesus into being more than a carpenter. When Jesus is twelve, Joseph tells Jesus about his miraculous birth.[4] After Jesus is lost on the trip back to Nazareth after visiting Jerusalem, Mary and Joseph find him in the temple speaking with the wise men. As in the gospel account, these men are impressed with Jesus' wisdom at such an age, so much so that Mary refuses to tell Jesus what he said when he was there, only that "[his] words were so holy she could not repeat them, no more than she could speak the name of the Lord aloud" (8). Jesus, however, forgets this story and forgets what Joseph has told him about his birth until he is praying at Joseph's funeral eighteen years later. It is at this point that Jesus begins to realize that he is called to be something more than a carpenter.

One of the main questions that comes up when people discuss the divinity of Christ is how or when he knew that he was the Son of God. Interestingly, Mailer's book uses Joseph as the means to that knowledge. It is difficult to believe, though, that anyone who hears such a story at twelve years old could truly forget that he was the Son of God. While it may be that Mailer's book is trying to offer a persuasive rationale for why it takes so long for Jesus to begin his ministry, the solution is awkward. It might have been simpler for Joseph to tell Jesus when Jesus is almost thirty and Joseph is about to die.

Ricci's view of Joseph is more balanced than that of either Burgess or Mailer. Here, Mary spends most of her married life believing she does not love Joseph, but after he dies, she mourns him when she realizes what a good husband he has been to her. She grieves for him and discovers that she loved

---

[4]While Mailer, a Jewish author, has a Joseph who seems to know much about Jesus, Reynolds Price, a Christian, presents a Joseph who does not even know Jesus is God's son, though he knows that Jesus is not his own (244).

him. He gave her a better life than she would have had otherwise. He was always good to her (272).

She even appreciates the way he has lived his life, despite what she has been unable or unwilling to do for him: "For here was a man who had worked all his days even to the final one, and who had known little comfort from his wife, whom he had married in disgrace, and yet somehow he had taken meaning from the things of his life, which was only in the birth of his sons and the thought of their prospering" (272).

Joseph is portrayed less positively than in his brief mention in the gospels, where he is willing to put Mary away quietly after she becomes pregnant, but he is also not portrayed negatively, as in some of the other novels. Instead, he is shown to be a typical Jewish man who seeks only an heir to keep his name alive, but who is also fair to those around him. This portrayal suggests a more righteous Joseph than do the others because it makes him more human. Rather than the ideal portrayal in Burgess' novel or as the cause of Jesus' knowledge of his divinity in Mailer's *Testament*, Joseph is a man simply trying to do what he believes is good, much like many readers. It is the humanizing of Joseph that truly makes this righteousness seem real.

The Gospel According to Jesus Christ adds more to the character of Joseph than do any of the other authors, straying the most from the more common portrayal of Joseph. When Mary and Joseph are in Bethlehem, Joseph gets a job working at the Temple in order to earn some money, as he and Mary cannot return to Nazareth for thirty days after Jesus' birth, while Mary is ceremonially unclean from the birth. One day, while Joseph is working, he overhears three soldiers discussing their latest assignment: they are to kill all the children under the age of three.

He immediately leaves work and runs to the cave where he and Mary have been living since their arrival in Bethlehem. Without telling Mary why, he tells her that they have to hide in the cave until morning, then leave before sunrise. Only later does he tell her why. Joseph's reaction seems credible, but later he is punished for what he did, or, more correctly, what he did not do.

Because he does not warn the other inhabitants of Bethlehem and thinks only of his own child, he is haunted by a nightmare every night for the rest of his life. The nightmare has a detachment of soldiers, "with Joseph himself riding in their midst, sometimes brandishing a sword above his head, and it is just at that moment, when terror overwhelms him, that the leader of the expedition asks, Where do you think you're going, carpenter. And the poor man, who would rather not say, resists with all his might, but the malignant spirits in the dream are too strong for him, and they prise open his mouth with hands of steel, reducing him to tears and despair as he confesses, I'm on my way to Bethlehem to kill my son" (96). McKendrick argues that Joseph's decision to save his son makes him a more interesting character: "Yet one of the most decisive twists given to the New Testament . . . is the guilt which Joseph feels, having overheard Herod's soldiers, for not having warned the parents of Bethlehem. The remorse which haunts Joseph, and which Jesus inherits, is what literally humanizes them" (31). From the first night of his having this dream, Joseph attempts to sleep as little as possible. Mary and the children get used to his thrashing around at night, but the nightmare never goes away.

The Gospel According to Jesus Christ changes how Joseph obtains the knowledge and, possibly, a bit of the knowledge itself in a different way. The biblical account shows Joseph's being warned in a dream that Herod was "going to search for the child to kill him" (Matt. 2:13). Clearly, the means of Joseph's receiving the information is not divine but human in Saramago's work. However, one piece of information is different, as well. In the biblical story, it is not clear if Joseph knows whether or not Herod will kill other children in an attempt to kill Jesus, but the implication is that he does not. By making Joseph aware of this knowledge, Saramago's book makes him guilty of not attempting to save the other children, enriching him as a character in the process.

Joseph's guilt also leads to his death, which may relate to his dream. Jesus, at least, thinks that it does, as does a being that appears to Mary (it is unclear at this point in the novel if the being is an angel, a demon or even the Devil):

> Herod's cruelty unsheathed those swords but your selfishness
> and cowardice were the cords that bound the victims'
> hands and feet. . . . You could not have done anything, for
> you found out too late, but the carpenter could have done
> something, he could have warned the villagers that the
> soldiers were coming to kill their children when there was
> still time for parents to gather them up and escape, to hide
> in the wilderness, for example, or flee to Egypt and wait for
> Herod's death, which is fast approaching. (88)

Because of his selfishness, then, Joseph dies, despite being innocent of the crime for which he is executed. Judas the Galilean is leading a revolt against the Romans, and the Romans strike back by crucifying all the followers they find. Joseph hears that his neighbor, Ananias, who has joined the rebels, has been injured, so Joseph seeks him out. When he is at the camp with Ananias, Roman soldiers come and crucify everyone they find there, despite everyone's believing Joseph is innocent.[5] His death by crucifixion at the age of thirty-three for a crime he did not commit foreshadows Jesus' death, as well. Further connecting the two is the fact that Jesus begins to have a nightmare the day Joseph is crucified. He has the same dream as Joseph, save that his is from his point of view. He sees Joseph coming to kill him, but he is a baby again, and, thus, he cannot defend himself.

Like the angel, Jesus believes his father deserves his death because of Joseph's failure to warn the inhabitants of Bethlehem: "Father murdered the children of Bethlehem. . . . No, Father was to blame, Joseph son of Eli was to blame, because he knew those children were to be killed and did nothing to warn their parents" (151–52). Jesus' view of Joseph's actions will later affect why he is willingly crucified, as well.

All of the authors' novels try to deal with the questions of Joseph and Mary's other offspring, as well as Joseph's absence from Jesus' adult life.

---

[5]Christopher Moore, in *Lamb*, also has Joseph being falsely accused, though the accusation in Moore's work is that he killed a Roman centurion. The two stories are related, though, as a member of the Sicarii actually killed the centurion. Thus, in both cases, a rebellion is involved with Joseph's being falsely accused. In Moore's work, however, Jesus (Joshua in Moore) saves his father from death.

Some, like Saramago's, present a negative view of Joseph and show him suffering for his inaction; others, like Burgess' and Mailer's, show Joseph as one who was loved by Jesus and Mary; Ricci's novel, however, attempts to create a realistic portrayal of Joseph, one who wanted what other men in his community wanted, but one who was also loving in his own way.

CHAPTER 5

ℐ Foil and a ℱorerunner

JOHN THE BAPTIST'S ROLE

In the gospels, john the baptist has one main role: forerunner to the Messiah, Jesus. John's actions may go beyond this, especially in his criticism of Herod, but this role remains the centerpiece of his character. While Burgess, Kazantzakis, and Mailer include this role in their portrayals of John, what each focuses on is John's life. Instead of simply proclaiming the coming of Jesus, he is also shown to have shaped Jesus' teaching. In fact, Ricci's novel shows him as Jesus' teacher. This change coincides with other "fictional transfigurations" of John, as Theodore Ziolkowski writes, "Equally popular is the figure of John the Baptist, who is sometimes represented as an evangelical figure . . . and sometimes more soberly as the teacher or tutor of the transfigured hero" (279). This development of John's character leads some critics to see him as a stronger character than Jesus: "The same romanticism which makes John a more vivid figure than Jesus in Rembrandt, Kazantzakis, and 'Godspell' makes him a more historical figure than Jesus in much contemporary scholarship, despite the complete lack of evidence deriving directly from John's own movement" (Chilton 26). Though there is a lack of historical evidence concerning John, another critic observes he "figures prominently in the New Testament, where he is mentioned about ninety times, exclusively in the gospels and in Acts; only Jesus, Peter, and Paul are mentioned more often" (Lienhard 197). However, "what two or all three synoptic gospels relate about John falls easily into three episodes" (Lienhard 197). John's actions and teachings still lead to a focus on Jesus, but they now take on more meaning as John and Jesus struggle to determine Jesus' path together.

Though a cult of John the Baptist developed as early as the fourth century (Lienhard 197), there are no significant legends from the early church.

There is evidence of the cult as a statue of John "stood in the baptistery of the Lateran basilica, put there in Constantine's time. The fourth-century building boom in Palestine included a settlement of monks at Aenon, where John the Baptist had exercised his ministry (cf. Jn 3:23), and baptisms were administered there" (Lienhard 197). Thus, authors who decide to portray John must rely on the gospel stories and their imaginations.

As with the gospel accounts, the five authors focus on different aspects of John's life. Only Mailer' and Burgess's novels, following Luke's description, mention John's birth and background. According to Luke, John's father is a priest named Zechariah who is serving at the temple when an angel appears to him, much in the same way the angel appears to Mary with an important message. The angel tells Zechariah that he and Elizabeth will have a child to be named John; this child "is never to take wine or other fermented drink, and he will be filled with the Holy Spirit even from birth. Many of the people of Israel will he bring back to the Lord their God" (Luke 1:15–16).

Zechariah, however, is not sure that this truly is an angel and questions him. The angel, in response, renders Zechariah unable to talk until the birth of the child. From his birth, then, people know that John is somehow different from other children, in direct contrast to the humble and quiet early years of Jesus.

The Gospel According to the Son's John the Baptist, as in Luke, is Jesus' cousin. In fact, it is while Mary is away visiting Elizabeth, John's mother, that Joseph hears a voice telling him that he should marry Mary, and, as in the gospel narratives, John leaps in the womb when he hears Mary's voice. John's father, Zacharias, however, has a slightly different role in society. He is still a priest, as he is in the gospel stories, but in Mailer's novel, he has been an Essene priest. Mailer's novel uses this fact to explain why Zacharias and Elizabeth have not had a child: "they believed that the body must be kept as a temple. Only a pure body could offer pure prayers in the struggle against the powers of evil. Therefore, they remained childless" (25). Thus, in Mailer's book, it is not barrenness that prevents Elizabeth from conceiving; it is piety.

However, Elizabeth regrets not having a child, and here Mailer uses the word "barren" to describe her condition. In light of what Mailer's book has already told the reader about Zacharias and Elizabeth's beliefs, though, "barren" must be interpreted as meaning, simply, not having children. For, she prays for a child, and her prayer is heard. When Gabriel tells Zacharias this news, he questions the angel, as in the gospels, and he is struck dumb for doubting God's power. However, later that day, "he was able to rise and give issue to Elizabeth," Mailer states (26). This event lessens the significance of the miracle from what it bears in the gospel accounts. By ascribing Elizabeth's inability to have children to Zacharias and Elizabeth's abstinence out of religious beliefs, Mailer's book implies that they could have had children at any time had they simply wanted to. Why Zacharias is surprised by the news of his wife's pregnancy, then, is inexplicable unless there is the possibility the angel is undermining religious teachings. That is out of the ordinary, but it is no miracle.

Mailer's novel also uses John's Essene background to explain his habits, unlike the gospel accounts, in which the angel tells Zechariah that John should take the Nazarite vows, which, according to Numbers 6:3–6, included not drinking any fermented drink, eating of anything that comes from the grape-vine, or cutting one's hair. Instead, according to Mailer's book, John's leanness is credited to his parents, based on their Essene beliefs, which diminishes any connection between John the Baptist and the Nazarites of the Old Testament and removes the connection the gospel accounts find for John as a continuation of the Old Testament prophetic tradition.

In Burgess' novel, also, John the Baptist's beginnings are similar to what is told in the gospel stories. Zacharias is performing his priestly duty when an angel appears to him, telling him that he and Elizabeth will have a son. Zacharias does not believe him, and he is struck dumb. When he arrives home, he writes out for Elizabeth what has happened, and they await the birth of their son, whom they believe to be special, perhaps even the Messiah. Burgess, as he often does, merely retells the gospel account with a bit more exposition, not adding anything to the characters as they are presented.

According to the gospels, when John becomes an adult, he begins to preach a message of repentance and preparation: "Produce fruit in keeping with repentance"; "Prepare the way for the Lord, make straight paths for him"; and "I baptize you with water. But one more powerful than I will come, the thongs of whose sandals I am not worthy to untie" (Luke 3:8, 4, 16). John clearly recognizes his place as a harbinger of the Messiah, but not as the Messiah himself. In fact, according to Matthew (and only Matthew, interestingly), John does not even feel that he should baptize Jesus: "I need to be baptized by you, and do you come to me?" (Matt. 3:14). Jesus refers to John as the one who was to come before the Messiah and sees John as the greatest in the kingdom of heaven (though the least in the kingdom is somehow greater than John): "For all the Prophets and the Law prophesied until John. And if you are willing to accept it, he is the Elijah who was to come" (Matt. 11:13–14).

Burgess' novel focuses on this role for John as the precursor of the Messiah, as do Kazantzakis' and Mailer's.[1] Saramago's book mentions John's baptizing Jesus, but it is an anticlimactic scene. In fact, all of these authors' works tend to treat the baptism scene as if they are checking off another item on a list that they must cover in presenting the story of Jesus.

Burgess, throughout his work, makes prophecies seem obvious to his characters. Thus, whenever they need to fulfill a prophecy, they go about it with a sense of duty. When Jesus approaches John to be baptized, "each permitted himself a smile of greeting" (107) before they exchange the words they know they have to say. The action is perfunctory and quick, with no explication at all. After Jesus is baptized, John tells Philip and Andrew, two of his disciples, that they should go to Nazareth, as that is where the ministry is to begin. This portrayal is consistent with Burgess' matter-of-fact methodology, as the outcomes always seem to be foreordained to those who

---

[1] Only Christopher Moore, in *Lamb*, has a John the Baptist who ever believes that he might be the Messiah. When they are teenagers and he has already begun baptizing people, he tells Joshua (Jesus), "You think you're the one, don't you? Well, you're not. My birth was announced by an angel as well. It was prophesied that I would lead. You're not the one" (87). It's easy to hear the teenaged voice coming through Moore's portrayal here, as it's clear that John wants to be the one, in typical teenaged mode. However, after John hears that Joshua can raise the dead and after Joshua heals John of a rash he acquired from spending too much time in the water baptizing people, he believes that Joshua is the Messiah.

know the story, and the characters, especially his Jesus, certainly already know the story.

John the Baptist is the harbinger of the Messiah in Kazantzakis' novel, but he is not introduced until halfway. He is mentioned earlier, as Andrew, Peter's brother, has been a follower of John before he comes to join Jesus. However, Jesus has already begun his ministry before he goes to talk to John, and he only does so then because he and Judas want to know if Jesus really is the Messiah or not, and they agree to let John decide.

John's message is just as it is in the gospels: "Repent! Repent! The day of the Lord has come! Roll on the ground, bite the dust, howl! The Lord of Hosts has said: 'On this day I shall command the sun to set at noon; I shall crush the horns of the new moon and spill darkness over heaven and earth. I shall reverse your laughter, turn it into tears, and your songs into lamentation. I shall blow, and all your finery—hands, feet, noses, ears, hair—will fall to the ground'" (237). It is not until after Jesus' baptism that Kazantzakis' novel begins to develop John more fully.

In Mailer's novel, people still mistake John for the Messiah. The High Priest sends Levites to John to ask him directly if he is the Messiah they have been expecting because he preaches with such force. John is even clearer in Mailer's work than he is in the New Testament in response to this question: "I baptize with water, no more. I am not the Messiah" (28).

Saramago's novel has a simple scene that makes the encounter with John nothing more than a step Jesus must pass before his crucifixion. John the Baptist is not mentioned here until about thirty pages before Jesus' crucifixion and the end of the book. John questions Jesus as to what he has been able to do, and Jesus responds with the answer that, in the Biblical versions, he gives to John's disciples who ask him if he is the one they are to expect: "the blind regain their sight and the lame walk, the lepers are made clean and the deaf hear, and the poor have the gospel preached to them" (356). John then baptizes Jesus and exits without saying anything more. This is the only encounter between the two of them, as Saramago's novel does not develop the family connections or give John any other role in Jesus' life.

In the novels where Jesus and John have more interaction, it seems that their relationship is strained, nowhere more so than in Kazantzakis' novel. There, Jesus and John disagree on the message that Jesus is supposed to bring. Until his encounter with John, Jesus' message had been one of love and love only. John, however, believes that anger and fire should be the message of the Messiah: "How can you love the unjust, the infamous and the shameless? Strike! One of man's greatest obligations is anger" (242). However, he does baptize Jesus despite having lingering doubts about Jesus as the Messiah. Before Jesus goes into the desert to wrestle with God and Satan, John gives Jesus some advice:

> Change your expression, strengthen your arms, make firm
> your heart. Your life is a heavy one. I see blood and thorns on
> your brow. Endure, my brother and superior, courage! Two
> roads open up in front of you: the road of man, which is level,
> and the road of God, which ascends. Take the more difficult
> road. Farewell! And don't feel afflicted at partings. Your duty
> is not to weep; it is to strike. Strike! and may you have a steady
> hand! That is your road. Both ways are the daughters of God,
> do not forget that. But Fire was born first and Love afterward.
> Let us begin therefore with Fire. (243)

It is not until his time in the desert and the death of John the Baptist, though, that Jesus does take up the ax that John has laid down. In fact, when the disciples see him after his time in the desert, it seems as if Jesus and John have somehow merged: "His forcefully clinched fist, his hair, cheeks and eyes were identical with those of the Baptist. The open-mouthed disciples looked at him silently. Could the two men have joined and become one? . . . The companions shuddered, for this was not his own voice; it was the voice of the fearful prophet, the Baptist" (294). For Kazantzakis' novel, Jesus needs John in order to be complete and to supply to his ministry the Fire needed for the mission on earth, even as he preaches the Love he feels that God is calling him to preach. The depiction of Jesus in the gospels is often taken to be nothing more than a messenger of love; however, many of Jesus' parables end with comments strikingly similar to John's, with people being cast out into darkness where there is weeping and gnashing of teeth. Kazantzakis' novel expands this idea to show John as the means behind that portion of the message, thus making more balanced a Jesus who combines mercy and justice, as opposed to conveying only the extreme message of John.

Burgess' novel also shows Jesus and John disagreeing about Jesus' message. It crafts a childhood event involving both John and Jesus to illustrate the main difference between their teachings. They are in Jerusalem for the Passover, and they are walking off by themselves, discussing ideas, such as whether to believe in fathers and what is the origin of mankind when a prostitute overhears them and joins in the discussion. Jesus is polite to her, though he turns down her offer; John tells him that he should "by rights have rebuked her. It is a sinful profession" (77). Jesus reminds John that he could have rebuked her, which John claims to have been doing with his stern expression. Jesus admits that her actions are sinful, but: "I liked the girl. She was not respectable. It is respectability that I hate, and yet respectability is not put among the sins." He tells John that if they have any true calling in the future, "it is among the sinners [they] must go," but John cannot accept with this. He believes that "to like sinners is to like sin." Jesus responds with what, in Burgess' novel, will become the cornerstone of his message: "Ah no, not at all. It is as much as to say that to cherish the sick is to cherish their sickness. Let me not say *like* either. *Love* is the needful word" (78).

In their ministries, John focuses on the repentance of sin, as he criticizes almost everyone he encounters, from the Pharisees to Herod. Jesus, however, presents a message of love to those who are unloved by the rest of the society, especially the religious leaders. He balances this message of love, though, with one of justice, especially in his criticism of the religious leaders, as he thinks they are more concerned with being respectable than with doing what is right.

This tension between John and Jesus is only implicit in the gospels. Some people try to compare Jesus and John, often through the actions of their disciples. Some Pharisees and teachers of the law say to Jesus, "John's disciples often fast and pray, and so do the disciples of the Pharisees, but yours go on eating and drinking" (Luke 5:33). Even in the book of Acts, there are those who have been baptized by John but have not heard about Jesus. In fact, there are still some who trace there religious heritage to John but do not claim him as Messiah. A small group of followers in Mesopotamia, called the Mandeans, attempt to continue John's movement. And one of John's disciples, briefly mentioned in the *Clementine Recognitions*, claims that John is actually the Messiah, not Jesus (Farmer 962).

Mailer's story goes beyond disagreement between Jesus and John to present a John who sees himself as a teacher and a Jesus as someone who needs to learn from this teacher. When Jesus seeks John, it is not for approval of his upcoming ministry; instead, he says that he is "one more pilgrim" (28). John, though, has been waiting for Jesus, expecting his arrival at any time. However, John treats him as just another pilgrim up until the baptism. John clearly implies that Jesus has sinned and needs to repent. Upon Jesus' protestations that he has few, small sins, John responds, "Well, you can still repent. Our sin is always more than we know" (31). John willingly baptizes Jesus, in direct contrast to the gospel account in which he believes he is unfit to baptize Jesus. In fact, in Mailer's version John seems eager to get his duty done, so that he can finish his life: "I have been told to wait for you, and I am tired. It is good that you are here" (29).

However, when Jesus comes out of the water, John either senses that Jesus is now different, or, perhaps, John at least hopes that is the case. He seems to want Jesus to be the Messiah, but he doesn't know if he is or not. Thus, John asks him, "Did the light of the Lord appear when you were immersed?" Jesus responds with a question of his own: "Is it not death and destruction to see Him?" (36). John knows at that moment that Jesus is the Messiah and simply responds, "For all but the Christ" (37). At that point, he simply tells Jesus that he has always known this day would come, and he leaves Jesus there. This portrayal of John is a combination of what is presented in the gospels, as Mailer's John has been waiting for Jesus, with a more modern skepticism, since John is not certain that Jesus is the Messiah even after he has baptized him. Rather than relying on a mystical feeling, he needs at least a minimum of empirical evidence to decide that Jesus is the Messiah.

Ricci's story takes the idea of John as Jesus' teacher even further. John is a teacher in the desert, and Jesus is one of his disciples.[2] John "went among the Jews preaching justice for the common people and condemning every sort of hypocrisy" (282). He is put to death by Herod for criticizing Herod's relationship with his brother's wife, and, thus, he sends his followers away from him. A man in a crowd accuses Jesus of deserting John at this time: "There are more who believe in him now because they saw he was ready to die when Herod took him. But some of those who were with him just ran off" (362).

Jesus, however, tells his disciples the true story of what happened. John tried to send all of his disciples away, but they refuse to leave. John says that six of them can stay, but six of them must leave; that way people will not say they were cowards, and there will also be some left to spread John's teaching. Jesus draws a short straw, so he must leave, which he does not want to do. Those who stay are butchered by the Romans, and, in fact, some of the six who are supposed to leave return and are also killed with John. Thus, Jesus says, ". . . it seemed cowardly that I'd gone. I didn't know if I could go on then. Here was my teacher in prison, and my friends dead, and I hadn't done anything" (368). This portrayal of John certainly raises his stature higher than what he merits in the other novels and in the gospels. John is much more in control of the situation, though neither he nor Jesus knows what the future holds. As such, this scene thereby lowers the stature of Jesus to someone who is much more human while elevating John to the level of spiritual teacher, though not beyond any humanly possible level of spiritual enlightenment.

In the gospels, as in Ricci's novel, John is ultimately killed by Herod because of a request by Herodias, his brother's wife. John criticizes Herod for his relationship with Herodias, but Herod is unwilling to put him to death for his criticism. However, Herodias, who is furious with John's comments,

---

[2]In *Lamb*, Christopher Moore shows John teaching Jesus for over a year, and, in fact, it is John who identifies the Divine Spark that Jesus has learned about as the Holy Ghost.

has her daughter dance for Herod. Herod is so enchanted with the dance that he offers the daughter anything, up to half his kingdom. She asks for the head of John the Baptist on a platter, and Herod must comply with this request (Matt. 14:1–12).

Like Ricci, almost all of these authors, with the exception of Kazantzakis, tell the story of John's death. In Burgess' novel, John becomes well-known for criticizing Herod for marrying his brother's wife. Herod and John, though, are actually distant cousins. Thus, when John presses through the crowd to confront Herod with his sin, he is allowed to get near enough to Herod to speak clearly: "The man you call your king is a sinner and a foul sinner. The woman he calls his wife is an adulteress and an incestuous fornicator. The sin is upon you all who abet the sin" (102). His constant rebuke of Herod eventually gets him thrown into prison, though at Herodias' insistence. Because of Herod's familial relationship with John, he is reluctant to do anything to John, including kill him. Thus, Herodias must trick Herod into committing himself to Salome so that she can ask for John's head. This is slightly different from the gospel stories in which Herod's reluctance to kill John comes from the people's perception of John and because Herod likes to listen to him. By making John and Herod relatives, Burgess' novel takes away an important dimension of Herod and of John, as Herod is no longer afraid of what the people think of John, and John ceases to have the power to sway the people including even Herod.

Mailer's book also follows the gospel accounts and shows John being thrown into prison for criticizing Herod and shows that he is later beheaded at the request of Salome, who dances so well for Herod that he promised her anything she asks, even up to half his kingdom. John's death leads to Jesus' anxieties about being killed, especially when his disciples tell him that the people are beginning to believe that Jesus is John resurrected. Thus, Jesus sends his disciples out, while he stays in a cave to deal with his fears: "I did not often sleep. Alone in my cave, I looked for solace in the thought that God was near while Herod Antipas was in his palace and far away" (113). Therefore, Jesus has to deal with the fear of his death even earlier than the night in the Garden of Gethsemane; Mailer evidently decides, then, to have

John's death serve as the catalyst of Jesus' fear. In the gospels, Jesus' reaction to John's imprisonment and death is to use John as an example of one who preaches the truth; this change shows a Jesus who struggles with human temptations throughout his ministry, not just at his death, thus providing readers with a Jesus who is more easily identified with.

What is also interesting is that the authors who do mention John's death at the hands of Herod rely on the gospel accounts, and not the historical record. John is put to death by Herod, as Josephus relates in *Antiquities*, but not for the reason given in the gospels. Instead, as Farmer writes, "John was arrested because Herod feared the political consequences of his popularity" (959). This does not mean that Herod did not have any ill will toward John for the criticism of Herod's lifestyle, but it should be noted that Herod probably would have seen those comments as treasonous more so than religious. Given these authors' propensities to salvage interesting character traits from history, it is surprising that none of them, especially Ricci, who draws heavily on historical criticism, develop this aspect of John's character.

Saramago's novel briefly mentions John's beheading by Herod just a few pages after John has criticized Herod's relationship with Herodias; however, Saramago merely summarizes the event. John does preach in the wilderness, but after Jesus has already begun his ministry; in fact, Jesus has performed most of his miracles and gathered all of his disciples before John is even introduced. John becomes an even more minor character in Saramago's presentation than in the gospels.

Other than Saramago, these authors' works show a John in tension with Jesus, trying to guide his teachings, much more so than is presented in the gospels. In fact, John's death by Herod is less important for what happens to John than to show how Jesus reacts. Thus, though John is not always shown to be a forerunner of Jesus, John's character is used to shift the focus to Jesus.

CHAPTER 6

Merely a Means of
Temptation, for Most

THE DEVIL'S ROLE

Contrary to what most people believe, there is little biblical information on Satan or the Devil. As Gary Galeotti points out, "there are fewer than 120 verses that refer directly to either Satan or the Devil" (72). Because of this paucity, these authors mainly focus on one aspect of the Devil that is presented in the gospels. For most of these authors, the Devil serves merely as a means of temptation for Jesus. These authors' works, however, do not make the Devil responsible for Judas' action[1]; instead, they focus on Jesus' struggles with his temptations. Burgess shows this through the scene of Jesus' temptation in the wilderness, though there does not seem to be much doubt that Jesus will prevail. Both Mailer's and Kazantzakis' books start with this scene, but they provide Jesus with other temptations by the Devil. Saramago's book creates a complex Devil who seems to know as much as God and who may somehow be connected to God, as well. Ricci's story, however, completely ignores the Devil, as he ignores most of the supernatural aspects of the gospels.

Almost all of these authors portray the Devil as the cause of some sort of temptation. Burgess', Mailer's, and Kazantzakis' novels all show Jesus being tempted by the Devil in the wilderness, and both Mailer's and Kazantzakis' show the Devil tempting Jesus at other times, as well. Saramago's novel creates a Devil who seems to be guiding Jesus throughout

---

[1]Margaret George's novel *Mary Called Magdalene* seems to have Judas become possessed by Satan, though it's never clear. While camping at Dan, a place with an evil history for the Israelites, Judas "felt its evil influence. In fact, this morning his eyes looked clouded, different" (434). This description suggests the depiction of Mary's eyes when she is possessed by the demons. After Mary learns of Judas' plan to betray Jesus, she thinks that Satan may be behind it: "Could Satan have entered into [Judas] back at that dreadful, haunted altar at Dan? Satan tried to get Jesus in the desert; he failed, but he got Judas instead at Dan" (487).

parts of his book, but who also seems to know as much as God. In fact, the Devil tempts God at the end, and Jesus seems to be at a loss as to which one to believe.

The Devil is notable in Ricci's book by his absence. There is no temptation scene in the wilderness, though Ricci indicates that Jesus spent time in the wilderness after Herod's soldiers came for John. There are no demons to cast out, only illnesses and injuries from which to be healed. Jesus seems to exist in a world with God, whom he talks about, but without the Devil, whom he never mentions. This approach is not surprising given Ricci's comment in his notes at the end of his novel that he drew a number of his ideas from the Jesus Seminar, a group of historians who seek to determine how the historical Jesus lived. They put little stock in anything supernatural, especially the Devil.

What is particularly interesting is that Ricci's approach comes closest of these authors to that of the early church, though for very different reasons. The early church seems to have largely ignored the Devil. As Robert Wernick writes, "It took three or four centuries of debate and speculation for the church to settle on a unified but not quite consistent picture of his history and functions." It developed the ideas that most people associate with the Devil: he has once been an angel who rebels against God, though the church is not clear as to why or even when; he has been cast into hell; and he will be judged, once and for all, on the Day of Judgment, and condemned to eternal torment (Wernick).

Wernick hypothesizes that one of the reasons the early church did not seem to be concerned with the Devil is that it had greater concerns at the time: "Perhaps the early Christians, members of a small persecuted sect faced with the daily possibility of meeting the representatives of the Roman state in the form of gladiators, lions and howling mobs in arenas, did not need to dream up faces for the Devil." Also, early Christians believed that Jesus had defeated the Devil and that Jesus was coming back very soon. Why, then, did they need to concern themselves with the Devil's role in the world when he was already defeated, and they would soon be with God in heaven? The early Christians seemed more concerned with understanding God and Jesus than they did with trying to understand the Devil.

Thus, Ricci's decision to ignore the Devil and focus on Jesus is similar to the early church's approach; however, Ricci seems to have made this decision out of a lack of belief while the early church accepted the reality of the Devil but did not take time to discuss him.

Burgess', Mailer's, and Kazantzakis' novels all present the Devil's tempting Jesus in the wilderness, following the gospels. In the Synoptic gospels the Devil (or Satan, as he is sometimes called in the gospels) shows up when Jesus goes into the wilderness to fast for forty days. He appears to Jesus there and presents him with three temptations: turning rocks into bread, throwing himself down from the temple where the angels should catch him, and receiving power in return for worshipping the Devil. Jesus, of course, resists these temptations, and the Devil leaves him to return at a more opportune time. Jesus also refers to the Devil quite a few times in his ministry, though he doesn't make a direct appearance again. In the parable of the sower, the Devil prevents some people from hearing the Word, and Satan has also kept a woman in physical bondage (she has been crippled for eighteen years) until Jesus heals her (Luke 13:16).

Burgess' Devil only shows up in the temptation scene at the beginning of Jesus' ministry. 74, as he presents himself to Jesus in a variety of images. The Devil takes on the shape of Jesus' mother Mary, calling Jesus to come home, claiming that she is sick. The Devil also pretends to be a beggar in the wilderness who questions whether or not evil is necessary, leading to a discussion of free will. Only at the end of Jesus' time in the wilderness does Satan present the three temptations found in the gospels.

However, Burgess' novel treats these temptations as if they are a mere formality for Jesus before beginning the ministry. There is never any question that Jesus will reject these temptations. In fact, the Devil seems to know which verses Jesus will quote in refutation, and he often provides the scripture references in the middle of Jesus' answer.

Thus, evil seems to be largely absent from Burgess' work. The focus is on Jesus' teachings concerning love, and evil seems to be something that exists nowhere near Jesus. Even the betrayals by Peter and Judas are shown to be mere slip-ups that are easily remedied, and the Pharisees' plotting is shown as simply something that must be done to accomplish God's plan. In Burgess' book, the world is well-controlled by God, and evil exists only to further God's plan, yet Jesus repeatedly emphasizes a free will that never seems to appear in Burgess' vision.

Burgess' approach ignores the gospel's focus on Judas as an instrument of Satan. The books of Luke and John both show Satan entering Judas, and in John Jesus refers to Judas as a Devil, not just a traitor (John 6:70). Whether the gospel writers mean that Judas is actually possessed at the time he betrays Jesus or whether they are simply trying to show the depth of evil involved in his act is unclear;[2] regardless, the fact that they use that term shows a recognition of evil that is markedly absent from Burgess' novel.

In Mailer's book, as in the gospel stories, the Devil doesn't make many appearances. His most important role is early in Jesus' life when he appears to Jesus in the wilderness to tempt him. Mailer uses Satan for that role, and he mainly expands Satan's knowledge of scripture to make a longer debate than in the gospels. Satan leads Jesus through the rejection of the temptations of turning stones to bread, throwing himself down from the Great Temple, and worshipping Satan to attain power. Jesus resists these temptations, but after his encounter with the Devil is over, he says, "Nor did I feel that I had escaped altogether" (56). This closing line is cryptic, and Mailer's novel never seems to return to it. Mailer may be referring to Luke 4:13, which says that the Devil left Jesus after the time in the wilderness "until an opportune time." Luke here seems to be reminding his readers that temptations are not just a one-time event, but that the Devil keeps coming, always at opportune times. Mailer may be referring to this verse to indicate that Jesus will face temptations later in his ministry, as Mailer depicts Satan's influence continuing in Jesus' life, in obvious temptations and more subtly.

---

[2]This description of Judas as a Devil is strikingly similar to Jesus' referring to Peter as "Satan" because he does not want Jesus to go to Jerusalem to be crucified (Matt. 16:23).

Kazantzakis' book also makes the Devil appear to Jesus in the desert, claiming that he feels sorry for Jesus who was crying out that he does not want to be alone. As in the Garden of Eden, the Devil appears in the guise of a snake, though this snake also has the "eyes and breasts of a woman" (255). Kazantzakis' Devil also presents Jesus with sexual temptation, not just through the description of the snake, but also through the snake's mentioning Mary Magdalene: ". . . it's Magdalene you must save! . . . Not the Earth—forget about the Earth. It's her, Magdalene, you must save!" (256). However, Kazantzakis' Devil tempts Jesus not just with sex with Mary Magdalene but with the idea of marrying her.

Unlike Burgess' story, though, Kazantzakis shows the Devil returning to tempt Jesus at the end of the novel when he, appearing as Jesus' guardian angel, tempts Jesus with a vision of his life as it could have been if he had not sacrificed himself on the cross. In the desert, Jesus thinks, "But thanks to Magdalene, God bless her, he would be cured; he would return to his workshop, take up once more his old beloved craft, once more make plows, cradles and troughs; he would have children and become a human being, the master of a household" (257). Jesus resists this temptation, though, by acknowledging that God's will shall be done, while in the desert, and through the support of Judas, as will be shown, when Jesus is tempted on the cross.

The other temptations that the Devil presents to Jesus are those of power and even of becoming God himself. The Devil appears to Jesus as a traveler in the desert and as an archangel, but Jesus recognizes him for who he actually is. In both guises, the Devil reminds Jesus of his childhood wish for power: "Do you remember when you were a small child still unable to walk, you clung to the door of your house and to your mother's clothes so that you would not fall, and shouted within yourself, shouted loudly, 'God, make me God! God, make me God! God, make me God!'" (263). The Devil even tells Jesus that the dove at his baptism called Jesus the son of God. Although this turns out to be true, the Devil is using the event here to cause Jesus to think of himself highly, putting pride before his mission of salvation. While most readers are unable to identify with Jesus' particular temptation of power, Kazantzakis reminds his readers that most of us have, at some point in our lives, craved power and that we may not have given up such childhood desires. The fact that the Devil exploits this desire when tempting Jesus is Kazantzakis' way of reminding readers that the Devil does the same to us.

The main, underlying temptation—the "last temptation" of the title—that runs throughout Kazantzakis' novel is the appearance of the Devil as Mary Magdalene. It is not just that Jesus is tempted sexually by the appearance of the Devil as Mary Magdalene; it is the fact that Jesus simply wants a normal life. The Devil preys upon this longing when Jesus is on the cross, and it is only thanks to Judas that Jesus does not succumb. This temptation reveals something about both Jesus and the Devil. It humanizes Jesus, making him more like the reader, someone who does not want to accomplish anything greater in life than just to live a simple, normal, happy life. For the Devil, however, the temptation expands the role he plays in the gospels and shows how he attacks one's weakest spot. Most of us cannot identify with the temptation to turn stones into bread or rule all the kingdoms of the world, but most readers can identify with the temptation not to do a hard task that is asked of us when there seems to be an easier alternative in sight.

Mailer's book, too, shows the Devil revisiting Jesus throughout his novel, even though Jesus resists the temptation in the wilderness. In fact, Jesus refers several times to things he learns from Satan or from the effect Satan has on him during that encounter. When he calls Peter and Andrew to be his disciples, Jesus says that "Between their eyes and mine passed an agreement across this space of water; I could feel how God had enabled me to steal a few skills from the Devil. In truth, I could now employ Satan's manner when speaking" (68). However, the exchange is not all for the good. Before Satan leaves Jesus, he wants to touch Jesus' hand, and Jesus let him: "And because I had wanted him to leave, I had touched my right hand to his, and knew in the same instant that I had surrendered a share of the Lord's protection. Only a small share. And I was certain that God had taken much back from Satan" (69).

Later, however, when Jesus relates the parable of the workers, a difficult parable for most people to accept, God chastises him: "Enough! In your speech is the seed of discontent. When you are without Me, the Devil is your companion." Jesus has to admit that he "no longer knew to whose voice [he] listened" (141). It is interesting that Mailer shows Jesus seemingly influenced by the Devil, especially in relationship to performing miracles, because, in the gospels, Jesus is compared to the Devil by the Pharisees for his ability to cast out demons. Jesus rightly points out how absurd such a notion is: "How can Satan drive out Satan? If a kingdom is divided against itself, that kingdom cannot stand. If a house is divided against itself, that house cannot stand. And if Satan opposes himself and is divided, he cannot stand; his end has come" (Mark 3:23–26). Mailer's portrayal of Satan here, though, is a reminder that evil has power, and he presents us a battle in which the outcome seems in doubt, unlike in Burgess' novel, in which Jesus' triumph is ordained.

In Mailer's novel, Satan also tempts Jesus when he first enters the Temple. Jesus is offended by the gross display of wealth that he sees there when the Devil appears to him. Immediately after Jesus tells the listeners that they cannot serve both God and Mammon, the Devil tells him that his followers will also give in to greed: "Before it is over, the rich will possess you as well. They will put your image on every wall. The alms raised in your name will swell the treasure of mighty churches; men will worship you most when you belong to me as much as to Him. Which is just. For I am His equal" (158–59). Mailer's Devil here invokes a popular temptation that draws on the history of the church: the idea that the followers of Jesus will succumb to exactly those things he preached against. Of course, in light of that history, the Devil's prediction is right, but Jesus is not hampered by this knowledge. Instead, he seems to believe that enough good will come out of his actions that he proceeds regardless, which becomes especially ironic in this version because Mailer's Jesus questions if his crucifixion serves any purpose at all.

The Devil's strongest temptation nonetheless occurs when Jesus is on the cross. A Roman soldier insults Jesus and says that he wishes Jesus were Barabbas, so he could wipe his filth on his face. The Devil appears to Jesus then and tells him to join him, so they can humiliate the soldier. The Devil then goes even further, though, and promises to take Jesus from the cross. Jesus is tempted, but he resists, and the Devil leaves. The temptation for revenge rings especially true for modern readers. The idea of Jesus as someone who turns the other cheek can be troubling, and the possibility that Jesus might step down from the cross to set someone straight is a strong temptation. However, as before, Mailer's Jesus is focused on what he sees as his mission, even though he later wonders if it does any good.

However, Jesus also believes that Satan inspires exaggeration; thus, the gospel writers have fallen prey to his influence, as well. By not relying on the truth of the story, he feels they have shown their lack of belief in him: "Many of those who had been near me were given to exaggeration; not one had believed in the Son or in the Father sufficiently to say no more than the truth. . . . When a man sees a wonder, Satan will enter his tale and multiply the wonder" (243). In the end, Jesus sees his followers still struggling with Satan, and, in many cases, they have simply given themselves over to him without knowing it: "There are many churches in my name and in the name of my apostles. The greatest and holiest is named after Peter; it is a place of great splendor in Rome. Nowhere can be found more gold. God and Mammon still grapple for the hearts of all men and all women. As yet, since the contest remains so equal, neither the Lord nor Satan can triumph" (247). It seems that the Devil's prediction of Jesus' followers and money has come true, yet Jesus does not seem to mourn this end much. Even though Jesus sees them losing many battles, he also sees them winning some, as well. The war may still seem up in the air, but Jesus thinks God has a plan somewhere.

Saramago, however, develops the Devil much more than do any of these other authors, though he does not follow any of the gospel stories in doing so. The Devil becomes a major character in Saramago's work, though the reader is not certain of who he is until late in the book. He first appears as a beggar at Mary and Joseph's door in the days early in Mary's pregnancy; in fact, he tells Mary that she is pregnant before she has told Joseph. He does not tell her anything about the uniqueness of her pregnancy, but he does fill a bowl with soil that glows. When the elders of the local synagogue suggest that Joseph bury the bowl behind their house, a plant grows from it. The plant is nothing but stalk and leaves, and they cannot kill it or prune it, no matter what they do, so they learn to live with it. The beggar returns years later, uproots the tree, and drags it after him as he walks away. Jesus has just left home to go and determine what happened in Bethlehem relating to his birth and his father. The beggar has also been seen walking beside Mary while she and Joseph are heading to Bethlehem for the census, and he is one of the shepherds who comes to provide the family with food after the birth of Jesus. At this point in the book, the beggar seems to be nothing more than an angel sent by God to look after Jesus. It is interesting that both Kazantzakis' and Saramago's works show Satan in a kindly guise, as a type of guardian angel. On one level, of course, this technique suggests simply that we often do not recognize evil when it is in our midst, but these stories go beyond this point to show a Jesus who does not recognize evil either. This certainly lessens the appearance of the divinity of Jesus, whose gospel persona always recognized the Devil and demons, and it seems to elevate the Devil to a level higher than what he occupies in the gospels. In the gospels, Jesus is always in control, while in both books by Kazantzakis and Saramago, the end result often seems in question.

After Jesus has discovered the truth about his birth in Bethlehem and the children who died there because of his father in Saramago's novel, the beggar appears to him and allows him to work with him as a shepherd. He tells Jesus that he should simply call him Pastor. Jesus works with Pastor for four years, though he almost leaves several times, mainly due to Pastor's blasphemy: Pastor does not perform any of the ceremonial cleansing rites, nor does he offer thanks at the appropriate times during the day, but Pastor's argument that he "wouldn't like to be a god who guides the dagger in the hand of the assassin while he offers the throat that is about to be cut" (193) is what causes Jesus to begin to leave. Because Pastor knows about Jesus' nightmares, though, Jesus stays to learn from him. The idea that Pastor knows more than Jesus and, seemingly, as much as God will become an

79

important theme that underlies his character throughout Saramago's work. It also presents a more Manichean worldview than any of the other authors do, with the Devil seemingly much more equal to God.

Pastor forces Jesus to leave after Jesus has seen God, though. Jesus tells him that God asked for a sheep to sacrifice, and Jesus willingly offers the lamb that he saved from being sacrificed for Passover a few years before. At that point, Pastor tells him, "You've learned nothing, begone with you" (222).

The Devil does not reenter the story until God appears to Jesus again to tell him exactly what will be expected of him. God and Jesus are out in a boat on a lake covered by mist when Pastor swims up to the boat and climbs in, which is when God tells Jesus clearly that Pastor is the Devil they had just been discussing. Jesus notices that "without God's beard they [God and the Devil] could have passed for twins, although the Devil was younger and less wrinkled" (310), which agrees with Saramago's assertion in the first chapter that "good and evil do not exist in themselves, each being merely the absence of each other" (6). This view of the Devil coincides with one of the main ways Satan was viewed by the early church: "One of the ways the early church chose to explain Satan was through the dualistic approach. Even before the New Testament the influence of dualistic thinking especially from Persia was spreading throughout the Ancient Near East. Zoroastrianism held to two primary powers. One was good and the other was evil" (Galeotti 74). This Manichean view of the universe gives Saramago's Devil as much information and power as his God.

In fact, the Devil seems to know everything that God knows, including God's plan to sacrifice Jesus for the good of humanity. The Devil, in fact, is somehow working with God: "The Devil . . . is condemned to eternal complicity in God's schemes, of which he is weary, and differs from God chiefly in his pity for the victims" (McKendrick 31). This portrayal of the Devil is strikingly similar to the Satan portrayed in the book of Job, as Harold Bloom points out, "Saramago seems to take us back to the unfallen Satan of the Book of Job, who goes to-and-fro on the earth, and walks up and down on it. And yet Job's Satan was an Accuser; Pastor is not" (158).

Saramago's Devil is similar to God in that he can also see the future, though he admits that he is often deceived in what he sees, as he believes his own lies and is unable to tell the true future from the false one. What is most interesting in this meeting, though, is that the Devil tries to prevent Jesus from having to go to the cross, not because he is afraid of what it will do to him, but because he does not want all the bloodshed that will come after Jesus' death (God had listed for Jesus all the martyrs and wars that will be fought in his name). He says to God,

> Today I use it [his heart] by acknowledging Your power and wishing that it spread to the ends of the earth without the need of so much death, and since You insist that whatever thwarts and denies You comes from the evil I represent and govern in this world, I propose that You receive me into Your heavenly kingdom, my past offenses redeemed by those I will not commit in future, that You accept my obedience as in those happy days when I was one of Your chosen angles, Lucifer You called me, bearer of light, before my ambition to become Your equal consumed my soul and made me rebel against You. (331)

The question that has to be asked here, of course, is whether or not Satan truly wants this to happen to avoid the future bloodshed or whether he sees his end in the sacrifice of Jesus and wants to protect himself. It appears that Saramago's novel is showing God as unforgiving and more willing to endure the sacrifice of his son and scores of humans than accept Satan back into heaven. Further complicating that idea, though, is one of Pastor's last comments before he leaves the boat: "Never let it be said the Devil didn't tempt God" (331). However, temptation does not always refer to sinning; we can be tempted to do something good, but refuse to give into that temptation. Given the gospel background of Satan's tempting Jesus in the wilderness, though, Satan is probably trying to trick God here. Saramago's novel, though, does not give God a defense, so he also ends up looking bad in this situation, reinforcing the idea that good and evil may be nothing more than two sides of the same coin. Harold Bloom argues that Saramago's Devil is "the only Devil who could be aesthetically and intellectually appropriate as we conclude the Second Millennium. Except that he cannot be crucified, this fallen angel has far more in common with Saramago's Jesus than with Saramago's God. They both are God's victims, suffering the tyranny of time, which God calls truth" (162).

The Devil remains an instrument for temptation, but only for Jesus, here. He does not enter Judas at any point, nor does he seem to tempt anyone else. Ricci's story, given his historical slant, ignores him completely, while Burgess', Mailer's, and Kazantzakis' novels show him tempting Jesus in the wilderness, and, with Mailer and Kazantzakis, at other times in their novels. Only Saramago's story develops the Devil into anything more than a test that Jesus must pass in order to be the Messiah.

CHAPTER 7

An Ordinary Man

PETER'S CONFESSION AND DENIAL

In many accounts, peter is mainly presented as a disciple with whom Christians can identify. He is brash, claiming that he will not deny Jesus, just hours before he does so, an action that reflects his human weakness. He has been a fisherman, not well-educated, but someone who becomes one of the leaders of the church after Jesus' death. His human fallibilities enable people to identify with him, while his ultimate rise from a seeming nobody to one of the most powerful people in the church corresponds to human desires to rise above their original station in life. Peter's reputation seems to be based on only two actions, as Theodore Ziolkowski points out: "the denial of Jesus and the attempt to defend him in Gethsemane" (278). These human characteristics are attractive to writers. The five authors present Peter as an ordinary man who struggles to understand Jesus, but who shares flaws with readers. Despite the high point he achieves when he recognizes Jesus as the Christ, which the five authors portray in different ways, they all also show him denying Jesus, though not always for the reason in the gospel accounts.

Peter's ordinary nature is usually evident from his being a fisherman, a common trade at the time, respectable enough, but certainly working class. Burgess focuses on Peter's ordinary nature more than any of the other writers under consideration. In his work, Peter (or Simon as he was known until Simon the Zealot joined the group around Jesus) is one of the first men to become a disciple, though he is not quite the first. Burgess' book focuses on Peter's ordinary background, his former trade of fishing, and his speech and actions to remind us of Jesus' mission to ordinary people. In fact, from the outset Peter tells Jesus that people like him aren't worth Jesus' time: "I know who you are, I think. . . . You're him. Well, I tell you straight—we're not worth it. We're nothing. Get away from us. We're only ordinary people. Leave us" (133). Peter's reaction here is an ordinary, human reaction, which surely resonates with most readers.

Jesus, of course, doesn't leave these folks, who end up following him. However, Peter is not initially presented as one who will become the greatest of Jesus' disciples, the rock upon which the church will be built. When four men try to lower a friend down to the room in which Jesus is teaching by removing the roof of Peter's house, Peter says, "God, hasn't a man a right to a damned roof over his head, damn you? Get him away there, damn the lot of you. God almighty, the damned insolence" (134). This language is not what most people would associate with the apostles, especially Peter, but, given his rough life up to this point, it should not be unexpected. Burgess' setting Peter up as a rough, ordinary fisherman makes his language perfectly appropriate and is used to remind readers that the disciples, even Peter, were far from saints, to begin with.

When Jesus sends the twelve disciples out to preach on their own, Peter's speech is simple, which is why he is successful. When he explains to them that a political revolution is not what they need, but a revolution of the heart, he says, "Now you don't put things right in this country or that country until you've put things right inside yourself, in here, here, do you get that? Do you see that now? You've got to stop hating, for one thing. It's no good hating the Romans or your mother-in-law or your wife's second cousin once removed. You've got to learn how to tolerate. You've got to learn how to love" (192). When someone asks Peter about justice, he responds by telling them the parable of the wheat and the tares. He reminds his listeners that their job is not to understand the theological implications of loving everyone; that job is God's: "You get on with loving and leave justice to God" (193). Peter is also the only apostle who is upset about having to get rid of his possessions when he chooses to follow Jesus, in marked contrast to Matthew, who gives up much more and does so willingly. Again, both Peter's plain speech to the people and his grumbling about having to surrender his possessions are consistent with the portrayal of Peter as an ordinary person, someone to whom readers can relate.

Peter plays a much smaller role in Saramago's novel than he does in the other works under consideration here or in the gospel accounts. He is still a fisherman, and Jesus spends a good deal of time with him, Andrew, James and John after he leaves Pastor. Peter is certainly not presented as the future head of the church, though his death by crucifixion (upside down) is mentioned. In fact, his named is changed from Simon to Peter, not because he is the rock, (petra) on which Jesus will build his church, as it is in the book of Matthew, but merely because there is another Simon, Simon the Zealot, who joins the group. Thus, Saramago's novel does not show Peter receiving his name because he recognizes Jesus as the Messiah; instead, it seems to be nothing more than a way to avoid confusion. As in Burgess' account, Peter is an ordinary man, but, in Saramago's work, he will remain such.

Mailer does not add much at all to the characterization of Peter, save for making him a bit less sure of himself and of Jesus than the gospels show. More than any of the other disciples, Peter is shown attempting to live up to the model Jesus sets for the disciples, but he constantly falls a bit short. When Jesus walks on the water, Peter is the disciple who tries to go out to him, but, as in the gospel stories, he is unable to. However, in Mailer's novel, Jesus does not rebuke him for his lack of faith; instead, it is then that Jesus recognizes that "Peter wanted to be loyal. Yet [he] also knew that there would come a time when he would have to fail [Jesus]. For his faith was in his mouth, not his legs" (123). Peter tries to be loyal to Jesus and do whatever it takes to be a good disciple.

As Mailer draws from the gospel stories of Peter's walking on the water, he also uses the episode when Jesus wants to wash the disciples' feet. In this instance, Peter originally does not want Jesus to wash his feet. When Jesus insists, Peter responds, "Then, Lord, not just my feet but my hands and my head as well" (John 13:9). In Mailer's novel, Peter also does not want Jesus to wash his feet, believing that this action is beneath Jesus. When Jesus tells Peter that this must be done or he can have no part of Jesus, Peter responds, "Then not only my feet, Lord, but my hands and my head" (207), almost an exact quote from the gospel of John.

However, Jesus is accurate in saying that Peter's faith is in his mouth. Though Peter is the only disciple who is allowed to protest that he will not deny Jesus, Peter is also the only one whose account of the denial of Jesus is shown. The others merely run off, but Peter denies Jesus three times in order to save himself. Mailer follows the gospels in showing Peter deny Jesus thrice. Earlier in the work, though, we see evidence of Peter's fear that blossoms in his denial of Jesus. After Jesus has healed Peter's mother-in-law, Peter encourages Jesus to leave, away from the people who will be seeking him the next morning: "People seek for you now, and I fear they will be many. I would warn you. They are curious. They wish to witness miracles," and when Jesus decides to move on to other cities, he says that he is now "thinking with the wisdom of Peter" (75). Here, Peter seems to be afraid that the people will expect too much of Jesus, that they will drain him of his power, or perhaps of the attention the miracles will draw. Regardless, he does not want Jesus in his house when anything happens.

Kazantzakis also follows the gospels in his presentation of Peter. When Kazantzakis first introduces Peter, Philip describes him as fickle:

> Forgive me, Peter, but you haven't developed good sense to match your white hairs. You flare up in a flash and burn out just as quickly, like kindling. Wasn't it you who roused us to come here in the first place? You ran like a madman from boat to boat and shouted, "Drop everything, brothers; a man sees a miracle only once in his life. Come on, let's go to Nazareth and see the miracle!" And now you're smacked once or twice on the back with a lance, and right away your mind turns upside down, you change your tune and shout, "Drop everything, brothers; let's go home!" You're not called "Weathercock" for nothing! (40)

Throughout the rest of the novel, Kazantzakis focuses on this aspect of Peter: his short-lived enthusiasm balanced by his fear. There are times when Peter lives up to Jesus' expectations of him. When all of the other disciples are talking about the places they will go to spread Jesus' message, Peter thinks of what they are going to eat for dinner. The other disciples chastise him, but Jesus says, "You have food on your mind, and you talk about food. When you have God on your mind you'll talk about God. Bravo! That's why men call you the Windmill. I choose you. You are the windmill which will grind the wheat into bread so that men may eat" (303). This scene is similar to Burgess' portrayal of Peter as an ordinary man who speaks plainly, and, in both novels, Jesus commends Peter for his honesty and simplicity. However, the books also take Peter beyond this point.

The authors all draw on the gospel portrayal of Peter as a leader of the disciples and use that to build to his confession of Jesus as the Messiah. In the gospels, Jesus includes Peter in a select group of disciples. Only Peter, James, and John witness Jesus' transfiguration (where Peter again says something that doesn't seem appropriate; Luke 9:28–32), and this same group accompanies Jesus farther into Gethsemane than do the other apostles (Matt. 26:37). Peter seems to be singled out even beyond this small group, however. When the temple tax collectors come to see why Jesus does not pay the temple tax, they address Peter, who then talks about the tax with Jesus (Matt. 17:24–25). When Jesus returns from praying in Gethsemane and finds the disciples sleeping, he addresses Peter, but not the other disciples, by name (Mark 14:37), and when he appears to the disciples after the resurrection, he again singles Peter out and tells him to feed his sheep or lambs (John 21:15–19).

Despite a focus on Peter as an ordinary man, in many cases not showing him to be the future head of the church, these novelists depict insight for which he is most known: recognizing Jesus as the Messiah. In the gospels, when Jesus asks the disciples who they believe him to be, it is Peter who answers with what would become known as the Great Confession: "You are the Christ, the Son of the living God" (Matt. 16:16). Each of these authors draws on this gospel scene in different ways.

Mailer's novel, for example, taints what is Peter's triumphant scene in the gospels. After Jesus has healed many people, he is exhausted and admits that there are some days he does not know who he is. Thus, he is prompted to ask his disciples, though he phrases the question as "Who do they say I am?" After they answer with the beliefs they have heard that he is Elijah or John the Baptist, Jesus asks them who they think he is, and Peter, [perhaps] "thinking of how [Jesus] had walked upon the water—asked gently: 'Can one say that you are the Christ?'" (130). Peter's grand declaration of Jesus as the Messiah is reduced to a question inspired solely by one miracle. Peter does not demonstrate belief that Jesus is the Christ; rather Peter voices the possibility that Jesus might be, and Peter seems to be asking for approval of such a thought rather than asserting it.

Oddly enough, however, that seems to be sufficient for Jesus: "Since I felt like an ordinary man in all ways but one, I could love Peter for the strength that his conviction gave me. Now I knew with more certainty than before that I must be the Son of God" (130). Despite Mailer's focus on Peter's doubts and fears, Jesus is still inspired by his loyalty, even if that loyalty is found only in his mouth. Not only does this scene in some ways diminish Peter, it also diminishes Jesus, showing him as someone who needs the approval of those around him, which, ultimately, makes him more human.

Saramago also shows Peter making the declaration that Jesus is the Messiah much less assuredly than is seen in the gospel narratives. In Saramago's work the declaration comes as a result of Thomas and Judas' reporting what John the Baptist has said, that someone would come who would baptize with fire and the Holy Ghost. When Peter does say, "So you are the Messiah whose coming John prophesies" (354), Jesus merely responds that it is Peter who said so, not Jesus. Peter is not rewarded for his insight as he is in the gospels, and the declaration does not carry the same weight. As in Mailer's novel, Peter here does not seem sure of what he is saying, though at least he does not quite frame it in the form of a question.

Some of these authors connect this confession to the Roman Catholic idea of Peter as the first pope. Burgess describes Peter two or three times in terms that can only be referred to as papal, and, given Burgess' background, this approach is not surprising. The first instance of this approach is a keystone passage for papal authority in the Roman Catholic church. When Jesus asks the disciples who he is, only Peter responds that he is the Messiah. Jesus then tells him that he will be the rock upon which the church will be built, and the one to whom "I give the keys of the kingdom of heaven" (200). However, Burgess does not leave it at that; he expands upon the Biblical account:

> [The church] must go on for ever. So there must be a body of men and women to hold the truth and teach the truth, and it must have a head or leader. This leader must, when he dies, pass on his authority to another leader. And so it must go on. It is easy for words to be distorted through time and ignorance and stupidity and, indeed, malice. But authority must prevail and say: the word means this. As all priests in the Old Law come from Aaron, so all priests in the New come from this blessed Peter. The authority shall not solely be to ensure that the message is passed on undefiled, but also to condemn and bless. Now there is a danger, long after our time yet perhaps again not so long, that men unchosen by our Peter here may believe that they and they only know the true meaning of the message, and they may set up, in good faith, churches pretending to teach the truth. But if they are not chosen by Peter or those that succeed him, they must merit condemnation. A church, you see, is no more than a body holding to the same faith, but it is false speaking to speak of a church, as it is false speaking to speak of a God, since there is only one God and only one church. (201)

The danger that Jesus refers to of those who would set up other churches clearly refers to both the schisms in the church and the Protestant reformation. Burgess seems to be criticizing those who question the authority of the Catholic church, merely using Peter's confession and Jesus' response as a springboard for his own theological/political views, rather than as a way to further develop Peter's and Jesus' characters.

Burgess uses Peter to exemplify later Christian practices near the end of the book, as well. When the disciples are separating to return to Galilee in the hopes of meeting Jesus there, "Awkwardly Peter sketched a blessing with his right hand. The shape of the gesture came to him without thought—hand down, hand across, hand across, a figure of four made out of a movement of three, a kind of mystery," and he tells them, "God and his blessed Son be with you. And the soul that belongs to both of them" (297). The obvious reference to the Holy Spirit at the end, though Peter does not know to whom he refers, completes what appears to be a typical, though early, Christian blessing. The fact that Peter does it naturally reinforces the idea that he is chosen by God to carry on the work that Jesus began.

Burgess, a former Roman Catholic, certainly is aware of how his church views Peter. The Roman Catholic church has long based the papal authority on Jesus' statement to Peter after his confession: Pheme Perkins writes, "Since the Reformation, Catholics have emphasized the Petrine foundation of papal authority in Matthew 16:17–20. The definitions of papal authority promulgated at Vatican I in Pastor Aeternus understand Jesus' words to Peter in John 1:42, Matthew 16:15–20, and John 21:15–16 as the historical transmission of a ruling power much as the Roman emperor might designate a successor" (3–4). Burgess sees Peter as the future head of the church, but certainly with flaws. Burgess may be acknowledging the church's humanity and its accompanying flaws, which is why his book suggests that Peter's denial of Jesus is worse than Judas' betrayal. The book may also be reminding the reader of Christian forgiveness: that the disciple who behaves the worst ultimately can become the leader of the church.

In contrast to Burgess, Michèle Roberts, in *The Wild Girl*, shows Peter after Jesus' resurrection as a leader who seeks to make the church's hierarchy patriarchal by removing the women from leadership, a criticism of Catholicism.[1] Roberts draws from the gnostic *Gospel of Mary* to show how Peter and the disciples initially turned to Mary to hear what she

[1]She also criticizes Catholicism by her depiction of a dream Mary has. Mary sees "a tall man in a stiff golden robe and with a high gold crown upon his head" who is leading the burning of women and books. He tells Mary that "these are the works of witchcraft, . . . and they shall burn, all the paper and the female flesh on which the devil writes his testament" (168–69), a reference to the Inquisition. Dan Brown echoes this critique in *The Da Vinci Code* when he writes, "Malleus Maleficarum—or *The Witches' Hammer*—indoctrinated the world to 'the dangers of freethinking women' and instructed the clergy how to locate, torture, and destroy them. Those deemed 'witches' by the church included all female scholars, priestesses, gypsies, mystics, nature lovers, herb gatherers, and any woman 'suspiciously attuned to the natural world.' Midwives also were killed for their heretical practice of using medical knowledge to ease the pain of childbirth—a suffering, the Church claimed, that was God's rightful punishment for Eve's partaking of the Apple of Knowledge, thus giving birth to the idea of Original Sin. During three hundred years of witch hunts, the Church burned at the stake an astounding five *million* women" (125).

had to teach them: "Sister, . . . we know that the Saviour loved you more than the rest of the women. . . . Therefore, if you have seen him, tell us the truth. Tell us all the words of the Saviour which you remember and which we have not heard" (107–08). However, Peter does not like what she teaches, so he calls her testimony into question: "Say what you like, . . . but I don't believe a word of this. I don't believe that the Saviour ever thought such things. If he had, he would have told them to us while he was still alive. Who ever heard such ridiculous teachings? Mary is raving. She has made them up" (111–12). In contrast to the *Gospel of Mary*, however, no male disciples come to her aid and allow her to speak the truth that Jesus has taught her. Instead, Peter becomes the leader of the church and keeps the women from preaching the gospel: "Mary, . . . listen. First of all we knew Jesus as Man. Now since his resurrection, we know him as God. The fact that God became Man, that the Word took flesh as Man, means that it is for men to come after him and baptise others and offer the bread and wine. It is as simple as that. You women have a different role. Not a lesser one: a different one" (131). In the same way that Burgess seems to use Peter to present a positive view of the Roman Catholic church and the papal leadership, Roberts uses Peter to show how the Roman Catholic church has barred women from serving as priests.

In *Mary Called Magdalene*, Margaret George effectively reverses this portrayal. Peter initially opposes Mary, especially in connection to her having special knowledge or visions, which would relate her to the gnostic portrayal of Mary. Peter even asks Jesus, "Why *do* you favor her? . . . What does she know and understand that the rest of us can't?" (422). When Peter has a vision, he will not allow her to help him interpret it until she proves that God has indeed chosen her to receive visions from him: "I cannot trust your interpretation, unless you can convince me that God *does* reveal things to you. So you must describe to me my vision" (431). After God shows Mary Peter's vision, though, Peter accepts her as an equal and treats her like that for the remainder of his life. However, Mary finds a church that believes that Peter has received a special role from Jesus, a reference to the later belief of Peter's role as the first pope. When a young person in the church asks about Peter's ability to forgive sins, a clear reference to the orthodox belief in absolution, Mary responds, "I have never heard Peter say that. . . . And I have spent a great deal of time in his presence. I don't think Jesus designated a successor. He knew we were all unworthy—or all equally worthy" (592–93). Thus, while it is clear that Peter's followers will succeed and develop into the Roman Catholic church with Peter as the first pope, George presents a Peter who does not seek such a position, nor does he ever claim it for himself, and a Mary who understands that about him and is not in conflict with him.

Kazantzakis also presents Peter as the future leader of the church, more affirmatively than Roberts, but much less so than Burgess. Peter has Matthew recount what Jesus has said to him when, as the disciples argue about who will be greater in the kingdom of God. Matthew grudgingly admits that Jesus told Peter, "You are Peter, and upon this rock I shall build my church"; and "And whatever you bind upon earth shall be bound in heaven; and whatever you loose on earth shall be loosed in heaven" (378). Despite the fact that raising this point shows a decided lack of humility, it also shows the greatness that Jesus has in mind for him. However, Kazantzakis does not develop this idea further, as his novel does not consider the church after Jesus' death. Thus, in contrast to the novels by Burgess and Roberts, it is unclear how Kazantzakis' novel sees Peter's role with respect to the papacy and the church hierarchy, in general.

These authors, however, play their portrayals of Peter as future church leader, as in the gospels, against his misunderstanding of Jesus' mission and his denial of Jesus. In the gospel of Matthew, Peter is shown to be flawed in his view of Jesus immediately after he has confessed him to be the Messiah. After he makes his confession of Jesus as the Christ, Jesus tries to explain to the disciples what he must suffer in Jerusalem, but Peter does not understand what Jesus' plan is, so Peter tries to stop him. In return, Jesus refers to Peter as Satan who does not "have in mind the things of God" (Matt. 16:23).

Burgess presents the most complicated portrayal of Peter in this regard, although it's unclear whether it is of Judas or Peter that Jesus speaks when he talks of someone's betraying him.[2] Jesus tells the disciples that he "must be betrayed, sold to the enemy—and by one of you here" (241). Peter does not "sell" Jesus, but Judas doesn't either; he does what he believes is a good thing, and it's only when the Jewish leaders give him the money that he realizes what's happened. The matter is further complicated by the question of who dips his bread in the bowl at the same time as Jesus. Jesus tells John, although none of the other disciples overhear, that "He who dips his bread in the dish of the juice of the meat when I dip mine—it shall be that one [who will betray him]" (241). Peter notices that Judas has not finished his bread, so he offers to help Judas get the rest of it down. He tells Judas that it's hard to eat when it's dry, so "he grabbed the bread that Judas held in limp fingers. . . . And he dipped it into the meat juice at the very same moment as Jesus. John drew in his breath in shock. Jesus warned him with a look to say, show nothing. Judas took the bread from Peter and, while Peter kindly watched, ate it" (243–44). Thus, both John and the reader are left to wonder over whom Jesus meant. He may have meant Judas since Judas ate the bread, but, literally, it should be Peter he is talking about.

An additional complication comes from the reaction of the people who accuse Peter of knowing Jesus, leading to his denial. As in the gospel stories, Peter denies Jesus three times before the cock crows. In Burgess' novel, Peter says he is where he is because he is waiting for some man to bring him money. Thus, when he denies Jesus for the last time and leaves crying, one of them says, "Crying, did you see that? Come to get some money, he said. You know what that'd be for, don't you? There's a word for that. There's some men as would sell their own mothers" (249).

Burgess' novel isn't arguing that Peter sells Jesus out, but it raises an important question about the characters of both Peter and Judas (and the reader), as well. Judas approaches the religious leaders in an honest effort to

---

[2]Most writers tend to let Judas off the hook when it comes to his betrayal of Jesus, but they do not usually do so for Peter. Christopher Moore is a notable exception to this approach. In *Lamb*, his Judas clearly betrays Jesus, but Joshua (Jesus) tells Peter, "You will deny me three times, Peter. I not only expect this, I command it. If they take you when they take me, then there is no one to take the good news to the people" (414). Moore's book doesn't show Peter's denial, but he does seem quite downcast after the crucifixion, so it's likely that he does exactly what Jesus commanded him to do.

help Jesus, but he is used by them to arrest Jesus, leading to the crucifixion. Peter, however, has no honest intentions when he denies Jesus; he is merely trying to protect himself. However, Judas is the one who has always been vilified as a result of the gospel stories. Burgess' novel asks the reader to examine motivation and action and to understand that good in one area does not always lead to or result from good in another area. At one point in the novel, Jesus is questioned by the religious leaders as to why the prostitutes and tax collectors are, according to Jesus, entering the kingdom of God first. Jesus responds with a story of two sons. When one is asked if he will work in the field, he replies that he will, but he does not. The other one, asked the same question, responds that he will not, but he does. Burgess' novel seems to echo this story in its depiction of the behavior of Judas and Peter: Peter says that he will not betray Jesus, yet he does; Judas seemingly betrays Jesus, but he perhaps doesn't. The readers can easily see themselves in both characters.

The other four authors under consideration present Peter as simply afraid, an understandable reaction, leading to his denial of Jesus. Kazantzakis' novel presents Peter as one of the most fearful disciples throughout his work. When Jesus is tempted in the wilderness, the disciples contemplate leaving Simon's tavern, where they are supposed to meet him. They have finally decided to leave when Jesus arrives, and he asks them whether or not they are leaving. Peter is the spokesman who tells Jesus, "John heard your footsteps in his heart and we were just going out to welcome you" (295). Jesus knows he is lying, but he chooses to ignore it at the time. This scene gives the reader an early indication of Peter's willingness to lie to protect himself. Also, when Jesus is speaking in Nazareth, after his time in the wilderness, his brothers come to try to physically drag him away, and they also attack the disciples. One of the townspeople grabs Peter around the throat and says, "It looks as if you're on his side, eh!" Peter, however, denies the accusation: "No! No! I'm not!" (310) while Judas is the one to support Jesus.

This denial prefigures Peter's denial after Jesus has been arrested, the culmination of Peter's fears. As in the gospel story, three different people comment that Peter was with Jesus, and he denies knowing Jesus every time. When the cock crows, he remembers Jesus' prophetic words concerning his denial, and he leaves the courtyard weeping. When the disciples visit Jesus during his temptation on the cross, Peter has deteriorated to the point where Jesus hardly recognizes him. Peter says, "The troubles of the world came upon me. I married, had children, received wounds, saw Jerusalem burn. . . . I'm human: all that broke me" (485). What really breaks Peter, however, is not having a chance to redeem himself after his denial of Jesus. In the gospel accounts, especially the gospel of John, Peter is one of the first disciples to believe in the resurrection, and, in the gospel of John, Jesus singles Peter out to tell him to "Feed my sheep" (John 21:18). These post-resurrection events are what enable Peter to be healed and to become the foremost apostle and the foundation of the church. Without those events, as in the scenario presented by the devil in the scene of the temptation on the cross, Peter simply becomes an old, broken man.

Ricci's Peter is as conflicted as the Peter in the gospels, complete with a denial, though a different one, and for completely different reasons. In the gospels, Peter fears for his life if he is associated with Jesus; thus, he denies knowing him. Ricci's Peter has this fear, too, but only after the crucifixion. Peter begins teaching, along with Jacob, Jesus' brother, after the crucifixion, but only after enough time has gone by so that Peter is no longer worried that the Romans are looking for anybody associated with Jesus. Thus, Ricci's Peter has still been afraid of being accused of guilt by association, a fear that exists at a different time from that of Peter of the gospels.

Instead, Peter denies Jesus while he is alive because he believes that Jesus is a bastard. Jesus has never told the disciples about his parentage, and he seemingly hadn't planned to. The truth emerges only because Zadok, one of the priests, confronts Jesus with this information in the presence of the disciples. He says to Jesus, "Though I hear the man isn't a Galilean at all but a Jerusalemite, at least on the mother's side. On the father's side it's not as clear. . . . Who was he, your father? . . . I might have known him" (408–9). Jesus doesn't respond, and the disciples are all shocked, but none more than Peter. Peter is the only disciple who speaks to Jesus about the matter, and all he can say to him is, "You cheated us" (412). The other disciples hoped that everyone would stay with Jesus, but after Peter declares his side openly, it becomes harder for them to do so.

As in the gospels, Peter later regrets abandoning Jesus. Peter is present at the cross, but that's where he tells Simon (the narrator), "I ought to have stood by him. . . . It was what he taught us." The narrator knows that that would have meant certain death, "But it seemed that was his point, that he'd rather be up there on the hill than watching from below" (448). Peter is finally able to admit that he should have been willing to give his life for Jesus, and he becomes willing to do so after Jesus' death and possible resurrection.

Peter begins to believe that even the crucifixion will be understood, given enough time: "We always came to understand the hardest things with him. . . . Maybe even this we'll come to understand" (449). In the end, he does come to some understanding of it, or at least he comes to enough of an understanding of it to begin spreading Jesus' teachings again. Simon of Gergesa believes that Peter needs to understand Jesus' illegitimacy as much as he needs to understand the crucifixion, and he understands why Peter never mentions that: "It wasn't for me to say he did anything wrong not to let out the truth, when often enough it happened that a truth of that sort, that didn't mean anything, stood in the way of one that did" (453). Thus, in Ricci's novel Peter ends up in much the same place as does the Peter of the gospels: he denies Jesus near the end; he comes to accept his denial and Jesus' death (which the Peter of the gospels also did not want to occur); and he spreads Jesus' teachings after Jesus' death.

Saramago's novel still shows Peter denying Jesus, but Jesus does not predict that Peter will do so, and, in fact, the Last Supper is markedly absent. Instead, when Jesus is being taken to Golgotha, three different people ask Peter if he has been with Jesus, and he denies that he has been all three times. There is no cock crow, nor does Peter show any remorse. Instead, the scene switches to the women who are also following Jesus. As with many of the other biblical accounts, Saramago's novel presents this episode matter-of-factly, as a scene that needs to be covered before moving on to other more important scenes. As such, the character of Peter is never fleshed out.

All five authors present Peter as a man with whom their readers might identify with. He is an ordinary fisherman who is afraid when he sees what happens to Jesus. He denies Jesus, and, in most cases, then feels remorse. In the novels by Burgess and Kazantzakis, there is a suggestion about the future leader of the church Peter will become, but the other novels leave their portrayal of Peter in the present.

CHAPTER 8

Friend or Foe? Nationalist or Innocent? Greed, Glory, or God?

JUDAS' BETRAYAL OF JESUS

O
f all the characters in the gospel story, Judas probably leaves the most for authors to develop. Judas' role in the life of Jesus and the disciples is the most well-known, the most problematic, but also the most necessary. As Theodore Ziolkowski writes in *Fictional Transfigurations of Jesus*, "The inevitable complement to Jesus is Judas, without whom the Passion cannot come to pass" (281). Because Judas is the most important secondary character in Jesus' story, the motivation for his betrayal becomes even more important. However, that motivation, biblically speaking, remains a mystery, though scholars have been struggling with it for centuries.[1] Concerning this mystery, Paul Casey writes, "The story of Judas Iscariot as it descends to us is almost entirely fictional, yet that does little to affect its status as myth. . . . What we know of Judas is paltry: we learn virtually nothing in the scriptures of his background or the meaning of his surname Iscariot" (102). This mythologization of Judas, combined with the lack of biblical knowledge, provides authors with a richer material source than most histories, giving them room to invent motivations and actions to explain Judas' character. Contemporary authors draw from these scholarly accounts and their imaginations, though they mainly let Judas off the hook, one way or another. In his discussion of modern stories of Judas, Hugh Pyper writes, "Rather than the demonic figure of the gospels driven

---

[1]Not only scholars have been struggling with it; creative writers have, as well. Paul Casey, in "Judas and His Role in Early Modern German Drama," points out that in the European Middle Ages, Judas was known as "a despicable traitor" (106) and, "As the German Middle Ages progressed, literary representations of Judas increasingly stressed solely the motive of avarice for his actions" (107). It is only in the Late Middle Ages that questions about Judas' motivation first began to be raised, as Richard Axton points out in "Interpretations of Judas in Middle English Literature" (a chapter in *Religion in the Poetry and Drama of the Late Middle Ages in England*).

by greed and envy,[2] the new Judas is represented either as choosing himself to bear the blame for handing over Christ in order to serve the higher good his actions may enable, or else as the victim of misunderstanding. His story becomes a tragedy in which he is cast either as a Promethean figure defying the God who dupes Jesus or else as a hapless yet conscious Kafkaesque pawn of an incomprehensible doom" (115). These authors add to that list a character who willingly goes along with Jesus' plan in order to help Jesus fulfill his destiny of crucifixion. Only Mailer creates a Judas who willingly, maliciously betrays Jesus. Burgess' novel shows an innocent Judas who accidentally delivers Jesus into the hands of those who would kill him, while Ricci's Judas is guilty for his name and his background as a Zealot. Saramago's Judas turns Jesus over to the authorities because Jesus asks him to.

As Judas is the most problematic character in the gospel stories, all of these authors have to struggle with Judas' motivation for betraying Jesus. Most do so by providing him with a background that leads him to the betrayal when the time comes. Burgess' novel shows him as well-educated, but also naïve, which leads him to trust the wrong people. Ricci, Kazantzakis, and Mailer depict Judas as part of a Jewish nationalist group, varying in degrees of violence, while Saramago's novel has Judas fulfill his role as betrayer because Jesus asks him to.

In Man of Nazareth Judas enters rather late, the last of the disciples to join Jesus. Here, in contrast to the gospel writers and most other re-tellers of the gospel stories, disciples join Jesus slowly, as they encounter him along their way. Thus, Judas is actually only in the book for less than the last half; however, as with the gospel stories, his impact is felt more than that of any of the others, including Peter.

This novel presents Judas as highly educated, yet terribly naïve. He is a young Pharisee, who is multilingual. Burgess comments about his Judas, "I had to remake Judas from scratch. I remade him first as a decent American college boy, well read in Latin, Greek and Hebrew, devoted to his widowed

---

[2]There is actually little evidence in the gospels to suggest that Judas acted out of greed, given the amount of money he received (see note 5) and there is no evidence at all that he acted out of envy.

mother, charmed at first by Jesus, later wholly convinced of his divinity, but so politically innocent that he runs to the Sanhedrin . . ." (YH 304). An interesting note is that Burgess has the narrator also work as a translator trained in Latin, Greek, and Hebrew, and this connection reminds the reader that many people are like Judas, though many would be hesitant to admit it. Making Judas educated also separates him from the typical characterizations of the disciples, the rest of whom are largely uneducated, except for Matthew the tax collector. Even though the novel does not develop the idea that his education makes him different from the rest of the disciples, this idea should occur to the reader.

Jesus is answering questions when Judas first meets him, and Judas asks one of his own. When Jesus tells the crowd that the second greatest commandment is to love our neighbor as ourselves, Judas is the person in the crowd who asks, "Who is my neighbor?" However, unlike the gospel account in which the teacher of the law is trying to justify his actions, Judas seems to be truly curious as to Jesus' answer: "The question he now asked was no carping question," and Jesus responds by saying, "Well asked" (171). Thus, from the outset, Judas is portrayed positively as one who is seeking truth. The contrast between Judas' attitude and that of the teacher of the law in the gospel accounts simply heightens the reader's surprise at seeing Judas as one truly interested in what Jesus is teaching.

In contrast to this presentation of Judas as a seeker of truth, the novels of Ricci, Kazantzakis, and Mailer portray him, from the outset, as a nationalist who seeks to overthrow Rome. We know that Judas' last name is Iscariot—or, as Luke says, he was "called Iscariot" (Luke 22:3)—and his name may have something to do with this portrayal. One theory concerning the name "Iscariot" is that it is related to *sikarios*, the Greek form of *sicarius*, which is Latin for "dagger-bearer."[3] Concerning this background, Barclay writes, "The *sicarii* were wild and fanatical nationalists, pledged not only to war against the Romans, but to murder and assassination at every opportunity.

---

[3]Two other meanings of Judas' name also fit with his character, in the gospels. It could simply mean "carrier of the leather bag," which would fit with his role as treasurer of the disciples (Blair 1006). However, it could also come from an Aramaic root which means "false one, liar, hypocrite" (Blair 1006).

If this is so, and it is by no means impossible, Judas was a violent Jewish nationalist, who had attached himself to Jesus in the hope that through Jesus his nationalist dreams might be realized" (74). Further evidence of Judas' possible involvement with the *sicarii* comes from Josephus, who, as William Klassen reports, "mentions nineteen men with the name Jude and thirteen with the name of Judas, most of them leaders in the Zealot-Sicarii group" (30). Klassen adds, "The fact that the name Judas was used by patriots may have influenced Jews who were known as Zealots and Sicarii to use it as well. Moreover, the image of Judah the Patriarch in the first century, as well as the *Testament of Judah* in *The Testament of the Twelve Patriarchs*, may have had a bearing" (31). While the fact that several leaders of the group bore the same name and that such a name was popular in the Zealot-Sicarii movement is certainly not conclusive evidence that Judas was a member of this group, it is enough to provide a creative writer with a basis for a character.

Christopher Moore, in *Lamb*, does not present Judas as a member of the *sicarii*, but he does show their role in Jewish society at that time. One of his minor characters belongs to the *sicarii*, who later turns out to be Mary Magdalene's (Maggie's) uncle. He appears in the book only a few times, but each time he is either killing someone or attempting to do so. Thus, Moore's book provides the reader with background about the *sicarii* without using Judas for that end. In this way, Moore's Judas can be a positive character in a book that indicates the violent nationalism that was rampant in first-century Israel.

There are two ways that Judas' background as a Jewish nationalist might have motivated him to betray Jesus. First, he may have been disappointed that Jesus does not live up to Judas' idea of a Messiah; thus, Judas might have turned Jesus over to the authorities (Blair 1007). Second, Judas may have been trying to force Jesus to act the part of his idea of a Messiah, believing that, faced with death, Jesus would cooperate. Barclay writes, "If that is so, the last thing in Judas' mind was any desire that Jesus should be crucified; the only thing in his mind was to create a situation in which Jesus would be compelled to unleash his power" (79).

Ricci uses this background to fashion a Judas who is part of a group that is planning a rebellion against the Romans; his group, in fact, can trace its roots to Judas the Galilean (who is briefly mentioned in the book of Acts). Judas shuttles back and forth between this group and Jesus' disciples throughout the book, torn between the two missions. He doesn't feel that he fits in with either group, and it is ultimately unclear which side he chooses. Wald-Hopkins observes that Judas is "a spy in the field when he first encounters Jesus . . . , he is indecisive and fearful, concerned with his own skin and more suited to whispering reports than taking action" (Wald-Hopkins EE-01).

Judas first meets Jesus when he is waiting for a contact in En Melakh. Jesus is squatting outside his lodging house, cold and hungry, but is doing nothing to remedy this situation. Judas feels sorry for Jesus, and so he gives him his cloak. This act does not feel natural to Judas: "What struck me as I draped the cloak over him was how peculiar this act of charity felt, how alien to my nature, as if I had now truly become a man whom I'd thought I merely feigned to be" (Ricci 6). This admission suggests that Judas has already grown as a person, just from a brief contact with Jesus, but the reader later sees that he did this as much to get credit as for any other reason: "And yet he did not think to thank me [for the cloak]. So it seemed I must wrestle him for my blessing" (Ricci 11). But Judas does buy Jesus food in the morning.

Testament's opening scene between Judas and Jesus sets up two themes. One is the idea that Jesus simply makes Judas feel uncomfortable. Judas does not know how to respond to Jesus, though he spends most of his time with Jesus trying to satisfy him. Judas is not used to trying to please someone who has no standing in his group or in society, yet he feels compelled to do so anyway. The other idea is related to that, in that Judas does things for Jesus, not just because he wants Jesus' approval, but because he wants people to see him as a person who does important things. No matter which group he is with Judas always wants the people around him to notice what he is doing. This underlying narcissism runs throughout the novel, but Judas' seeking of approval keeps it in check and certainly keeps him from doing anything to purposefully betray Jesus.

Kazantzakis is more interested in Judas than in any of the other characters in his novel, save for Jesus. Like Testament, *The Last Temptation of Christ* shows Judas as a Zealot, which supplies a political motivation for his interest in Jesus. Judas knows Jesus before the ministry, and he seeks to have Jesus join his group, though he is repulsed by Jesus, who spends his time making crosses the Romans use to crucify the Zealots whom Judas believes might be the Messiah. He is so disgusted by Jesus, in fact, that the group of Zealots to which he belongs sends him to kill Jesus for making the crosses. Despite their long acquaintance, Judas is willing to kill Jesus for the cause of independence. Michael Antonakes writes, "Kazantzakis's Judas is . . . filled with a violent hatred for the Romans and believes that force is the solution for the people of Israel. Even though he has intimations that Jesus is not an ordinary man, he tries to convince him that armed conflict is the way to restore freedom" (98). Sending Judas to kill Jesus echoes the biblical idea of Judas' action leading to the death of Jesus. But this echo sets up a conventional expectation of the role of Judas that will be challenged as the novel progresses.

When Judas confronts Jesus, he is unable to kill him because Jesus is willing to die. Judas is accustomed to killing those who resist him, so he is puzzled by a willing victim. Judas' culpability in the execution of Jesus remains in force in this novel with Jesus' willingness to die at the hands of Judas; this scene should remind the reader of Jesus' sending Judas out to betray him and of his willingness to die on the cross. However, after talking with Jesus, Judas is unable to kill him because he begins to see that Jesus might be the Messiah: "The halo of light around the youth's head grew brighter; his sad, wasted face flashed like lightening and his large, jet-black eyes seduced Judas with the unutterable sweetness. The redbeard felt troubled and lowered his eyes. I wouldn't kill him, he thought, if I were sure he would go out to speak and rouse the hearts of the Israelites, rouse them to attack the Romans" (158). Instead of showing the reader a Judas who betrays Jesus because he is the Messiah, this novel reminds the reader that it would be difficult for a Jew, especially a Zealot who sought the overthrow of the Romans, to kill anyone who might be the Messiah, who might be the one to deliver Israel from the Roman occupation.

The Gospel According to the Son also makes Judas a nationalist, but one focused on social justice. Oddly enough, Jesus doesn't trust Judas, yet he chooses him anyway: "I wished him to be among my twelve even if I could not see what was in his heart. His eyes were too full of fire. Indeed, I felt blinded by the blaze of his spirit. Notwithstanding, I welcomed him" (Mailer 84). And Jesus notes that Judas' problem is that he "could not be taught. He was too proud" (85). In fact, Jesus believes that Judas may be "Satan's gift" to him (84).

Regardless of his understanding of Judas' character, Jesus selects him to be his disciple. In Mailer's book, Judas is concerned for the poor, so much so that he is willing to put aside his doubts about Jesus because Judas sees Jesus as someone who will help the poor, no matter what else he may do. When he and Jesus discuss why Judas even bothers to follow Jesus, Judas tells him, "Having grown up among [the rich], I know what is in their hearts, and I detest them. They continue to believe they are good. They see themselves as rich in charity, in piety, and in loyalty to their people. So I scorn them. They not only tolerate the great distance between the rich and the poor, they increase it" (143).

Judas' emphasis on social justice for the poor makes him the perfect disciple to protest the woman who anoints Jesus with spikenard shortly before the arrest. The gospel of John tells us that Judas keeps the money for the group (John 13:29), primarily in a negative fashion. When Jesus is anointed by a woman (Mary of Bethany in John's account), the disciples object to the waste involved, as the perfume was quite expensive, and the money should have been given to the poor. In the book of John, only Judas raises this objection, and it is not the poor he has in mind; rather, "he was a thief; as keeper of the money bag, he used to help himself to what was put into it" (John 12:6). Thus, John sets up Judas' negative character early on. However, the explanation in Mailer's book goes farther than even the Synoptics do to make Judas' protest look noble. Now, he is protesting that the poor need help for their own sake, not so that he can line his pockets.

Mailer's book adds one other component to Judas' character. It completely omits Simon the Zealot from the narrative, other than a brief mention in listing all the disciples and explaining why Jesus changed Simon Peter's name to just Peter. Judas takes the place of Simon the Zealot to advocate an overthrow of Rome. Not only does Judas hate the rich, he also believes that the gap between the rich and the poor cannot be overcome while the Jews are enslaved by the Romans: "Before the Jews could come to know the brotherhood of man, they must be free of the Romans. . . . That was the only way, he declared to all of us, that the Jews could be free of the shame that kept them apart, some few rich, so many poor, and all subservient to the Romans" (222–23). The combination of an interest in social justice with a dedication to Zealotry creates a Judas who is richer than one with a single focus. Not only does this portrayal help explain Judas' protest over the spikenard, it also helps give his opposition of the Romans a convincing backstory.

This Jesus initially distrusts Judas, but when Jesus is in the dungeon, awaiting his hearing before Caiaphas, he wishes for Judas' advice. He knows that Judas understands the political system much better than he does. Judas, of all the disciples, "had been the wisest in explaining how our priests went about arranging matters with the Romans" (221). But Judas has already committed suicide, though Jesus does not know it at this point. Thus, Jesus learns for himself how the priests arrange matters with Rome. He has not heeded Judas' advice because he "did not feel subservient to the Romans. They might hold us in their grip here on earth, but they were as nothing compared to the Kingdom of Heaven" (223). Judas cannot accept this idea; instead, he believes they must overthrow the Romans and restore social justice; Jesus, however, believes in a kingdom that is beyond this world. It is that conflict that leads Judas to betray Jesus.

Unlike both Ricci's and Kazantzakis' Judases, who doubt that Jesus is the Messiah, Burgess' Judas, after joining Jesus, seems convinced that Jesus is the Messiah from the outset. When Jesus asks the disciples who they think he is, Judas concurs with the answer that Peter gives. This book seems to imply that Judas operates on the same level of understanding as Peter, but he's not quite as willing to speak out as Peter is. However, Judas is not well-suited to the ministry to which Jesus has called his disciples. When the disciples are sent out to teach, Judas strikes people as overly educated, and, thus, they do not listen to him as they do to the others. This effect is in stark contrast to Peter's who speaks with simple language, and, thus, is successful in reaching the people.

Burgess' novel portrays Judas as one who is so convinced that Jesus is the Messiah that he is willing to do anything to help bring that kingdom about; however, he also is presented as rather naïve about what it is, exactly, that Jesus is doing. Samuel Coale writes of Judas' innocence, "In his [Burgess'] portrayal of Judas as a political idealist and innocent . . . he creates a valid and interesting character. Burgess' Judas thinks that Christ wants both an earthly kingship and a spiritual rule within it" (181). After witnessing Lazarus' resurrection, Judas goes to Jerusalem ahead of the other disciples and Jesus. Thinking of the gospel, the reader expects that he is going to turn Jesus in. In the book, Judas seeks out Zerah, a former student who has become quite powerful as a Pharisee. Judas is afraid of Jesus' talk that he must be killed when he comes to Jerusalem. He wants Zerah to convince the other Pharisees of Jesus' Messiahship and also not to do anything to Jesus but to help bring Jesus' kingdom to fruition. Coale comments, "He betrays Christ to the priests, because he thinks they will keep him safe until the appointed hour of his triumph" (181).

This idea of Judas as naïve and innocent is compelling in that, in the gospels, none of the disciples, including Judas, seem to believe that Jesus could possibly be crucified. In fact, they all seem baffled whenever he talks of going to Jerusalem and being put to death: William Klassen writes, "The Gospel accounts also agree in affirming that not one of the disciples thought for a moment that Jesus would be crucified. There is, then, no reason to believe that Judas thought he would assist in bringing about Jesus' death when he brought Jesus and the authorities together. . . . It may well be that Judas believed most strongly that in any confrontation between Jesus and his enemies, Jesus would triumph" (45). Thus, Judas in *Man of Nazareth* simply does not believe that Jesus could possibly be executed by the Jewish leaders; instead, he thinks that Jesus will convince them that he is the Messiah and bring his kingdom to the people. It is precisely his belief in Jesus as Messiah that provokes him to this action.

The Last Temptation of Christ, in contrast, shows a conflicted Judas who, even after he refuses to kill Jesus because he might be the Messiah, struggles with that idea. Judas ultimately joins Jesus, though it is clear he still does not believe Jesus is the Messiah, nor does he even believe much of what Jesus says: "Judas listened to him and knit his brows. He was not interested in the kingdom of heaven. His great concern was for the kingdom of the earth—and not the whole earth, either, but only the land of Israel, which was made of men and stones, not of prayer and clouds. The Romans—those barbarians, those heathens—the Romans were trampling over this land. First they must be expelled; then we can worry about kingdoms of heaven" (196).

In fact, not only does Judas not believe everything Jesus teaches, he seems to be leading Jesus, rather than following him: "Watch out, son of Mary. I've said it once and I say it again: watch out, take the road I tell you. Why do you think I go along with you? Well, you had better learn: it's to show you your way" (204). However, since Judas believes that Jesus might be the Messiah, even when Judas doubts, he has reason enough to follow Jesus: "I don't want to rush into this and kill the Saviour; no, I don't want that! . . . He might not even know it himself, I said. Best be patient and let him live awhile, let him live so that we can see what he says and does; and if he isn't the One we're waiting for, there's always plenty of time to get rid of him" (205).

Here Jesus seems to be the one who is confused, not Judas. Jesus is the one who asks Judas what they can do to solve the problem of Jesus' identity, and it is Judas who comes up with the idea of going to John the Baptist to discover whether or not Jesus is the Messiah. Leavitt comments, "Judas is the one disciple to understand and oppose his master's new teaching: The Savior he seeks carries an ax and not a flowering branch. Ordered by the Zealots to kill the maker of crosses, Judas becomes his follower instead, for he suspects before anyone else that his childhood friend may be the Messiah" (70–71). Judas has the answers, while Jesus only has questions. This portrayal of Judas, though it diminishes the presentation of Jesus—making him seem wishy-washy and almost spineless—is consistent with a Judas who has a background as a Zealot, and who is a killer, at that. He is not used to taking direction from anyone else; he is used to giving it, and he expects Jesus to follow him rather than vice versa.

However, after Jesus' time in the wilderness, the relationship reverses, especially when it comes to Jesus' death. Jesus believes that the only way he can fulfill the mission of the Messiah is to offer himself up as a sacrifice on the cross. However, he needs one of the disciples to help him do so; he needs someone to betray him. He chooses Judas because he is the only disciple he can rely on. Judas, however, questions Jesus: "I've asked you before, Rabbi—is there no other way?" and it is now Jesus who has the answer to the question: "No, Judas, my brother. I too should have liked one; I too hoped and waited for one until now—but in vain. No, there is no other way. The end of the world is here. This world, this kingdom of the Devil, will be destroyed and the kingdom of heaven will come. I shall bring it. How? By dying. There is no other way. Do not quiver, Judas, my brother. In three days I shall rise again" (420).

This change in the relationship does not mean that Judas no longer questions Jesus. When Jesus heals the daughter of a Roman centurion, Judas' zealo-try flares up again: "You dissipate your strength on unbelievers. You help our enemies. Is this the end of the world you've brought up? Are these the flames?" (Kazantzakis 324). Says Leavitt, it seems that "this Judas is disturbed by his friend's seeming passivity, by the forgiveness which he preaches, above all by his refusal to lead their rebellion" (68). Judas does, however, fulfill his mission, and he betrays Jesus so that Jesus can be crucified.

It is not surprising that Judas' betrayal of Jesus is the one aspect of his character that is consistent in all four authors, as even people who are unfamiliar with much of the Bible know the role that Judas plays in the gospel story. In fact, the authors of the gospels tell little about Judas beyond the fact that he betrays Jesus.[4] While there are narratives about how many other disciples come to join Jesus, especially the major apostles, such as Peter, Judas simply appears in the list of the twelve, though the authors of the Synoptics make sure to mention that he is the one who betrayed Jesus (Matt. 10:4, Mark 3:19, Luke 6:16). Similarly, *Man of Nazareth* shows a Judas who accidentally

---

[4]Reynolds Price stays so close to the gospel accounts, for example, that his Judas lacks any interest at all. He betrays Jesus, but Price gives him no motivation for doing so (275), and his Judas also commits suicide by hanging himself. Jesus does appear to Judas before Judas hangs himself, but all he does is touch Judas on the wrist.

sends Jesus to his death, while the novels by Kazantzakis and Saramago show Judas merely doing what Jesus wants him to do. Ricci's novel depicts Judas betraying Jesus in smaller ways, not by a one-time betrayal that leads to death. Only *The Gospel According to the Son* offers a malicious Judas who goes to the authorities because of something Jesus does.[5]

In an interesting departure from these authors, Christopher Moore, in *Lamb*, makes it unclear whether or not Judas is doing what Jesus wants him to or not. When Joshua (Jesus) first meets Judas, he says, "I know who you are. . . . I've been waiting for you," which clearly shows that Jesus knows the importance of the role Judas will play (365). However, when they are at the Last Supper, he whispers something to Judas that no one else hears. He then says, "One of you will betray me this very night. . . . Won't you, Judas?" (414). Judas is surprised by this accusation, but, when no one comes to his defense, he flees. When Biff comes to kill Judas, Judas tells him, "He knew he had to die. . . . How do you think I knew he'd be at Gethsemane, not at Simon's? He told me!" (434). Thus, it seems that Joshua tells Judas where he will be because he knows that Judas will go and tell the Pharisees. Joshua knows that Judas is going to betray him, so he gives him and no one else the information. In a sense, then, he sets Judas up to be able to betray him when he very well could have avoided it. Judas even says to Biff, "I had to do it. Someone did" (435). However, he adds that Joshua would have "just reminded us of what we'll never be" (435), which seems to be another reason for Judas' betrayal. It's not just that Joshua admitted that he would never overthrow the Romans, which Judas, as a Zealot, would have wanted. Instead, Joshua's mere existence would have shown the rest of humanity how far we are from perfection; thus, he had to die. Because he does not feel any guilt over what he has done, he does not commit suicide; instead, Biff kills him, and it only appears that he hanged himself.

---

[5]It is interesting to note, though, that none of the authors choose the most obvious and simple motivation: Judas is simply greedy. Barclay points out that, if Judas betrayed Jesus for this reason, then he "struck one of the most dreadful bargains in history when he betrayed Jesus for thirty pieces of silver, about fourteen dollars, the normal value of a slave" (79). E.P. Blair points out that "the sum of money appears trivial for a treachery so heinous, and the motive superficial" (1007). Paul Casey also reminds the reader that "the conclusion that Judas betrayed Christ for less than half the price of the ointment [used by Mary of Bethany to anoint Jesus' feet] ought to spark some skepticism as to the sufficiency of the financial motive" (107).

The only two gospel accounts to give a reason for the betrayal at all (Luke and John) simply say that Satan entered Judas.[6] Burgess' novel rejects this idea, but still gives a motivation for the betrayal: idealistic innocence: "And so the arrest in the garden, Judas' shocking loss of innocence, his suicide following his awareness of involuntary betrayal of the one he would never wish to betray. That was my first Judas. The final Judas was a palimpsest of Judas as sweet innocent, as higher zealot, as indiscreet babbler, as disappointed idealist. But the devil did not enter him" (*YH* 304). Judas simply does not understand the political climate of the situation. Coale observes, "Judas operates in a carefully drawn political landscape, which Burgess describes well: the Zealots willing to overthrow Rome, Pontius Pilate hoping to remain neutral as the procurator of Judea, and the priests attempting to prove Christ's apparent blasphemy as actual treason in their successful effort to transfer the act and responsibility of Christ's death from their hands to the state's" (181–82).

Burgess creates a Judas who presents Jesus to the authorities in an effort to protect him, not to betray him. Unfortunately, Zerah, a Pharisee, is not a person Judas should trust, and he and Caiaphas prey on Judas' innocence to arrest Jesus. Caiaphas tells Judas, "There is only one way out, as I see it. . . . He must be delivered into the hands of his friends—those of his friends, I mean, who are best able to protect him. Forgive me, my son, for implying that you and your companions are powerless. Powerful in grace you may be, but grace cannot contend with stones and swords and hangman's nooses" (240). Because of his innocence and misplaced trust, Judas agrees to this plan, giving Caiaphas and Zerah the information they need to arrest Jesus.

When they arrive to do so, they hand Judas the thirty silver pieces, and Zerah says, "Jesus of Nazareth, you stand under arrest on a charge of

---

[6]*Mary Called Magdalene* is the only book here to allude to the idea of Satanic possession, as it seems to relate Judas' becoming possessed by Satan, though it's never clear. When they are camping at Dan, a place with an evil history for the Israelites, Judas "felt its evil influence. In fact, this morning his eyes looked clouded, different" (434). This description is reminiscent of Mary's eyes when she is possessed by the demons. After Mary learns of Judas' plan to betray Jesus, she thinks that Satan may be behind it: "Could Satan have entered into [Judas] back at that dreadful, haunted altar at Dan? Satan tried to get Jesus in the desert; he failed, but he got Judas instead at Dan" (487).

blasphemy. The charge comes from the mouth of your own disciple here. He sold you" (246). Judas becomes like a wild animal, running around the garden until he finally flees, looking for rope with which he can hang himself. Judas suffered from too much innocence, as Zerah sees it: "You have taught innocence, so I hear, Jesus of Nazareth. You had a good pupil here in my old fellow-student, ever ready to learn. Good at Greek, good at innocence. The innocence of one who wished to see the salvation of the world" (247). Klassen argues that, from the perspective of the Bible, Judas' suicide also shows his innocence in turning over Jesus to the authorities: "Matthew reports that Judas changed when he saw that Jesus was being handed over to Pilate. The implication is clear: this is not what he had intended" (161–62).

It then becomes hard to fault Judas for believing too much in the salvation of the world and in Jesus as the means by which that might be accomplished. Burgess' novel raises the question of intentions and actions by presenting Judas in this manner, in addition to merely providing a motive for Judas' actions. Humans often do horrible actions for truly good reasons, which is a way to let Judas off the hook.

In a similar manner, Margaret George, in *Mary Called Magdalene*, seems to create a Judas who betrays Jesus in an attempt to protect him, only to see him executed instead. After Herod's soldiers have warned Jesus about his gatherings, Mary and Judas talk about protecting Jesus from himself, though Mary is much less sure of this than Judas. To her, it sounds as if she is "disloyal" and "conspiratorial," but she is relieved when Judas says that they will prevent him "by persuasion" and that Jesus' "mother would help [them]" (408). Even though Mary has visions of what will happen to Jesus in Jerusalem, she does not attempt to protect him from himself, and she does talk to him of what might come. Judas, on the other hand, meets with Herod, Annas, and Caiaphas to let them know where they can capture Jesus quietly. While he insists on being paid for his information, he tells Annas, "I think he should be protected from himself. . . . He has raised enormous expectations that he can never fulfill. When he cannot, people will turn on him. This should give him a chance to think, before it is too late" (477). In the Garden of Gethsemane, he tells Mary that Jesus will be taken "to the house of Annas, and thence to Caiaphas's palace. Jesus will be examined and questioned there, and detained until after the crowds have left Jerusalem. Then he can go back to Galilee with his faithful, peaceful, . . . brave, loyal . . . followers" (508). It is only when he hears Jesus' sentence pronounced that he realizes what he has done: "Oh, God, you lied! I have sinned, sinned in betraying innocent blood" (520).

However, *Mary Called Magdalene* may offer another reason for Judas' betrayal, though it is never explicitly stated. Shortly after Judas joins the group of disciples, he begins showing an interest in Mary passing beyond that which the other disciples show. He is the first to sympathize with Mary after Joel's death, and he volunteers to take care of the money that she has recently inherited so that she will not have to deal with it. When Peter accuses Mary of being Jesus' favorite disciple, Judas is the only disciple who defends her. When Jesus is leading them toward Dan, which the disciples perceive as dangerous, he tells Mary, "As a woman, . . . surely you must be concerned for your safety," and then he moves "closer to Mary, implying his protection" (427). Just before that, when asked why he has followed Jesus, he states that Jesus "seemed to have all the answers," but his response is so quick that it "was obviously rehearsed" (427). Judas seems to be following Jesus only to be close to Mary. He confirms this when they arrive at Dan, and he proposes to Mary after asking her to visit his family with him. She rejects both offers. It might be this rejection, not Satan's possession, that causes his eyes to darken and leads him to betray Jesus. Because it has been evident to all of the disciples that Mary cares for Jesus, Judas may simply be betraying Jesus to get back at Mary for rejecting him. Even without Mary's affection for Jesus, betraying Jesus would ruin Mary's life, which may be reason enough for Judas to turn him over to the religious leaders. This motive, more than the possession by Satan, would make Judas a more human character, one whom readers could more easily identify with.

In *The Last Temptation of Christ*, Judas betrays Jesus, but only because it is his mission to do so; in fact, Jesus encourages him to do so. Antonakes comments, "Kazantzakis presents Judas as a collaborator of Jesus in his effort to carry out the divine plan. However, it is not made clear how the divine plan serves Judas's initial revolutionary plan" (98). Klassen argues that such an interpretation of Judas might well fit with what actually happens. He points out that "what our earliest sources do say is that Judas did nothing until Jesus told him to do it. Later, the final editors of the Gospels, beginning with Luke, Matthew, and John, found this possibility so difficult to swallow that they felt they had no choice but to ascribe dark motives to the actions of Judas. Yet they never imputed one saying to Jesus that actually criticized Judas, nor did they ever imply that Jesus considered what Judas was doing to be a sin" (45). Kazantzakis' novel draws on this idea of Jesus as the one behind Judas' betrayal and presents a Judas who goes to the authorities reluctantly, only because he clearly believes Jesus is the Messiah, and Jesus is asking this one action of Judas.

Not surprisingly, then, especially given his earlier role as the driving force in their relationship, Judas seems to be the one who saves Jesus from his temptation and forces him to go through with what Jesus asked Judas to begin. In the vision of marital bliss that the Devil presents to Jesus on the cross, it is only Judas, of the disciples, who criticizes him for leaving the cross. Writes Leavitt, Judas is

> the only realist in a crowd of self-seekers and dreamers, and he is the one disciple able to act, a colossus stronger than the master himself. Thus it is he who must betray Jesus, to enable him to fulfill his mission, perhaps to become the Messiah . . . When Jesus dreams on the cross that his crucifixion has never occurred, that he has lived instead a pedestrian life, it is his uncompromising disciple who compels him to return to his mission, to awake on the cross and call out to God. (71)

He will no longer even acknowledge him as Rabbi, let alone Messiah: "As he faced the cross this fake Messiah went dizzy and fainted. Then the ladies got hold of him and installed him to manufacture children for them. He says he fought, fought courageously. Yes, he swaggers about like the cock of the roost. But your post, deserter, was on the cross, and you know it. Others can reclaim barren lands and barren women. Your duty was to mount the cross—that's what I say" (Kazantzakis 491). In fact, Leavitt observes, "In both [visions, the one at the beginning of the novel and the one at the end], it is Judas the patriot who compels his younger and weaker friend to fulfill his mission, to save . . . what? Himself? Israel? Mankind? Neither is sure" (Leavitt 64).

Jesus needs Judas as much as Israel needs Jesus. Without him, he cannot fulfill his mission. In fact, Jesus believes that Judas has the harder path. Judas asks him if he can betray his master, and Jesus replies, "No, I do not think I would be able to. That is why God pitied me and gave me the easier task: to be crucified" (421). Jesus has to rely on Judas, then, trusting him to help with the completion of his mission.

Judas plays a lesser role in Saramago's work than he does in other narratives, both gospel and adaptations. He is, however, still the person who turns Jesus in to the authorities, but here, as in Kazantzakis' work, it is Jesus who asks him to do so. Jesus is trying to avoid being sacrificed as the Son of God, so he decides that, if he can be crucified as the King of the Jews, he will thwart God's plan, which will result in so much bloodshed to come. However, he needs someone to help him execute his plan, and Judas is the only disciple who volunteers. The others, in fact, draw their daggers and threaten to kill him to prevent his doing so, but Jesus has them put away their weapons and encourages Judas to go quickly.

Judas does not take any money from the authorities for his information, but he still hangs himself for what he does. In fact, he hangs himself at a place where Jesus will pass, and his body is still warm when the authorities examine it while they are taking Jesus to Golgotha. Saramago's book does not make it clear why Judas commits suicide, but the reader may infer that he expects that Jesus' plan will fail, that God will succeed in the end, and that he will be the means of that sacrifice and, thus, vilified for all eternity. Saramago's Judas seems at least to want to remind Jesus of the sacrifice he is making for Jesus' sake.

Judas in *Testament* attempts to earn Jesus' approval, and that ultimately leads to Jesus' death, even though he does not intend that result. Judas takes part in a riot after Pilate put up Roman standards near the Jewish Temple; the Jews are highly offended, interpreting the standards as idolatry. Judas joins this protest because he feels that he has been idle from his Zealot group for too long. Pilate lures the group of protesters into a stadium under the pretense of talking to them, but he surrounds them with soldiers, instead. Rather than fearing for their lives, the Jews, one by one, kneel down and bare their necks to be struck by the soldiers; Judas joins them in this action. This action begins to change his view on how to work against the Roman government: "The object, in this case, was our freedom, which I had always imagined was a thing that had to be wrested away from our enemies like a trophy or prize. But in the stadium, when we'd been kneeling there, it had seemed something more subtle than that, not to be captured or won but somehow called into being, conjured up like a spirit" (73). Jesus does not praise him for what he has done: "I began to speak to him of the events in Caesarea but he was strangely distant and cool, treating me as if I had betrayed him by going off or by daring to learn things that might compete with his own teaching" (77). This is the type of betrayal that Judas is described as doing in Ricci's novel, not the proactive betrayal of Jesus that leads to his crucifixion, as in the gospels. Instead, it is the minor, day-to-day betrayals that loom so large to Ricci's Jesus.

Judas' association with this group is what directly leads to Jesus' death. After a riot in the Temple, Aram (a follower of Jesus who splits from him for a while but who ultimately returns) tells the examiners in the jail that Judas is often with Jesus; the examiner seems more interested in this news than any other that Aram shares. The authorities believe that Jesus is somehow associated with a rebel group that seeks to overthrow the Roman government. Because they do not understand Greek, Peter and Simon the Canaanite, believe that Judas has betrayed Jesus:

> The truth was that neither of them had followed the trial well, not speaking much Greek. They hadn't gathered that it was Aram who'd betrayed Jesus and assumed it was Judas, since his was the name they'd made out during the charges—I

> [Simon of Gergesa] ought to have set them straight then but didn't
> want to admit that I'd knelt there beside Aram while he'd
> sealed Jesus's fate, and hadn't done anything. (435)

This approach is similar to what several scholars have hypothesized about Judas, which Klassen summarizes: "In order to protect Jesus and Judas from making serious mistakes of judgment several scholars have even conjectured that Judas was taken captive by the high priests during the time of the Temple action and he was then forced to reveal where Jesus could be apprehended" (51). While Ricci's Judas is not forced to tell them where Jesus can be apprehended, Judas' being imprisoned because of the events in the Temple directly leads to Jesus' arrest.

It is not surprising that the disciples would assume Judas would betray Jesus, as they have not liked him from the outset. One of the reasons for this dislike may have been his geographical background. Ricci's Judas is the only disciple from Judea, an idea that probably stems from Judas' name. "Iscariot" could mean "the man from Kerioth." If so, then, even according to the gospels, Judas would have been the only disciple from Judea (Blair 1007). This Judean background may play into the betrayal later, but it would also possibly have made him feel an outcast among the disciples.[7] Concerning Judas' role as outsider because of his heritage, Casey writes, "This hypothesis makes him by heritage an outsider, whose ancestry distances him from the rest of the disciples: it underscores the detachment of the other disciples from his deed" (103). Barclay even argues that the Judean background may have helped Judas see Jesus' chances of succeeding in Jerusalem much more clearly than do the other disciples, or even Jesus. Because he sees Jesus losing against Rome and the Jewish leaders, he turns Jesus over in an effort to protect him from getting killed (77). However, Ricci uses this background only to reinforce the difference between Judas and the other disciples.

Judas recognizes fairly quickly that he does not fit in, though, from his point of view, his lack of acceptance is due to what he would see as positive

---

[7]*Mary Called Magdalene* also shows Judas as the only disciple from Judea, which makes him an outsider among the disciples.

causes: "From the outset it was clear that I was not well accepted by the other in Yeshua's [Jesus'] inner circle. My education marked me, and my accent; but chiefly it was my willingness to challenge Yeshua's views, which Yeshua applauded, saying it kept his mind sharp for his critics, but which in the men of the group brought out a brooding discomfort and in the women a fairly open hostility" (43–44). It is easy to see, because of his intelligence and education, why Judas, according to Hand, "is viewed with suspicion by the fishermen, masons, farmers and women who accompany Yeshua on his travels. Through one of *Testament*'s neater twists, we see how the gossip and mistrust rampant among Yeshua's own camp cause the innocent Yihuda to become the now-familiar betrayer Judas" (Hand T6).

It is true that the women, especially Mary Magdalene, do not like Judas. She ascribes a number of problems to Judas: "By the following morning it was clear that along with the stranger [Judas] had come an evil influence. We awoke to the news of the prophet Yohanan's [John's] death—in Migdal the word came through at dawn, out of Tiberias"; and "While we were waiting, however, I saw the stranger approaching from the far gates, which led out to the Roman camp, and not long afterwards a contingent of soldiers arrived. I didn't know what to make of this except that he was a spy who had been sent to us and had called the soldiers in the hope of provoking a riot, so that Yeshua [Jesus] might be arrested as the cause of it" (Ricci 158).

What is most interesting about Ricci's portrayal, though, is that his book never shows us Judas' reaction to Jesus' arrest or crucifixion, and the reader never knows whether or not Judas knows that he has any role in Jesus' death. In fact, Judas leaves Jesus a few weeks before Passover, even though his group wants Judas to reinfiltrate the disciples and report back whenever they arrive in Jerusalem. Judas, however, does not do this. Instead, he ends his narrative section by merely reflecting on Jesus, and it seems that he has been dramatically changed by his encounter with Jesus, perhaps more so than the other characters: "But there was in Yeshua [Jesus] that quality that made one feel there was something, still, some bit of hope, some secret he might reveal that would help make this world over. Tell me your secret, I wanted to say to him, tell me, make me new. And even now, though I had left him, I often saw him beckoning before me as towards a doorway he would have had me pass through, from darkness to light" (122). Perhaps Judas never attains the truth that Jesus has for him that would make him new. Or perhaps he sees Jesus more clearly than any of the others do. Ricci leaves the reader with a Judas who merely walks away, never to be heard from again.

Mailer's Judas has warned Jesus earlier of what would happen if Jesus ceases to advocate for the poor: "I would turn against you. A man who is ready to walk away from the poor by a little is soon ready to depart from them by a lot" (144). Thus, Jesus is not surprised when he looks up and notices that Judas has left: "If he loved me, so did he also love me no longer" (201). Thus, his betrayal of Jesus comes as no surprise. Because he believes Jesus has turned against the poor, he turns against Jesus and turns him in. However, he suffers the same remorse he suffers in the gospel accounts, returns the thirty pieces of silver, and commits suicide. Jesus, however, does not understand what motivates Judas to this action: "How could I comprehend? Of what had Judas repented? Of his lack of belief in my Father? Or his lack of loyalty to me? No, I could not speak. Nor did I dare" (225). While Mailer's novel gives the readers a clear reason for Judas' betrayal of Jesus, he leaves the readers in the same situation as Jesus regarding Judas' change of heart and suicide. We, like Jesus, simply wonder why he would do it, given how he felt about Jesus' actions.

The books, with that by Saramago a notable exception, show a complex Judas who struggles with who Jesus is and how he is to relate. Soren Kierkegaard wrote in his Journals, "One will get a deep insight into the state of Christianity in each age by seeing how it interprets Judas" (qtd. in Pyper 115). In these authors' works, Judas becomes more human, someone readers can relate to, rather than the abstraction of the gospels who betrays Jesus merely because Satan entered him. Burgess represents one extreme, presenting him as an innocent, while Mailer shows the other extreme, an angry nationalist who reacts to Jesus' ignoring the poor by betraying him to the authorities. The other authors fill in the middle, providing readers with a wide spectrum of interpretations concerning Judas, although almost all leave him innocent. In the second half of the late twentieth and early twenty-first centuries, rather than condemning Judas, authors and readers seem to be looking for ways to excuse his behavior, much as we would like our own betrayals explained away.

CHAPTER 9

'Tis Pity She's a Whore

THE REVISION OF MARY MAGDALENE

Though the information the bible presents concerning Mary Magdalene is thin, artists and religious leaders have long been fascinated by her. In her review of research on Mary Magdalene since 1975, Pamela Thimmes writes, "Apart from the other Mary, Mary the mother of Jesus, no other woman character in the Christian Scriptures has received as much attention. What makes this interest so extraordinary is that Mary Magdalene is a character found in all of the canonical gospels, but nowhere else in the New Testament. However, she is a character in 11 gnostic/apocryphal works, where sometimes she is a major character" (193). Galen Knutson observes, "However, if a count is made more narrowly of the passion, death and resurrection narratives, only Peter who denied Jesus and Judas who betrayed Jesus are mentioned more frequently" (207). However, that attention has not always been positive; in fact, for most of the past two thousand years, Mary has been portrayed as a prostitute, a sinner who was in need of redemption, rather than as the first witness to Jesus' resurrection. Although there have been gains made in the critical evaluation of Mary Magdalene, Mary Rose D'Angelo is too optimistic when she writes, "Feminist interpretation has debunked the image of the fallen and repentant Magdalene, substituting the figure of Mary Magdalene as the intrepid and faithful disciple of Jesus, an apostle with the twelve and a witness to the resurrection" (105). In fiction, rather than in the theological realm, Mary has largely moved from an apostle in the early church to a redeemed prostitute to the main cause of Jesus' sexual temptation, depending on whose version of the story one reads. Contemporary authors retell Jesus' story and use Mary Magdalene to reinforce themes of redemption or temptation in their works through how they present her: whether or not she was a prostitute, how she lived her life

121

with Jesus, and whether or not she had any role in the spreading of the story of the resurrection.

Most authors focus on the Mary Magdalene of legend, the prostitute. As Thimmes writes, "Based on the strategy that sex sells, Andrew Lloyd Webber and Tim Rice's rock opera *Jesus Christ Superstar* (1969) and Nikos Kazantzakis' books, *The Last Temptation of Christ* (1960, and the subsequent film in 1988) and Report to Greco (1965) built their fictionalized portrayals of Mary Magdalene as a prostitute and the lover of Jesus from conflated and erroneous biblical interpretations, popular legends and Christian art" (194). Through her, they show the sexual temptation that Jesus faces (and gives into in Saramago's book, though it does not show that action as negative), but they also use her to show the idea of redemption and Jesus' acceptance of those whom society does not accept. Even Ricci's book, which does not present Mary as a prostitute, still makes her an outcast.[1]

It is not surprising, given the number of legends and the teaching of the early church concerning Mary Magdalene, that almost all writers who deal with her draw on her mythical past as a prostitute. She had been seen as an equal to the apostles—the "apostle to the apostles,"[2] in fact—but that changed on September 21, 591, when Pope Gregory presented a homily where he stated, "We believe that this woman whom Luke calls a female sinner, whom John calls Mary, is the same Mary from whom Mark says seven demons were cast out" (qtd. in Jansen 32–33).[3] Gregory connects Mary Magdalene to Mary of Bethany, but he also connects her to the woman mentioned in Luke

---

[1]Only a writer such as Reynolds Price whose slim gospel seems to simply tell the gospel story of the Bible, has Mary as the minor character she is in the gospel accounts. He shows her having the seven demons cast out of her, at the cross when Jesus is crucified, and at the empty tomb where Jesus appears to her, but nothing more.

[2]Thimmes writes, "it is significant to note that Hippolytus, bishop of Rome (c. 170–235) . . . was the first to grant to Mary Magdalene the title *'Apostola Apostolorum'* (apostle to the apostles). In his commentary on *Canticle of Canticles* he associates her with the bride and with the Bride of Christ, a symbol of the Church" (220–21). According to Lucy Winkett, "The ancient tradition of Mary of Magdala as apostola apostolorum ('apostle of the apostles') is used today by Pope John Paul II" (26).

[3]There was evidence of this change coming before Gregory preached his homily. Thimmes writes, "The origins of the 'invented' Mary Magdalene traditions are so elusive and obscure that a source cannot be posited, although some suggest that the writings of Ephraim the Syrian (306–373 CE) provide a clue to the origins of this ruse, for he identifies the Mary Magdalene of Lk. 8.1–3 with the unnamed woman of Lk. 7.36–50" (221).

who anoints Jesus' feet with perfume.[4] It is not explicitly stated that this woman is a prostitute, but it is clearly implied:

> Although the Greek word for a harlot, *porin*, which appears elsewhere in Luke (15:30), is not used in this account, the emphasis given to Luke's phrase "a sinner in the city," and the word "sinner" used by the Pharisee, both seem to indicate the latter's conviction that the woman's "sin" is sexual, that she is a prostitute. That the woman wears her hair loose is another sign of her fallen status, as only prostitutes wore their hair thus in public. (Haskins 18)

The influence Gregory has on the later interpretation of Mary is difficult to overstate: "Gregory's influence in this matter can be seen in later centuries when his sermons were highly praised in the eight [*sic*] and ninth centuries (they were more popular than Augustine's), and his composite Mary Magdalene rode into the Middle Ages, where the legends grew and the myth endured" (Thimmes 221). And so, "by the 10th century Mary Magdalene the holy harlot was fully formed. Abbot Odo at Cluny Abbey wrote that after an existence devoted to 'sensual pleasures' Mary Magdalene helps, by a reformed life and zealous ministrations to the daily needs of Jesus, to rescue females from the condemnation Eve brought upon women at the beginning" (Winkett 21–22).

There are a few other contributions to the longevity of this idea. Magdala, Mary's hometown and from whence she derives her name, was known for its immorality, especially relating to sexuality; rabbis, in fact, blamed the fall of the city on the inhabitants' behavior (Blair 288). A purported autobiography

---

[4]Lisa Bellan-Boyer argues that Gregory did this "to conflate all the women who supported and participated in the life and ministry of Jesus into as few women as possible, making the many Marys into one honorable Mary and one Mary who bore the mark of shame. Mary, the mother of Jesus, like her son, become less and less Jewish and more and more divinized. She became increasingly separated from other women,'blessed among women' so as to become ostracized from them, or they from her. One can never be as good as the Blessed Virgin Mary, no matter how unassailable one's bodily purity may be or how selfless a mother. You could be 'as good' as Mary Magdalene, though" (55–57). What Bellan-Boyer does not point out in this assertion, though, is why Gregory would have conflated Mary of Bethany, certainly one of the "good" Marys with Mary Magdalene, who became the representative of the "bad" Marys.

of Mary, of which there were many, now referred to as the *vita eremitca*, shows Mary going to Egypt to live be a hermit for thirty years. The true Mary of Egypt, whose story is combined with Mary Magdalene's in this work, had been a prostitute before she is converted (Jansen 37–38).

Mary is also loosely connected to the woman caught in adultery in John 8. Haskins writes, "The links between Mary Magdalen [*sic*] and both the woman of Samaria and the woman taken in adultery are even more tenuous than those between the Magdalen and Luke's sinner and Mary of Bethany. They owe their origins, however, to the conflated creature which Mary of Magdala became from the sixth century on—the repentant whore" (26). The Catholic Church officially held Gregory's position until 1969 (Jansen 35), and it is clear that this idea is still held, though no longer officially.[5] The lingering effects still exist, as Lucy Winkett points out: "Mary Magdalene has given her name to homes for fallen women, to the Magdalen laundries; popular as workhouses for, among others, women pregnant with the children of priests (with all the attendant imagery of sin and stain). She has given her name to a charity which currently exists to assist women who have had or who are having relationships with priests who have committed themselves to celibacy" (20). Galen Knutson adds to this list, "This mythic image of a sainted 'sinner' even led to a pornographic movement in nineteenth-century England, where poor women were manipulated into posing for 'Magdalene photos'" (206).

It is understandable, also, why people might cling to the idea of Mary as a prostitute, even outside of the stories and legends that have accumulated. It is an appealing picture because a Mary who is a sinner is much more human than a Mary who does nothing more than support Jesus' ministry, witness his resurrection, and spread the gospel like the rest of the apostles. In the same way that Peter's denial humanizes him, Mary's role as a prostitute humanizes her. Karen King points out the metaphorical importance of these legends: "Yet the role of repentant

---

[5]*The Da Vinci Code* has Leigh Teabing argue that the church purposefully labeled Mary as a prostitute to discredit her: "Magdalene was no such thing [a prostitute]. That unfortunate misconception is the legacy of a smear campaign launched by the early Church. The Church needed to defame Mary Magdalene in order to cover up her dangerous secret—her role as the Holy Grail" (244).

prostitute is symbolically appealing in its own right, and not just because the other options were closed off. It has proven itself to be a much more evocative figure than that of Mary as Jesus' wife or lover. The image of Mary as the redeemed sinner has nourished a deep empathy that resonates with our human imperfection, frailty, and mortality. A fallen redeemer has enormous power to redeem" (153). While it is easy to understand why the myth of Mary Magdalene has had such staying power, modern scholarship has recently tried to rescue or re-vision Mary, focusing on her role as a witness to the resurrection and attempting to correct the legends that have accrued around her. However, reviewing film versions of the gospel stories, Jane Schaberg states quite clearly how this attempt has failed: "So much for modern scholarship which tries to undo the conflation between the Christian Testament figure and the nameless women of other stories—the conflation which became the essential aspect of her image" (35). Other than Ricci, all of the authors under consideration continue this conflation and turn Mary into a prostitute.

Burgess' presentation of Mary seems quite simple, as he, like most of the other authors, presents her as a prostitute; he does not, however, equate her with the woman in John 8 who is accused of adultery. His novel also ignores the main scriptural reference to Mary's past that shows that Jesus had cast out seven demons from her.[6] Burgess' book does provide an interesting twist to Mary's character. Despite the fact that she is clearly breaking Jewish law by engaging in prostitution, she refuses to work on the Sabbath, no matter what her madam thinks. Thus, she is presented as someone who seems to do what she must to survive but who does not willingly disobey the Jewish laws. It is this observance of the law, despite her profession, that lays the

---

[6]Many authors seem to ignore this fact, which is odd, considering it is one of the few clear references to Mary in the Bible. Perhaps it is our scientific world's discomfort with the idea of demon possession that makes authors skip past this information. Margaret George, though, in *Mary Called Magdalene*, actually devotes almost the first third of her book to describing how Mary becomes possessed with the seven demons and how she unsuccessfully tries to rid herself of them. It seems that there has been a wide variety of opinions as to what the demons were, as well, often reflecting the interpretation of Mary at that particular time. Winkett says, "Each age has tried to explain them: Medieval theologians interpreted them as the seven deadly sins, with emphasis on lust. Martin Luther interpreted them as the seven devils. Modern theologians interpret them as convulsions, similar to the man who lived among the tombs, a form of disability. Others write of a goddess cult contemporary with Jesus, which had seven steps of initiation" (23).

groundwork for Mary's interest in Jesus even before she encounters him. This presentation also further humanizes Mary, as her attempt at observing orthodoxy in a matter that many modern readers (though not Orthodox Jews) would consider minor is in direct contradiction of what could be a major transgression.

When one of her customers tells her of Jesus, calling him "friend" because of the way Jesus speaks of the forgiveness of sins, Mary decides to seek him. Jesus is speaking of the day of judgment, and a Pharisee points to Mary and asks if she will be included in the wheat (the holy people) who will enter paradise. Jesus protects Mary as he responds to his interrogator, though Jesus seems to address his comment to Mary, "Have no fear, daughter. For the sins of the body are quickly purged. But the fire is a strong one that will burn out the sin in the soul" (177). It is understandable, then, why Mary would want to follow someone who clearly accepts her as she is. She has been trying to follow the law but needs to make a living; Jesus shows Mary that she is closer to the truth than she could have ever imagined and that the law may be less relevant than the intentions of her heart.

Thus, Mary joins Jesus and follows him, though Jesus makes her and the other women travel separately. He reminds her that his disciples are merely men who are trying to resist temptation. Jesus, however, seems not to be tempted by Mary in the least, treating her more as a kindly father would. Through this separation, the book reminds the reader of the role of women in Jewish society at the time but does not seem to critique it. Instead, the situation is merely presented as a fact, an inconvenience that must be dealt with and nothing more.

Kazantzakis' novel also depicts Mary Magdalene as a prostitute; however, unlike Burgess', it presents Jesus as the reason behind Mary's employment.[7] When Jesus is twenty years old, he travels to Cana to choose a wife. He sees Mary holding a rose, and he knows immediately that he wants her, but "ten claws nailed themselves into his head and two frenzied wings beat above

---

[7] It might be argued that God is the reason behind Mary's choice of careers, as he is behind Jesus' reaction. However, Mary is unaware of God's role at this time, as is Jesus. Thus, Mary sees Jesus as the cause, and Jesus feels guilty for causing it, though he certainly had no control over his actions then.

him, tightly covering his temples. He shrieked and fell down on his face, frothing at the mouth" (26). God will not allow Jesus to marry, it seems. It is unclear why this event drives Mary to prostitution, but it seems perhaps to be a way for Mary to retaliate against Jesus. In the same way in this novel that Jesus seems to rebel against God's calling him to be the Messiah by building crosses, Mary rebels against the typical role for women in Jewish society by going to an extreme.

Simeon, Mary's father, does not know that Jesus is the cause of Mary's decision; he merely knows that "one day, after she returned from a festival in Cana, she wept and declared she wished to kill herself, and afterward she burst into fits of laughter, painted her cheeks, donned all her jewelry and began to walk to the streets" (38). Not only is she rebelling against Jesus by her action she is rebelling against her family and its expectations, as well. It has done nothing to deserve this, though, and the members of her family suffer needlessly because of her decision.

Jesus goes to Mary to ask her forgiveness and to try to save her from her behavior, but she does not want him to save her. She believes that she will find salvation in "the mud: shame, filth, this bed, this body of mine, covered as it is with bites and smeared with the whole world's drivel, sweat and slime!" (90). However, when Jesus leaves, she weeps, and it is clear she still loves him. She does not follow him as she believes that he will come back for her. He does come back, and this time he saves not just her soul, but her body as well.

She had practiced her trade on the Sabbath, which angered many of the Zealots. Barabbas and others went to her house to stone her. Here, Kazantzakis takes the story of the woman caught in adultery from John 8 and adapts it to fit Mary Magdalene. Barabbas and men and women from Magdala and Capernaum are preparing to stone Mary when Jesus comes through the crowd and physically restrains Barabbas' arm, asking him, "Barabbas . . . have you never disobeyed one of God's commandments? In your whole life have you never stolen, murdered, committed adultery or told a lie?" (176). From this point on, Mary ceases to be a prostitute, and she follows Jesus until the end. As in Burgess' novel, it is easy to see how such acceptance would appeal to someone in Mary's position. Both novels by Burgess and Kazantzakis show Jesus accepting Mary publicly, not behind closed doors. This acceptance gives her a public standing that a prostitute (or even a woman) could not have imagined in the society of the time.

Mary plays a very minor role in Mailer's novel. It does draw on the gospel account of Jesus' casting seven demons out of Mary, as the reason for her support of his ministry (Luke 8:1–2). In the gospels, the reader does not know when she encounters Jesus and when he cast the demons out, and there are no explanations for how she had the money to support his ministry. Mailer's novel does provide an explanation for the demons, and it also presents her as a prostitute: "The bones of her face were delicate, and her hair flowed down her back. With art, she had painted her eyes. She was gentle even as her mouth was proud and foolish" (183). Jesus refers to her as a harlot, and he remembers scriptures that condemn prostitution. Mary's role in Mailer's novel seems to be nothing more than a means to highlight attributes of Jesus. Since Jesus thinks of scriptures that condemn prostitution when he sees Mary, but moves beyond those scriptures to accept her, the novel poses an implicit criticism of those who cannot move beyond such attitudes. However, this remains implied, and it does not help with the characterization of Mary much at all.

Like *The Last Temptation of Christ*, The Gospel According to the Son takes Mary beyond being a common prostitute and turns her into the woman caught in adultery who is brought before Jesus for judgment. Jesus first thinks of many scriptures which condemn such behavior, but he ultimately lets her go with one of his most famous sayings: "He that is without sin among you, let him cast the first stone" (184). However, he does not send her away until he has cast the demons out of her. Again, this scene seems to be included more to demonstrate the development of Jesus' character than Mary's. Jesus struggles with Mary's role in society, yet he forgives her and casts the demons out of her, and that is all.

Mary Magdalene in *The Gospel According to Jesus Christ*, also a prostitute, is allowed more range than is evident in the other novels. Here her house is on the outskirts of town because of the lack of official acceptance for what she does, though enough men come to visit her to show that there was plenty of unofficial acceptance. Jesus stops to visit her because he has a sore foot, and he needs some medical attention. Jesus seems a bit naïve initially, as he is not even certain that she's a prostitute:

> The woman reeks of perfume, but Jesus, who may be innocent, has learned certain facts of life by watching the mating of goats and rams, he also has enough common sense to know that just because a woman uses perfume, it does not necessarily mean she is a whore. A whore should smell of the men she lies with, just as the goatherd smells of goat and the fishermen of fish, but who knows, perhaps these women perfume themselves heavily because they want to conceal, disguise, or even forget the odor of a man's body. (233)

After taking care of Jesus' foot, Mary invites Jesus to bed. Jesus initially resists by quoting verses concerning lust, but he ends up quoting the Song of Solomon: "Your thighs are like jewels, your navel is like a round goblet filled with scented wine, your belly is like a heap of wheat set about with lilies, your breasts are like two fawns that are the twins of a gazelle" (236). They live together for the next week with Mary instructing Jesus in the bedroom.[8]

After a week, when his foot has had time to heal, Jesus leaves Mary to return home. When his family does not believe that he has seen God, he returns to Mary to see if she will believe him. She has given up prostitution and promised herself to him alone, and she begins to travel with him, even though it seems she already knows who he is. When they are talking one night, Mary tells him that she will be at his side whenever she is needed. Jesus responds, "Who am I to deserve this?" Mary answers, "Don't you know who you are?" (240). She seems able to intuit how important he is and his impending death, but she chooses to accompany him anyway.

---

[8]Though this book goes farther than any of the others in granting Jesus and Mary an open, sexual relationship, even he does not suggest marriage. Oddly enough, one author notes that "Martin Luther believed that Jesus and Magdalene were married, as did Mormon patriarch Brigham Young" (Van Biema).

Even though Saramago is the most unorthodox of all the authors, his book does hint at Mary's ultimate role as the "apostle to the apostles." Since she recognizes who Jesus is even before he does, it makes sense that she might also understand the possibility for resurrection as well as, if not better than, any of the other disciples. While this book does not take the story to the resurrection, this portrayal of Mary is certainly more consistent with the gospels than many of the others, even though its author is an atheist.

It is interesting to note that other authors who write about Mary Magdalene, even when they are ultimately trying to rescue her reputation, still present her as a prostitute. For example, Marianne Fredriksson's *According to Mary Magdalene* is clearly trying to show Mary as a positive character and as a foil to the rest of the disciples. Twice in the opening twenty pages, the novel shows Mary remembering parts of her life in language almost verbatim from the gnostic *Gospel of Mary*.[9] In this section, the apostles ask Mary Magdalene to "Give [them] the words [Jesus] spoke to [her] and which [they] do not know" (3). Throughout the work, the novel refers to Mary's (and women's) role in Jesus' ministry. When Paul visits her after Jesus' death to find out what she knows, she tells him, "We were equal numbers of men and women disciples, and women constantly surrounded him. Right up until Golgotha, when most of his apostles deserted him. Around the cross we stood, his mother, Susanna, Salome, Mary, Clopas' wife, and me" (98).

However, Mary also sees that men have controlled women's lives and attempt to control religion. Thinking back to her mother's life, she remembers her mother's smile, only because it was so rare. What she saw more often was the pain of her mother's life: "But the clearest pictures were of her mother's sorrow. And her exhaustion, her body sucked dry from childbearing, bowed, its beauty gone, and the clenched hand pressed to her back to ease the pain. It was slavery, she thought" (26). Mary sees this same control of women taking root in the new religion of Christianity. Speaking

---

[9]In *The Wild Girl*, Michèle Roberts also quotes from both the gnostic *Gospel of Mary* and the *Gospel of Philip*, though more to talk about Peter than about Mary Magdalene. However, the novel does reference the *Gospel of Philip* by having disciples call Mary "the companion of the Saviour" (49).

to the priestess at the temple of Isis, she says, "Nothing will change. . . . The apostles are Jews, rooted in ancient prejudices that woman has no soul and man is the only human being." The priestess replies, "It's not just the Jews. The ancient goddess lost power all over our world. People free themselves from agriculture, from childbirth, and from the flow of life" (86–87).

Margaret George's *Mary Called Magdalene* also uses Mary to illustrate the limitations women have in a patriarchal society. When she is younger, she realizes that "girls could not attend the school, since they could have no official place in religion." In fact, her father quotes a rabbinical statement, "It would be better to see the Torah burnt than to hear its words upon the lips of women" (8). And, when it comes to selecting a husband, her friend Keziah says, "We are women. . . . In the end, we have so few choices" (80). However, what truly angers Mary about Jewish law is the description of women as unclean. After the birth of her daughter, she is not allowed to touch her for sixty-six days because of her unclean state. Though Joel lightly jokes about it in public and allows her to break the law in private, for Mary, "it was a painful reminder that in every way women were considered so much lower than men" (122). This book's choice of the Hebrew law to represent the repression of women leads into Jesus' questioning of the law later. In light of Mary's feelings about the hindrances placed on women, not just by her society, but also by her religion, it makes sense that Jesus' questioning of that law would appeal to her and encourage her to leave her family to follow him.

Since Fredriksson, like George, creates a Mary Magdalene who is obviously hemmed in by a culture that does not give women much freedom, why, then, would a woman who points out the importance of Mary Magdalene and women, in general, depict a Mary who is a prostitute?[10] One reason might be to show society's role in women's limited choices of profession. When Mary was little, she often hears her father pray, "Praise

[10]It is especially interesting that Fredriksson draws on the legend of Mary as a prostitute, just as she uses the idea that Jesus cast seven demons out of Mary, which is biblical, to show how myths arise about Jesus. Peter tells Mary that the disciples believes that about her, but she tells Paul, "You see how the myths already flourished even when he was alive. I was not possessed by any demons. I was happy because of the spring, the flowering fields" (109).

be to Thee, oh Lord, King of the Universe, for not creating me a woman" (17). She notices that her father, her mother's brother, and the neighbors all act as if she does not exist. She understands "that it was a curse to be born a girl, and in addition the firstborn" (18). When she arrives at Euphrosyne's brothel, she finds out about Miriam, who obviously does not want to be a prostitute; however, "she was raped by a soldier and gave birth to a child in secret. Her parents put the child out and drove Miriam away" (37). It is no surprise when Miriam later commits suicide.

However, Mary willingly chooses to become a prostitute, unlike Miriam, and it is this contrast that the novel draws between Mary and many women of her time. Mary does not become a prostitute because she has to. Even though she leaves home because she thinks she is a bastard and even though she believes that Leonidas is dead, she never feels any compulsion to turn to prostitution as a way to make a living. In fact, Euphrosyne has no plans for her to become a prostitute. What changes is that Mary has sex with Quintus, even though it's clear that she does not love him (but she thinks she does). She tells Euphrosyne what she plans to do, and Euphrosyne tries to prevent her, but Mary "liked men, their purposeful striving to achieve pleasure, and their bodies nearly always so tense and hard. She learned a lot and always had the courage to show how she wanted it—she was both inventive and demanding" (78).

Although Mary turns to a life of prostitution in Fredriksson's novel, it is for very different reasons than what the male authors present. Kazantzakis' novel shows Jesus (or God) as the reason behind Mary's choice of professions, while the other books show Mary as a prostitute almost solely to provide Jesus with a temptation. Mary in *According to Mary Magdalene* tempts Jesus, but not with sex (they do have sex, many times, it seems); instead, it is along the lines of Kazantzakis' Mary, who tempts Jesus with a normal life: "After she had cleared and washed the dishes, she realized why he had spoken about his mother as a great temptation. It was not only the devouring mother threatening him—it was her, too, the woman who loved him" (150). However, this novel's presentation shares characteristics with Saramago's Mary who provides Jesus with physical pleasure and becomes one of his closest disciples, and from Kazantzakis' portrayal of Mary as a temptation for Jesus to live a normal life.

Michèle Roberts' *The Wild Girl* also uses Mary to raise the issues of the role of women at that time, but Mary is forced into prostitution to illustrate the low standing of women. Roberts is clearly aware that the portrayal of Mary as a prostitute is not accurate, as she writes in an author's note:

> Medieval and later tradition in art, hagiography, legends, poems and plays collapses the figure of Mary Magdalene, briefly mentioned in the Gospels, into that of Mary of Bethany, the sister of Martha and Lazarus, and also into that of the sinful woman who anoints Christ. Although many modern scholars distinguish separate figures in the Gospel accounts, I have chosen to follow the tradition of centuries, the spinning of stories around a composite character. (9)

As with Fredriksson, the choice to continue this mingling of stories of Marys is conscious, though for a different reason. Where Fredriksson wants to show a Mary who chooses to be a prostitute because she enjoys men, thus giving her a choice in her future, Roberts wants to show the low status of women in Jewish society at that time and thus present the limited options women had, especially physical relationships. Early in the novel, Roberts shows Mary's struggle with her position in society: "My brother Lazarus was encouraged to study the ancient books of our religion, but not I. I learned about our faith through the words of men. God was mediated to me, as to my older sister Martha, through the words of my father and brother in the confines of our home, and, outside, through the authority of our village priests and rulers. I sulked under this triple yoke, but for a long time expressed no rebellion" (12–13). This subordination ultimately forces her to leave her home in search of a free life, but, along the way, she is raped. When she returns home after her father's death, knowing no man will marry her as she now is, she turns to prostitution to help earn money for the family: "Then it became obvious that I could employ my newly acquired identity as a means of augmenting the meagre income of our family, so long as I remained discreet and careful in my manner of doing so and avoided any possibility of open scandal" (28). Because she lives in a society where men can frequent prostitutes and still be able to marry, but women cannot marry after they have been raped or had sex, Mary has to embrace her fallen status in order to earn money for the family.

Ricci's book, however, differs greatly from the others under consideration, for it does not present Mary as either a prostitute or some sort of sexual temptation to Jesus. Writes a reviewer, "The Mary Magdalene painted here has neither the immorality nor the madness sometimes attributed to her. The thin, plain daughter of a Jewish fish merchant and his Syrian wife, she accounts herself fortunate not to be bound to someone in marriage" (Wald-Hopkins EE-01). Mary does still have an interest in Jesus beyond his teachings. She loves Jesus, but in a motherly, protective sort of way, certainly mixed with romantic love, as Simon of Gergesa notes:

> But I would sooner have put myself in the way of any of Jesus's men than in hers, for all that a good wind would have knocked her down. All sorts of stories about her went through the camp, that she was the one who'd poisoned the pregnant girl we'd heard about, out of jealousy, or that she tried to put enmity between Jesus and those she didn't like. But it was just that she wanted to possess the man—you saw that in how she never let him from her sight, and protected him, and was the one who stood guard to see he had his moment of peace. (365)

Mary is definitely not a sexual temptress as she describes herself as plain, and she has no interest in marriage, even after her father works to find some men willing to marry her. Not only is she not attractive, she is young and innocent, about as far from a sexual temptress as she can be. She is the most naïve of Ricci's four narrators and the only one who believes that Jesus can actually heal merely by touching people: ". . . I could see that his healing was no mere magic or enchantment but a sort of power that flowed through him in his very touch, and that surely must have sprung from the Lord. Sometimes he need only lay his palm on a sick child's brow for the fever to lift, or move his hands over a crippled leg for the bones to find their place, and the lame to walk again" (146). It is not surprising that this Mary is one of the two women who go to the tomb and claim to find it empty, for this book seeks to show how believers manipulate genuine events into the events presented in the gospels.

Christopher Moore's *Lamb* also does not make Maggie (Mary Magdalene) into a prostitute; however, it draws on almost all the other legends about Mary that lead to her reputation as a prostitute. Moore, in effect follows the example of Pope Gregory who combined the various Marys from the Bible into one woman. Maggie has a sister Martha and a brother Simon (who is called Lazarus) whom Joshua (Jesus) raises from the dead. When it becomes clear to Maggie that Joshua is going to Jerusalem where he and his followers know he will be killed, she goes out and buys an alabaster box containing ointment that she uses to anoint his feet, just as the woman in Matthew 26 and Mark 14 does. Thus is combined the sister of Martha and Lazarus with the woman who anoints Jesus' feet with Mary Magdalene, yet she is not a prostitute here. In the Afterword to *Lamb*, Moore writes,

> Although I've glossed over many events that are chronicled in the Gospels, there are numerous elements which many people think are there, which simply are not. One is that Mary Magdalene was a prostitute. She's always portrayed that way in movies, but it doesn't ever say that she is in the Bible. She is mentioned by name eleven times in the synoptic Gospels (Matthew, Luke, Mark). Most references to her talk about her preparation for the burial of Jesus, and then being the first witness of his resurrection. It also says that Jesus cured her of evil spirits. No whore references, period. There are 'Marys' without surnames all over the Gospels, and some of them, I suspect, may refer to the Magdalene, specifically the Mary who, soon before his death, anoints Jesus' feet with expensive ointment and wipes them with her hair, certainly one of the most tender moments in the Gospels and the primary basis for my rendering of Maggie's character. (442)

Moore seems to have no knowledge of Pope Gregory's combination of Marys; instead, he seems to have come to this conclusion on his own. He believes that the confusion of Mary as a prostitute comes from the early church: "We know from letters that many of the leaders of the early church were women, but in first-century Israel, a woman who struck out on her own without a husband was not only considered uppity, but was likely referred to as a harlot (as was a woman who was divorced). That could be where the myth originated" (442). Though there is no scholarly evidence to support Moore's hypothesis, it makes a good deal of sense, given the low status of women in that society.

In *Mary Called Magdalene*, Margaret George also draws on this idea in her presentation of Mary. George does not portray Mary as a prostitute, nor does she even have any of her characters clearly state that she is, but she does have a couple of characters point out that Mary might be perceived as one.[11] While Jesus is being tempted in the wilderness, some of his followers begin to discuss whether or not they will stay with him. Nathanael, a student of the Law, tells Mary that she can't stay: "You can't join him anyway. . . . You're a woman. You can't be a disciple. There is no such thing as a woman disciple. Did you see any with John? And even if there were, you're married. You can't leave your family. Then you'd surely be stoned, as a prostitute. Jesus couldn't have meant it when he invited you. He just meant it in some symbolic sense" (213). Of course, Nathanael is wrong; Jesus did mean it in a literal sense. However, he is right in that the popular interpretation of Mary's actions will be that she is a prostitute.[12]

Unlike George, after all of his research Moore changes one of the few facts we know about Mary from the gospels. When Joshua casts seven demons out of Maggie, it is nothing more than a ruse to get her away from her husband Jakan, who is a leader of the Pharisees and, thus, will now divorce her. It is

---

[11]While it is clear that members of Mary's family feel that she has behaved as a whore with the male disciples, and possibly Jesus, as well, they never call her a prostitute. Her father Nathan even says, "She's a whore! . . . People will account her one" (258). The implication is that whether or not she had sex with the disciples, people will assume she does. However, if she does have sex with the disciples, she does so for free, which would make her a whore, not a prostitute.

[12]And, like Moore, George argues in her afterword that "there is no scriptural or historical basis for the ideas that she was ever a prostitute, the sinful woman who washed Jesus's feet with her hair, or the same person as Mary of Bethany" (628).

not that Moore's Joshua could not do such a thing, but Moore seems to want to present his Mary Magdalene as someone who is strong and who would never be possessed with demons in the first place. Instead, from the first time Maggie is introduced, she is different from the other Jewish girls. She wants to be a fisherman. Thus, it is not surprising that he also does not make her a prostitute.

Though the Mary in *The Gospel According to Jesus Christ* is a prostitute, she is, like Mary in *Lamb*, a strong woman; she is seen as a positive influence on Jesus' life, at least by his family, but she also affects one of Jesus' miracles. In fact, Harold Bloom writes that Jesus' "principal relationship in his life, as Saramago sees it and tells it, is to neither of his fathers, nor to the devil, nor to Mary his mother, but to the whore Mary Magdalene" (164). In meeting Jesus' mother at the wedding at Cana, she attempts to work out a peace among the family members. She even earns the respect of Jesus' mother, who tells her, "You will always have my blessing and gratitude for all the good you have done my son Jesus," and when Mary Magdalene kisses her shoulder out of respect, "Mary threw her arms around her and held her tight, and there they remained for some moments, embracing each other in silence before returning to the kitchen" (290). Mary Magdalene seems to have some type of healing effect on Jesus that his mother notices because on his first night home after having spent a week with Mary Magdalene his nightmares cease, and he never experiences them again.

Saramago's Mary Magdalene, in contrast, prevents Jesus from performing one of his greatest miracles. Saramago's novel shows Mary in keeping with the biblical Mary whose sister is Martha and whose brother is Lazarus. Lazarus has some sort of breathing problem, choking as if his heart were about to stop beating, and he turns pale. When Jesus and Mary are visiting her family, Jesus heals Lazarus while they are sitting outside one night: "You are cured, Jesus murmured softly, taking him by the hand. And Lazarus felt the sickness drain from his body like murky water absorbed by the sun. His breathing became easier, his pulse stronger, and he asked nervously, puzzled by what was happening, What's going on, his voice hoarse with alarm, Who are you?" (348).

However, when Jesus and his disciples are gone to Jerusalem, Lazarus dies, but the novel does not say from what Lazarus died, leaving unclear, then, whether or not Jesus' healing powers were powerful enough or whether Lazarus died of something unrelated to his previous illness. Regardless, just as Jesus is preparing to raise Lazarus from the dead, Mary stops him: ". . . but at the very last minute Mary Magdalene placed a hand on Jesus' shoulder and said, No one has committed so much sin in his life that he deserves to die twice" (362). This Mary clearly passes beyond a sexual tempter to one who might influence which miracles Jesus performs and which ones he does not.

Testament differs from the other books that present Mary as a prostitute, drawing on recent scholarship that has attempted to reclaim Mary. This approach comes from the biblical scholarship that actually begins at about the same time that Kazantzakis' writes. Pamela Thimmes notes,

> Coinciding with the publication of Kazantzakis's novels and Lloyd Webber and Tim Rice's opera were the early years of feminism, the Second Vatican Council in Catholicism and the development and use of new biblical methods in the Academy. The convergence of these religious, cultural, political and academic factors as well as an injection of new scholars and pastors—and for the first time, significant numbers of women—suggested that both the Academy and the Church would revisit the biblical texts, looking for texts about women, investigating women characters and so on. (194)

Since *Testament*'s Mary is not a prostitute, Ricci must find another way to create a character who is an outcast. Not only is she a woman who travels with Jesus, but she also has a mother who is not Jewish. Her mother seems to be descended from one of the many tribes that occupied what was, in Jesus' time, Israel before the arrival of the Jews: "Her own people, she said, had lived on these lands since the world was created, and had got on very well long before the Jews arrived with their one true God" (125). Mary becomes so desperate to rid herself and Jesus of Judas that she turns to her mother's religion and attempts to invoke a pagan curse against him. It seems to be working, but when she returns to the man who performed the curse for her, she finds him near death; in the end, she brings Jesus to him to heal him, and the man, Simon the Canaanite, becomes one of Jesus' disciples. She is forgiven by Jesus for what she has done in trying to hurt Judas, and she realizes that "it was as if after much struggle and despair [she] had suddenly reached the pinnacle of some high mountain, from where everything was visible" (176), and she believes that this sequence of events was all part of God's plan to lead Simon to Jesus. Of course, this scene does not merely show her as an outsider, not completely Jewish; it also reveals her naïveté and her complete faith in Jesus as part of God's plan.

Perhaps because Mary is forgiven, or maybe because she has taken Jesus' teachings to heart, she later treats Judas with immense kindness while they are traveling. They make a long, hard trek to Jericho, and Judas' feet have become blistered. Judas sits down to massage his feet "when Mary came, though with a face like a mourner's, and offered to rub oil on them . . . and it was the strangest thing then, watching how gently she rubbed his sores and knowing it cost her to do it" (375–76). Despite her aversion to Judas, she treats him as she would like to be treated, following the core of Jesus' teaching. This scene echoes the biblical scene of the woman who anoints Jesus' feet, and it illustrates that Mary treats Judas even as she would treat Jesus. Thus, *Testament* can use Mary to illustrate the theme of redemption, though he does so without turning her into a prostitute.

Mary's role as the first witness of Jesus' resurrection is almost completely ignored by these books, partly because they ignore the resurrection altogether. This omission is particularly interesting, as it is one of only three things we know about her from the gospels. In the gospel accounts, she goes to the tomb to either look at the tomb (according to Matthew) or to properly prepare his body for burial, as she and the other women have not had time to do so because of the Sabbath (Luke 23:55–24:1). According to John, after the disciples have gone back home after they have been to see the tomb, Jesus appears uniquely to Mary (John 20:10–18). Mark, too, mentions that Jesus appeared to Mary first (Mark 16:9). Even though she is not given prominence in the books of Matthew and Luke, she is the only woman all four gospels indicate has gone to the tomb. Saramago, however, does not take his story that far, and Kazantzakis' story ends with the crucifixion completed after Jesus' last temptation. In this temptation, Jesus marries Mary Magdalene, but she dies when they are both still young. Oddly enough, the idea of being married to Mary is not enough for his temptation; instead, he must move on to a more domestic scene with Mary and Martha, the sisters of Lazarus.

Man of Nazareth shows Mary in attendance at Jesus' crucifixion with Mary, Jesus' mother, and Salome, who has also joined the women who are following Jesus, and this Mary is present when the tomb is discovered to be empty. However, here the resurrected Jesus appears to Salome, not to Mary. In fact, Mary is barely mentioned at the tomb, and she is never mentioned afterward. This book, then, has completely robbed Mary of her role as "apostle to the apostles," much in the same way that Gregory did in his homily. She is turned into nothing more than the Mary of legend, the prostitute who represents the repentant sinner.

In *The Gospel According to the Son*, Mary appears at Jesus' tomb, but Jesus, as narrator, is not sure if that story is correct or not. He believes that the story that she and his mother come to the tomb may be true, but he is unable to confirm it. Thus, Mary exists mainly in Mailer's novel as she does in Burgess': a prostitute in need of cleansing and forgiveness.

Testament, which does not present Mary as a prostitute, does show her following Jesus to the end. Mary is, in fact, one of the few who stay with Jesus all the way to the cross. Almost all of his followers have abandoned him, except Mary Magdalene, Mary the mother, Jesus' brothers, a few disciples, and Salome. The other disciples come back after the stories of his resurrection, and Peter becomes a great preacher, but Mary is the only one who remains with him from her first exposure to him when he stayed at her father's house to the cross and, in her mind, after his resurrection.

This positive portrayal of Mary, especially in comparison to Peter, who becomes the head of the church, has its background in the writings of the early church and again shows Ricci's reliance on contemporary scholarship. In the earliest church writings, Mary is presented as, if not equal to the other apostles, then just a step below them. According to Jansen, the *Gospel of Mary* presents her as "both a prophet and the moral conscience of the disciples. She exhorts the other apostles to act on the Lord's precepts and reveals a vision in which Christ extols her constancy of faith" (25). She was, it should be remembered, the first person to take the news of the risen Christ to the disciples, making her the first to proclaim the gospel. *The Song of Songs*, a book once thought to have been written by Hippolytus, refers to Mary as the first witness, and it calls her an apostle. However, it also confuses Mary Magdalene with Mary of Bethany, which becomes a recurring problem (Jansen 28–29).

Other early writings also portray Mary positively. Elaine Pagels points out that "the *Gospel of Mary* depicts Mary Magdalene . . . as the one favored with visions and insight that far surpass Peter's. The *Dialogue of the Savior* praises her not only as a visionary, but as the apostle who excels all the rest. She is the "woman who knew the All" (22). Karen King reminds us that "the second-century work, *First Apocalypse of James*, suggests that James should turn to Mary and the other women for instruction" (143) and that in "the *Sophia of Jesus Christ*, also from the second century, . . . Mary is included among those special disciples to whom Jesus entrusted his most elevated teaching, and she is commissioned along with the other disciples to preach the gospel" (144). In the *Pistis Sophia*, Jesus speaks directly to Mary: "Excellent, Maria. Thou are blessed beyond all women upon the earth. . . . Speak openly and do not fear. I will reveal all things that thou seekest" (Jansen 25). In the same work, he also says that "Mary Magdalene and John the Virgin will be superior to all my disciples" (Maisch 21). And rather than confusing Mary Magdalene with a prostitute, as later writings do, the hymns of Ephram the Syrian hymns combine Mary Magdalene with Mary, the mother of Jesus, thus focusing on her virginal aspect (Jansen 30–31). Thimmes sums up these apocryphal views of Mary: "For most scholars, the arguments, while diverse, are quite simple—Mary Magdalene represents in gnostic texts a leader, one who receives revelations, who correctly interprets revelations, one with Jesus' authority to teach the disciples, and one who is spiritually mature (has gnosis). In these texts she is the leadership/authority figure that Peter represents in the canonical texts" (216).

Eastern Christianity also shows Mary positively, not succumbing to the portrayal of her that arises in the West. Knutson writes, "In the *Didascalia Apostolorum*, from the first half of the third century in northern Syria, Mary Magdalene is associated with women deacons who serve as baptismal ministers" (210–11). He also relates what Modestus, the Patriarch of Jerusalem who died in 634, wrote about Mary: "After the death of Our Lord, the mother of God and Mary Magdalen [*sic*] joined John, the well-beloved disciples, at Ephesus. It is there that the myrrhophore ended her apostolic career through her martyrdom, not wishing to the very end to be separated from John the apostle and the virgin" (qtd. in Knutson 212). What is especially interesting about this comment is that Modestus associates Mary with the women who anointed Jesus' feet with myrrh (whether the unnamed woman from Matthew 26 or Mary of Bethany), yet he does not connect her with prostitution at all. In fact, he later claimed that she "remained a virgin always" (qtd. in Knutson 212). Thus, as Knutson comments, "The divergence [between the two portrayals of Mary] cannot be more stark. In the west, Mary Magdalene was being portrayed as a penitent prostitute, while in the east she was believed to have lived with Mary, the mother of Jesus, and with John, was a teacher of holiness and was herself a virgin. In the east, the feast of Saint Mary Magdalene is focused on her as myrrh bearer and equal to the apostles" (212–13).[13]

Dan Brown takes this positive portrayal of Mary to its utmost extreme in *The Da Vinci Code*. Drawing on the Merovingian legends,[14] *The DaVinci Code* historians, Teabing and Langdon, tell Sophie that Mary was married to Jesus, and she gave birth to a daughter, Sarah, after she had fled to France. Because Mary was of royal descent, as was Jesus, since he was descended from the line of David, this bloodline could claim the throne of Israel. Teabing goes even

---

[13]Lisa Bellan-Boyer points out that Mary and John, in the Eastern Church's tradition, are said "to have traveled together as partner-evangelists" (53).

[14]As David Van Biema points out in *Time*, "The notion that Magdalene was pregnant by Jesus at his Crucifixion became especially entrenched in France, which already had a tradition of her immigration in a rudderless boat, bearing the Holy Grail, his chalice at the Last Supper into which his blood later fell. Several French kings promoted the legend that descendants of Magdalene's child founded the Merovingian line of European royalty, a story revived by Richard Wagner in his opera *Parsifal* and again in connection with Diana, Princess of Wales, who reportedly had some Merovingian blood."

farther, though, when he tells Sophie, "The quest for the Holy Grail is literally the quest to kneel before the bones of Mary Magdalene. A journey to pray at the feet of the outcast one, the lost sacred feminine" (257).[15]

Brown's book, like Michèle Roberts' *The Wild Girl*, is an argument that the church has lost the balance between masculine and feminine that Christ sought by focusing exclusively on the male aspects, largely represented by the Roman Catholic church via Peter; Mary Magdalene, then, becomes the representative of the feminine, what the church has lost, for both authors.[16]

Though all of these books make significant changes to what the biblical record preserves of Mary, drawing on the legends where it fits, mostly, they seem to give her a good deal of power while Jesus is alive, yet try to take it away from her in the end. Perhaps this results from how her story has been told over the years, or perhaps it is so that the reader can focus on Mary as a symbol of redemption. Either way, the changes reflect a trend to use Mary's ever-evolving story as each generation has need of it.

---

[15]This idea is not new, as David Van Biema points out: "The idea that Magdalene herself was the Holy Grail—the human receptacle for Jesus' blood line—popped up in a 1986 best seller, *Holy Blood, Holy Grail.*"

[16]Margaret George, in *Mary Called Magdalene*, is much more generous to Peter than either Brown or Roberts. The book shows Peter's followers claiming that Peter has been given primacy, but Mary, who has spent a great deal of time with Peter, argues that she has never heard him claim anything along those lines.

CHAPTER 10

Who Was Responsible for the Crucifixion of Jesus?

CAIAPHAS, PONTIUS PILATE, AND THE HERODS

The question of who is responsible for putting Jesus to death has been argued and re-argued on a regular basis. Those who read the gospel accounts literally assign the blame largely to the Jews, led by Caiaphas, and see Pilate as someone who unwillingly went along with their demands. Current scholarship points toward Pilate and the Romans who were seeking to prevent a riot, though Caiaphas and the other Jewish leaders might have encouraged such a view.[1] Herod is mentioned in the gospels in relation to Jesus' death only because Pilate sees him as a way to avoid responsibility. Historically, Herod probably had nothing to do with Jesus' death, though he did put John the Baptist to death, whether to prevent a rebellion or because of John's criticism of his marriage. The books of three of the five authors here—Burgess, Ricci, and Kazantzakis—divide the blame between the Romans, led by Pilate, and the Jews, led by Caiaphas. Mailer's novel puts the burden completely on the Jews, while Ricci's does the same for the Romans. All five writers draw on the gospels and noncanonical writings and legends in crafting their characterizations of Caiaphas, Pilate, and Herod.

CAIAPHAS

Burgess' novel develops Caiaphas much more fully than do any of the other books. The novels by Kazantzakis, Ricci, and Saramago barely mention him, as does Mailer's, though Mailer's lack of mention means much more than those of the others.

---

[1]John Dominic Crossan's *Who Killed Jesus?* is a good example of this argument, as are most books by members of the Jesus Seminar.

Although the early parts of *Man of Nazareth* seem to deviate from the gospel portrayal of Caiaphas, the book eventually follows it completely, and then even makes Caiaphas seem worse than he is in the gospel accounts. In the gospels, both Luke and Mark largely ignore Caiaphas; Luke mentions him in passing, and Mark shows Jesus being taken to the high priest, but he is not named. John gives the fullest description of Caiaphas, especially with respect a meeting of the Sanhedrin. There, Caiaphas says, "You do not realize that it is better for you that one man die for the people than that the whole nation perish" (John 11:50). As if this portrayal of Caiaphas is not negative enough, John adds: "He did not say this on his own, but as high priest that year he prophesied that Jesus would die for the Jewish nation, and not only for that nation but also for the scattered children of God, to bring them together and make them one" (John 11:51–52). Thus, John's Caiaphas does not merely want to kill Jesus because Jesus claims to be the King of the Jews or because of the trouble he is causing but because Caiaphas has said that Jesus will die as a sacrifice, and he must make that happen.

Of course, Caiaphas does make it happen by striking a bargain with Judas to capture Jesus without any crowds around. Then, according to Matthew, he asks Jesus outright if he is the Son of God because the accusers have been unable to get enough testimony to condemn Jesus. Once they have his confession, they are able to take him to Pilate who will be able to execute him. Caiaphas, however, does not accompany any of the other Jewish leaders on the visit to Pilate, allowing them to speak on his behalf as to what they expect from Pilate.

Burgess' novel originally presents Caiaphas to the reader as one who seems to see no threat in Jesus' ministry. In fact, when he first speaks of Jesus, he talks of the beneficial actions that Jesus has been performing. Ultimately, when one of the leaders suggests that Jesus be killed, Caiaphas does raise the idea for which he is most famous in the gospel accounts that "it is meet that one man die for the people" (233). However, in the face of resistance to this idea, he reminds the council that it does not have the power to put anyone to death, and Caiaphas concludes the meeting by saying that they may meet again after Passover. However, after the meeting, his feelings concerning Jesus are exposed. Almost immediately after everyone has left, Caiaphas tells Zerah, another of the religious leaders, "There is an area where blasphemy and treason become one. The Romans, as we know, regularly use blasphemy to compound treason. Speak against the Emperor, and you are also speaking against God. For us, it is a question of making *our* blasphemy *their* treason" (234). Thus, Zerah and Caiaphas plot to get Judas to say that Jesus has claimed to be God. Judas, in Burgess' work, is innocent and naïve, and, thus, the two plan to take advantage of that innocence. By altering Caiaphas' behavior among the Sanhedrin, Burgess' novel renders him duplicitous, as he even tricks other members of the Sanhedrin who may believe as he has. With this change, Caiaphas seems more evil, acknowledging the good that Jesus does, yet seeking to put him to death anyway, more along the lines of John's presentation. The other gospels are less clear about Caiaphas' motivation, but here it is clear that he knows exactly what he is doing.

Not only does Caiaphas recognize Jesus' positive actions, Caiaphas also understands Jesus' ultimate purpose more clearly than anybody else in the novel. Caiaphas goes to Pilate after Jesus' death, and the two discuss Caiaphas' reasoning for wanting Jesus dead. Caiaphas tells Pilate, "Let me say this only—that if God *did* decide to create a new aspect of himself, confining his entire spiritual essence within the body of a human being, then it would be for one purpose only: that he might sacrifice himself to himself, achieving the supreme expiation of man's sins" (283). However, this is not the reason for Caiaphas' wanting Jesus dead. Rather, Caiaphas says, "The Messiah—of the Jewish people— that is a very different notion. And the time of the Messiah is not yet" (284). However, he willingly admits that Gentiles might very well believe in such an idea of the Messiah. The implication here is that the Jews have missed the coming of the Messiah, but the Gentiles, because of their different understanding of the Messiah, see it clearly. This novel follows an orthodox Christian view that the Jews completely missed Jesus' role as Messiah, which provides support for the case that the Jews are completely responsible for Jesus' death. Since the Romans are Gentiles who might ultimately understand Jesus, they are portrayed in this reading as much more innocent of the crucifixion, but the Jews, according to Burgess, have no hope of ever understanding.

The novels of Kazantzakis, Ricci, and Saramago largely ignore Caiaphas, which is not surprising since, apart from the gospel stories, Caiaphas is seldom discussed. Josephus mentions that he was appointed to the rank of high priest by Valerius Gratus and that he was later removed from the office by the Procurator Vitellius. He served from approximately 18 CE to 36 or 37 CE (Sandmel, "Caiaphas" 481). And that is the extent of the record.

The Last Temptation of Christ mentions Caiaphas very briefly and only in passing. Caiaphas is one of the main perpetrators behind Jesus' death; however, this novel does not show the reader any of Caiaphas' actions or thoughts. Instead, it merely relates that Caiaphas is involved. Oddly enough, the only time it shows Caiaphas to the reader is when Jesus is leaving Pilate for the first time. As Jesus exits, he sees Caiaphas, who is "so fat that globs of blubber formed cocoons around his eyes." When he sees Jesus, he asks him, "What do you want here, rebel?" to which Jesus severely responds, "I'm not afraid of you, high priest of Satan" (385). Kazantzakis' novel does show Caiaphas pampered, carried on a litter, and his obesity is certainly intended to show how gluttonous (beyond merely food) members of the priesthood have become. Otherwise, however, Caiaphas is left out of Kazantzakis's novel.

Caiaphas is not even given a name in *The Gospel According to Jesus Christ*, referred to merely as the high priest. He encourages Pilate to have Jesus executed, but he does little else in the novel. There is no plotting behind the scenes to have Jesus killed; in fact, it is not made clear exactly why the high priest sees Jesus as such a threat. It is clear that he believes Jesus is guilty of blasphemy, but nowhere does the reader get the impression that Jesus is much of a threat to the religious establishment other than when he overturns the tables in the temple.

Testament does not mention Caiaphas at all, and it lays all of the responsibility for Jesus' death at the feet of the Romans. Judas is aligned with a rebel group who wants to overthrow the Romans, and it is this connection that leads to Jesus' being crucified for treason. It is not anything Jesus says that angers the Jews enough to want him dead; in fact, almost no one in Jerusalem knows who he is. Given Ricci's admission that he spent time reading the writings of the Jesus Seminar, this approach makes sense. Scholars who have tried to find the historical Jesus tend to the argument that the Romans were probably responsible for Jesus' death, as the Jews had little power under Roman rule. Thus, Ricci's novel completely omits mention of the Jews in this instance and provides only the political connections between Judas' group and the Romans as the reason for Jesus' death. The exact opposite is true of Mailer's novel, which blames the Jews for Jesus' death.

The Gospel According to the Son gives Caiaphas less mention than Herod or Pilate, yet his actions may be more telling. Mailer's novel does not show Caiaphas meeting with any other Jewish leaders, planning what must be done to Jesus; instead, it tells us that Jesus imagines what they were saying, that one man must die for the good of all the Jews. The first time the reader sees Caiaphas in this novel is when he is questioning Jesus in an attempt to find him guilty of something meriting capital punishment. Caiaphas asks him outright if he is the Christ, and Jesus responds that what Caiaphas has said is true. Then Caiaphas rips Jesus' clothes and takes Jesus to Pilate for execution. The only other appearance of Caiaphas is when Pilate needs to know there will be a reward for Jesus' death, and Caiaphas smiles in agreement.

However, the book makes clear that it is the Jews who are responsible for Jesus' death, not the Romans. While this approach certainly coincides with the literal, Biblical accounts, numerous theologians in the twentieth century have argued that the Romans are much more responsible than are the Jews. Mailer's approach becomes even more interesting when we recall that Mailer is Jewish. David Gelernter comments, "Don't conclude that, because Mailer doesn't tell this story like a Christian, he tells it like a Jew. Jewish scholars have long rejected as impossible the Gospel account of the legal proceedings culminating in the Crucifixion, and Mailer is scrupulously faithful to the Gospels" (55). Mailer himself, though, says,

> What came over me as I began to write the book was how very
> Jewish he is. One has to come to think of him as probably

the greatest Jew who ever lived. So, no, I was—I'm Jewish. So, you know, for me it was most interesting to recognize, as you begin to study it closely, how very Jewish he is. One has to face the fact that the New Testament is intensely anti-Semitic, particularly the Gospel of Luke. And it seemed to me the way to diminish the anti-Semitism implicit in the question is to deal with the intensity of how Jewish Jesus is. ("The Gospel According to Mailer")

However, by mirroring the gospel accounts of the death of Jesus, Mailer's account is just as critical of the Jews.

Mailer's Jesus realizes early in his ministry that he might have to counter his own people in order to convey his message to those who need to hear. He comes to this realization about the Pharisees when he is healing a man on the Sabbath. Most of the Pharisees who are there leave after this action, and Jesus thinks, "I had to conclude that a time might come when I would go to war with some of my own people" (88). He also realizes that he must contend with the Jewish idea of the Messiah, the idea that the Christ would be a king like David who would lead his followers to political freedom. When he enters Jerusalem for the second time, some of the people called him King, but "they did not know that [his] kingdom . . . would be in heaven. They were looking for a monarch who would restore the greatness we had known in Israel under King David" (180). On his first entrance into the temple, Jesus has a long debate with a scribe about healing on the Sabbath, which ultimately leads to a discussion of the gentiles. The scribe finally asks Jesus, "Are you saying that you would give a light to the gentiles?" to which Jesus in the end responds clearly, "But He [God] also said, 'I will give you a light to the gentiles in order that you may be My salvation unto all the ends of the Earth'" (171). The scribe believes this statement is blasphemy, so he and many of the others who were listening leave. Jesus, however, believes that he must battle the Temple and all that it represents. Mailer's book completely ignores the presence of the Romans and the threat that Jesus may have posed to them. Instead, it focuses completely on Jesus' interactions with the Jews, not exploring what Jesus' Jewishness truly meant.

PILATE

The novels of Kazantzakis and Ricci both focus heavily on Pontius Pilate, the first on Pilate's question of truth and the second, showing him as a cruel ruler who angers the Jews at every opportunity. The novels of Burgess, Mailer, and Saramago barely develop Pilate beyond his portrayal in the gospels.

The accounts of Matthew, Mark, and Luke follow the same pattern: Jesus is accused by the chief priests; he does not defend himself, which surprises Pilate who tries to let Jesus go, but the chief priests (either on their own or via the crowd) convince Pilate to have him crucified. John's portrayal of Pilate follows much the same pattern, but both Pilate and Jesus have more to say. Pilate is still portrayed as hesitant to crucify Jesus, and, in fact, goes to greater lengths to avoid doing so than in the Synoptics; however, he is also shown to be more cynical and concerned with his own power. When Jesus says that he testifies to the truth, Pilate responds, "What is truth?" (John 18:37–38). And when Jesus finally refuses to talk to Pilate, he comments, "Don't you realize I have power either to free you or to crucify you?" (John 19:10).

Kazantzakis' novel draws on John's account to consider Pilate's view of the inability to know truth, his relativism, even before Jesus is brought before him to be crucified. Pilate calls Jesus to him in order to warn him, to discourage him from following his current plan of action. The first description of Pilate shows his nihilism: "He believed neither in gods nor in men—nor in Pontius Pilate, nor in anything. Constantly suspended around his neck on a fine golden chain was a sharpened razor which he kept in order to open his veins when he became weary of eating, drinking and governing, or when the emperor exiled him" (380). He returns to this nihilism when Jesus is brought before him. Jesus simply states that he has proclaimed the truth, but Pilate responds, "What truth? What does *truth* mean?" Jesus sees Pilate here as representing the world: "Jesus' heart constricted with sorrow. This was the world, these the rulers of the world. They ask what truth is, and laugh" (437). Since Kazantzakis says in his introduction that he writes his book so that people may know Jesus, Pilate works as a foil here to the truth that Jesus brings. Kazantzakis sees the modern world as one that has lost the concept of any kind of truth, but especially spiritual truth that Jesus represents. By creating a Pilate who is an extreme representation of the world's relativism and nihilism, Kazantzakis further highlights the hope that Jesus brings to the world. However, Jesus does not have a chance to respond, as Pilate's comment ends the discussion he and Jesus are having, and he allows the crowd to choose Barabbas to be freed.

In their earlier meeting, though, Pilate shows himself to be both compassionate and prescient. He has called Jesus before him on behalf of his wife, who has been dreaming about Jesus on a regular basis. He seems to honestly want to help Jesus avoid trouble: "Well, she fell at my feet to make me call you and tell you to go away and save yourself. Jesus of Nazareth, the air of Jerusalem isn't good for your health. Return to Galilee! I don't want to use force—I'm telling you as a friend. Return to Galilee!" (383). When Jesus will not listen, though, Pilate washes his hands, as he will later do after condemning Jesus to death.

Pilate, though, accurately foresees what will happen to Jesus if he continues on his present path. He even sees beyond Jesus' crucifixion to the disciples and what they will tell others: "You insult Rome in order to make me angry, so that I'll crucify you and you'll swell the ranks of the heroes. You prepared everything very cleverly. You've even started, I hear, to revive the dead: yes, you're clearing the road. Later on, in the same way, your disciples will spread the word that you didn't die, that you were resurrected and ascended to heaven." However, Pilate claims that he will have no part in Jesus' plans: "I'm not going to kill you, I'm not going to make a hero out of you. You're not going to become God—so get the idea of your head" (382). Of course, Pilate does crucify him and make a hero out of him, and Jesus either is or becomes God through that crucifixion. Kazantzakis' Pilate here is similar to Burgess' Caiaphas who can see Jesus' ultimate mission yet seeks to prevent it. The idea of Pilate's ever being convinced of Jesus' message is never presented, and the implication seems to be that someone who embraces such nihilism and relativism is not open to such a message. Whether or not Pilate is unable or unwilling to prevent Jesus' ultimate plan remains unclear. Since he sees the result clearly, he should be able to find another way to remove Jesus, but he does not do so.

Unlike the compassion that Kazantzakis' Pilate shows, Ricci's novel creates a Pilate who is shown early in the work to be a man of extreme cruelty and one who angers the Jews simply because he can do so. He puts his standards near the temple, which the Jews view as idolatrous, so they begin to riot in the streets. Pilate ignores them for a while, but he finally agrees to meet with them. His soldiers direct all of the protesting Jews into a stadium, so he can address them. When they are all in the stadium, he has his soldiers surround them, and he tells them to stop their protests and return home and they won't be killed, and his soldiers all unsheathe their swords. The Jews ultimately win the protest by baring their necks to the soldiers, showing that they are not afraid to die; however, the incident illustrates Pilate's disregard for the Jewish faith and his cruelty.[2]

Ricci seems to draw this event from one that occurred in Caesarea. According to Brian McGing, Pilate introduced soldiers with the military standards almost immediately after he took over in Judea. The Jews protested and went to Caesarea to complain, but Pilate refused to negotiate on the issue of the standards, as he claimed that removing them would be an insult to the emperor. The Jews protested for five days until he made a decision to surround them with troops with the order to put them to the sword if they did not move. The Jews "stayed where they were and showed themselves quite unwilling to back down. Pilate was the one who backed down; the standards were removed from Jerusalem" (428–29). As McGing comments, "The episode shows in Pilate a curious mixture of (apparent) provocation, indecision, stubbornness, and finally weakness, a willingness to give in. Not for the last time we observe Pilate getting himself into an awkward situation

---

[2]Margaret George's *Mary Called Magdalene* has Pilate kills pilgrims from Galilee in the Temple, for no particular reason, also showing his cruelty. However, when Pilate gives in to the Jewish leaders' demands for Jesus' crucifixion, Mary describes him as "cruel as his reputation," but also as "frightened" of the Jewish leaders. Thus, we get a Pilate who is more in line with the biblical portrayal of him, but with the historical, cruel background, as well.

over the matter of loyalty to the emperor" (429). Thus, the historical Pilate and Ricci's Pilate are much more complex than the Pilate of the gospels who seems merely weak-willed and willing to give in to the demands of the Jewish leaders.

Pilate also angers the Jews merely by being present at their festivals. He parades through the streets with his Samaritan soldiers, reminding the Jews that they are under Roman rule. On one of these parades, he passes Jesus and three of his disciples, foreshadowing Jesus' encounter with him in the prison.

This portrayal of Pilate fits in well with many of the accounts we have of him. In non-Christian works, he is shown to be ruthless and cruel. Philo accuses him of rape and murder, while Josephus recounts several accounts of Pilate's ordering troops to disperse large groups, sometimes merely by show of force, but sometimes by execution of leaders of those groups (Sandmel, "Pilate, Pontius" 811). Brian McGing gives an interesting interpretation for why the gospel writers portray Pilate as much more benign than historians: "In the Gospels the Jews get all the blame for forcing a reluctant Roman governor to execute an innocent man. In reality, so it is argued, Jesus was executed unhesitatingly by Pilate as a rebel, because he was a rebel, or something very like it. Representing the young Christian sect in a hostile Roman empire, the evangelists could afford neither to admit Jesus' guilt as a terrorist, nor to lay the responsibility for his death on the Romans, hence the reasonably favorable (but incorrect) portrait of Pilate" (418). He adds, "And the Jewish involvement in Jesus' end was merely a Christian construct designed to provide a scapegoat for the Messiah's death, and to disguise the Roman responsibility for it. In truth Pilate behaved with the pragmatic ruthlessness displayed so consistently by Roman officials in their dealings with people like Jesus, and displayed, according to Philo and Josephus, by Pilate himself in other incidents of his governorship" (422).

However, Philo and Josephus' portrayal of Pilate may not be quite complete, either. As McGing writes, Philo merely speaks of Pilate in "very general terms," with few examples to back up his portrayal. "The only hard evidence Philo . . . puts forward is the one incident with the golden shields.

The rest is a string of insults which looks highly rhetorical in nature. . . . If he had other evidence for his assertions, he does not give it to us. Modern writers have perhaps been too influenced by aspects of Philo's rhetoric" (431). Ricci's account may, then, be one of those highly influenced by Philo.

Ricci also draws on the gospel of John, though, in Pilate's questioning of Jesus. Jesus is arrested for a misunderstanding; a riot begins in the temple when Andrew begins wailing, and Jesus and several of his disciples are arrested, as the Roman soldiers are on guard for a rebellion they have heard could happen during Passover. Pilate encounters Jesus in the prison, where he is reviewing the prisoners to see who will die and who will be set free. Jesus is the only prisoner who talks back to Pilate, telling him that he is a fool for believing what he has heard to be the truth. Pilate asks the guard to ask him (not knowing that Jesus knows Greek), "Ask the man what he means to say by the truth," the equivalent of the question Pilate asks Jesus in the book of John. Jesus responds in Greek, "Don't ask for something you can't understand" (432). From then on, Jesus refuses to answer Pilate, leading Pilate to condemn him for treason for his association with Judas.

Pilate condemns Jesus without any hesitation, nor does he have to be persuaded to issue the death sentence, as in the gospel accounts. Pilate is presented as bloodthirsty and disrespectful of Judaism, more in line with Philo's portrayal, and he needs little reason to sentence Jesus to death.

Pilate serves only this one role in the gospels: he must give his assent to the crucifixion of Jesus. He is characterized as not being particularly willing to do so, yet he is led into this action either by the Jewish leaders or the crowd, depending on the gospel. In all the accounts, for whatever reason, Pilate seems to be on Jesus' side much more so than on the side of the chief priests. However, in the end, he bends to their pressure and has Jesus crucified.

Overall, the novels by Burgess, Mailer, and Saramago follow this general outline and create a Pilate who fulfills the role of ordering Jesus' crucifixion, though each adds one or two aspects. In Burgess' novel, though, Pilate does see through the Jewish leaders' reasons for wanting Jesus executed. As he says to his deputy, Quintilius, "It sounds to me as if they have reasons for getting rid of him which have nothing to do with what they call treason.

Slimy lot, these Jews" (261). In fact, it seems as if Jesus has to convince Pilate not to let him go, to actually give the order for the crucifixion. And, Pilate tries to allow the crowd to give him a way out of the execution. However, the crowd is made up of Zealots, whom Jesus has angered by healing a Roman and eating at the house of a centurion; thus, they call for Jesus' crucifixion as both Jesus and the Jewish leaders knew they would.

In the end, Pilate falls back on a procedural answer in that he renders himself officially absent. His deputy, then, having been bribed by the Jewish leaders, gives the order for the crucifixion. Pilate stops a young boy carrying water, and it is then that he physically washes his hands of this decision. Thus, Burgess' novel shows Pilate quite unwilling to participate in the death of Jesus and as one who does almost everything he can to get out of it. However, he does not send Jesus to Herod, as in the gospel accounts, nor does he let him go outright. He is still politically savvy, and he knows that he does what he must do in order to keep the peace. Thus, Burgess' novel adds to the portrayal of Pilate in the gospels to make him appear even a bit more cowardly by means of the official absence that he uses to remove himself from the decision. In the gospels, he seems afraid of the crowd, but, in Burgess' work, it seems he is just as influenced by the Jewish leaders as he is by the Zealots who want to see Jesus die.

Mailer's Pilate is fairly consistent with the gospel accounts: Pilate is willing to work with the Jewish leaders in order to keep the peace, but he also lets them know that he is in charge of the situation. He doesn't seem particularly unwilling to kill Jesus, but he wants to know that he will be repaid for this action. When the people express their willingness to have Barabbas released rather than Jesus, Pilate smiles. Caiaphas returns his smile, as if to say, "I have the strength to bear this burden" because Pilate knows that "it would cost the Temple a goodly sum to free a Jew who had killed a Roman soldier" (229). As in the gospel stories, Pilate questions Jesus, tries to send him on to Herod, but then ultimately washes his hands of the entire situation and allows Jesus to be put to death. Mailer's portrayal of Pilate is more in line with McGing's ultimate understanding of Pilate as one for whom "opposition and eventual capitulation are remarkably consistent with the Pilate we know from Philo and Josephus" (437). Thus, Mailer's presentation of Pilate shifts the blame back to the Jews for their behind-the-scenes conspiracy that results in Jesus' death.

Pilate is barely mentioned in *The Gospel According to Jesus Christ*, serving the role of ordering the crucifixion after interrogating Jesus briefly, but doing little more. There is no attempt to pardon Jesus, though Pilate does regret having sentenced him, but that is due more to the high priest's annoying Pilate than it is to his belief in Jesus' innocence. Pilate, in fact, seems to be quite indifferent throughout the entire account.

What is interesting is that none of the authors draw from the Christian legends surrounding Pilate after his death. A Christian version of *Acta Pilati* (*Memoirs of Pilate*) was published, probably around 425 CE, wherein Pilate is "depicted as treating [Jesus] with great consideration. . . . Pilate is described as consulting Jesus as to what he should do with him" (Brandon 154). Pilate ultimately blames a list of Jewish leaders, including Herod, Archelus, and Caiaphas, for Jesus' death (Brandon 155). Justin Martyr cites the *Acts of Pontius Pilate* much earlier, saying that that work attests to the miracles of Jesus. Tertullian accuses the Jews of having coerced Pilate (who was "himself in his secret heart already a Christian") into handing Jesus over to them, and Pilate then presents his report to the Emperor, Tiberius, in such a way that Tiberius is convinced of Jesus' divinity. Origen does not hold Pilate responsible for the crucifixion at all; instead, he largely blames Caiaphas, though he also includes Herod in his attacks (Brandon 155). Because of these positive portrayals Pilate is eventually honored as a saint and martyr by the Coptic church (Sandmel, "Pilate, Pontius" 813).

However, the Christian view of Pilate ultimately changes. Eusebius relates that Pilate committed suicide sometime during the reign of Gaius. Another legend has Tiberius cast his corpse into the Tiber. However, the mere presence of the corpse attracted so many demons that it was moved to Vienne. It was then moved to Lausanne where demonic activity continued, leading ultimately to his body being put in either a well or lake (depending on the legend), where the demons continued to seek it out (Brandon 156).

In the end, probably none of these views of Pilate, including the gospel portrayal, are completely accurate. Sandmel writes, "Neither the Christian nor the Jewish depiction of Pilate is historical, but each is a product of varied and varying biases" ("Pilate, Pontius" 812). Simon Légasse agrees, "[Pilate] does not deserve the merciless picture which Philo paints of him, nor the features of a weak-willed person yielding to the pressure of the crowd, as the Synoptic Gospels suggest" (62). As in most cases, the truth must lie somewhere between these extremes, and these authors, save for Saramago, try to plot out a course in this middle ground.

Herod Antipas

In the gospels, Herod Antipas only encounters Jesus once, but he plays an important role in that encounter. According to Luke, Herod meets Jesus near the end of Jesus' life. In an effort to avoid responsibility for Jesus' death, Pilate sends Jesus to Herod, as Herod has long wanted to see Jesus and Jesus is under Herod's jurisdiction. However, Jesus refuses to answer any of Herod's questions, so Herod and his soldiers mock Jesus and send him back to Pilate (Luke 23:6–12).

Historically, though, whether or not he is involved in Jesus' trial is questionable. The Gospel of Luke mentions that he is, but "the absence of a comparable passage in Mark, Matthew, and John suggests strongly that this passage is legendary" (Sandmel, "Herod" 593). Brandon adds, "It is conceivably possible that Pilate might have consulted Herod (Antipas), the tetrarch of Galilee, about a Galilean accused of sedition, if he requested more information about him. However, according to Luke, this was not what Pilate did; he implies, instead, that Pilate handed the case over to Herod, which seems to be very improbable in view of the fact that Jesus was accused of seditious action also within Pilate's area of jurisdiction" (121).

Not surprisingly, due to this lack of historical evidence and scant mention in the gospels, these authors largely overlook Herod's involvement in Jesus' trial (only Mailer's novel gives him any mention there at all, and his role is reduced greatly). Margaret George's *Mary Called Magdalene* seems to be the only exception. While Herod is far from a major character in this work, he does actively participate in the death of Jesus. Before Jesus even arrives in Jerusalem, Herod sends troops to warn Jesus because of his large gatherings: "But we will be watching. And the first wrong thing you do . . . you will go straight to Antipas" (421). Later, when Jesus is in Jerusalem, Herod sends his spymaster to watch him: "Eliud! Antipas's spymaster. . . . But it means that Antipas is having Jesus followed. That incident with the money-changers— although he wasn't arrested, it means he will be kept under surveillance from now on" (470). However, what clearly shows Herod's involvement in Jesus' death is that Caiaphas, Annas, and Judas all meet at Herod's residence to discuss Judas' betrayal. While Herod says little in this exchange, it is clear that he is involved, given his previous warnings to Jesus and that he allows them to use his dwelling for their meeting. This approach shifts the blame back to the Jews, as it shows Herod not merely as a means for Pilate to escape responsibility, but as someone who is involved with the plot from the outset. Even though the Jews are not fond of Herod, he is still Jewish; thus, the meeting at his house is clearly portrayed as a meeting of Jewish leaders, and there are no Romans present.

Matthew and Mark recount Herod's other appearance: his order to behead John the Baptist (Luke merely mentions it in passing). According to Matthew, Herod wants to kill John, as John has criticized his relationship with Herodias, his brother Philip's wife; however, he is afraid of the people, so he simply lets John languish in prison (Matthew 13). Mark, however, points out that Herod likes to listen to John, which is why he does not kill him (Mark 6). Regardless, Herodias wants John dead. Thus, she has her daughter dance for Herod, and he enjoys her performance so much that he offers her anything she wants, up to half his kingdom. She demands, as requested by her mother, the head of John the Baptist on a platter. Herod has no choice: "The king was greatly distressed, but because of his oaths and his dinner guests, he did not want to refuse her. So he immediately sent an executioner with orders to bring John's head" (Mark 6:26–27).

In contrast to George's book, the novels by these male authors mention Herod, only in terms of his involvement with John the Baptist. Burgess, in fact, is the only author whose book develops the character Herod Antipas (or Antipater, as he calls him). Mailer's book mentions him more than does Ricci's and Kazantzakis', whose books merely mention him in passing.

Man of Nazareth draws on Matthew and Mark's account of Herod's execution of John the Baptist. Here Herod is much more hesitant, but the event is used to foreground Herod's sexual perversions that lead him to be easily swayed by Salome's dancing. Herod is described as having "in youth worn out the possibilities of normal sensual gratification and, in maturity, had to exploit such fantastic variations on the basic theme of coition as a fevered imagination could suggest to him" (101). In fact, it is the incestuous nature of his marriage to his brother's wife Herodias that appeals to him at all. Salome's youth also is given as a reason he is drawn to this union:

> For he had reached a stage in his libidinous odyssey when he could only attain erotic purgation through contact with very young flesh of either sex, and the flesh of Salome was very young, though undoubtedly female, flesh. Herod Antipater did not demand coition at this phase of his anabasis towards eventual impotence: it was enough that his eyes be excited by the sight of a young body unclothed, half-clothed, progressively and somewhat slowly divested of its clothes with, if possible, an accompaniment of precociously wanton writhings, leers, poutings, pantings, the movements of simulated rut. (101)

Thus, Herodias exploits this weakness and encourages Salome to dance for him, though it seems that Salome is unaware of what her mother will ask for. In Burgess' account, it is Herodias that speaks to Herod, not Salome and, later, Salome flees the temple, realizing that she is responsible for the death of John. Burgess, thus, gives an explanation of why Herodias would have her daughter perform a dance of seduction for her relatively new husband and why Herod might demand such a thing. By providing Herod with a background of perversion, his promise to Salome makes more sense.

Herod, however, has already let John go. He has first merely told John that he will not execute him if for no other reason than to "spite that bitch of a queen of mine" (157). He then sends John back to prison, but Herodias

160

comes in complaining of a crowd outside the palace calling her an adulteress. Thus, Herod agrees to exile John, though not kill him, and Herodias accepts this arrangement, knowing of her plan with Salome. Herod believes that Herodias will have John killed once he is out of prison, so he sends troops to protect him on his journey to Egypt. Before he arrives, Herodias sends a message for his head to be severed on the spot, and Herod signs the papers because of his promise. Thus, even though John ultimately dies, this extra scene develops Herod's unwillingness to kill John further than the gospel stories do. Herod is presented as someone who may be perverted but who does not wish to kill a prophet.

It is not surprising that Burgess would be so concerned with Herod's connection with John the Baptist because that is the one aspect of Herod from the gospels that can be verified by other sources. While it is true that Herod divorced his first wife and married Herodias, the wife of one of his half brothers, Herod II, and that Herod had John the Baptist executed, Josephus gives the reason as Herod's fear of John's leading a rebellion, not his relationship to Herodias (Sandmel, "Herod" 591). Brian McGing supports the interpretation that John's beheading was political, not merely the granting of a birthday wish: "According to Josephus, Herod Antipas was afraid that John's eloquence might lead to civil disorder. So Antipas forestalled the trouble and had John executed; it was a political execution" (422–23).

The focus of *The Gospel According to the Son* seems to be on Jesus, ignoring most of the minor characters in the story, especially those associated with Jesus' death. The novel mentions Herod early in relation to the execution of John the Baptist, so the reader expects him to be more important than he is. Jesus is afraid of Herod because of what Herod has done, but when Jesus appears before Herod, Herod says only a few words to him. He does provide Jesus with a purple robe that better suits a king, or "a robe fit at least for the officers of a king" (227). Other than this action, though, Herod is merely shown as being distracted by a beautiful woman. This distraction harkens back to John's execution, finally caused by Salome's dancing. Accordingly, Jesus is sent back to Pilate without even being asked to perform a miracle, which is what Pilate expects Herod would ask him to do.

The Last Temptation of Christ doesn't much mention Herod. Instead, it covers the gospel accounts. The reader finds out that Salome dances for Herod, and he gives her what she wants: the head of John the Baptist on a platter. However, it also gives us an intimation of Herod's cruelty: "One night Herod the aged king of Judea—a wicked, damnable traitor!—had smeared forty adolescents with tar and ignited them as torches because they had pulled down the golden eagle he had fastened to the previously unsoiled lintel of the Temple" (36). In this instance, Herod sounds much more like the typical presentation of Pilate: brutal, cold, and unforgiving.

The only other appearance of Herod is in relation to the resurrection of Lazarus. The old rabbi, Simeon, cannot understand why Jesus has raised Lazarus from the dead, and he confesses that the one thing he cannot stand is the smell of a rotting body. In anticipating Herod's disgusting death, Simeon points out that Herod's problem may stem from his not having a soul as much as from the problems of his body: "Is this a king? I asked myself. Is this what man is: filth and stench? And where is the soul to put things in order?" (396). This novel does show that Herod seems to lack a soul, but that is not connected with the earlier cruelty. Rather than having Jesus appear before Herod and reminding the reader of this cruelty, the book lets it drop.

Herod is not a major character in *Testament*, but he does arrest and kill John the Baptist for criticizing his relationship with his brother's wife. Otherwise he is mostly neglected. He employed Mary's father as a clerk, which changes Mary's status from that of a peasant as in the gospels to someone more courtly, but Herod has no other connection with her. Given this book's historical approach, it is not surprising that Herod is largely ignored, as he probably did not have any connection to Jesus' crucifixion.

The changes these five writers introduce to the characters responsible for Jesus' death show biases or historical leanings with respect to the crucifixion. Ricci relies on historical research so that his book blames the Romans for Jesus' death, while Mailer's book focuses on the Jews and completely ignores the Romans. The remaining three books distribute the blame between Pilate and Caiaphas, usually ignoring Herod Antipas, save for his role in the death of John the Baptist, much as the gospel accounts do.

CHAPTER 11

*J*ust a Man . . . or
More Than a *M*an?

JESUS' HUMANITY AND DIVINITY

Most writers who attempt to retell the gospel stories struggle with the interplay of the humanity and divinity of Jesus. Helena Kaufman writes about "the symbolic as well as conceptual duality inherent in the Christ figure: the historical (rational) and the legendary (supernatural); the human and the divine; the Son of Man and the Son of God. Around this essential tension core are built some of the most famous literary Christ figures, such as Jesus from *The Last Temptation of Christ* (1953) by Nikos Kazantzakis" (451). Not surprisingly, in a more secular, rational age than the one in which the gospels were written, authors focus much more on the humanity of Jesus than on his divinity. Though they struggle, they largely end up creating a Jesus whom readers can identify with, someone much more like us.

In the same way that authors struggle with this dichotomy, the early church also struggled with the idea of Jesus as human and divine. The apostles, however, did not have this struggle, as they would have thought of him first as human because they had spent time with a very human Jesus. Thus, as Knox argues, "we shall not expect to find that his humanity constituted any problem for the earliest Church or was at first invested with any special theological significance. He would have been thought of simply as the human being he was" (5). As the church grew, though, the issue of Jesus' divinity began to gain influence. The first stage is adoptionist theology, which sees Jesus as human until God resurrected him when he was exalted to the right hand of God and made into the Messiah (Knox 6–8). Later, but before Paul's letters were written, Jesus' divinity was more definitive. God would not have simply waited around for a man to appear whom he could raise to the level of the Messiah; instead, God must have preordained Jesus' presence on earth (Knox 10–11). From there, the next idea is *kenosis* or "emptying." Knox writes, "A pre-existing divine being 'emptied' himself and became a man—precisely that man who because he was 'obedient to death, even the cross,' was 'highly exalted' and given the name of Lord" (12). This understanding marks Paul's writings; however, it did not remain the only idea of how to interpret Jesus.

In reaction to this view, Docetism arose. Docetism, writes Knox, argues that Jesus "*seemed* to be [human]—and it was important for our salvation that he should have *appeared* as such—but actually he was not. He was actually the divine being he had always been and, in the nature of the case, could not have ceased to be. His humanity was a disguise he wore for a while or, better perhaps, a role he played" (16). This idea is most prevalent in the writings of the Gnostics. Basilides, for example, wrote that Jesus

> did not suffer, but a certain Simon of Cyrene was impressed to carry his cross for him and because of ignorance and error was crucified, transformed by him so that he might be thought to be Jesus. Jesus himself took on the form of Simon and stood there deriding them. Since he was the incorporated Power and Mind of the ungenerated Father, he was transformed as he wished and thus ascended to him who had sent him, deriding them, since he could not be held and was invisible to all. (qtd. in Grant 49)

Accordingly, Jesus was never a corporeal being; instead, he was the Power and Mind of God and, thus, could not have been a human being and could not have been crucified.

Ignatius of Antioch countered this type of Christology with the reasoning that would come to represent orthodox theology. He wrote, "Be deaf when anyone speaks to you apart from Jesus Christ, who was of the stock of David, who was from Mary, who was truly born, ate, and drank, was truly persecuted under Pontius Pilate, was truly crucified and died in the sight of beings heavenly, earthly, and under the earth, who also was truly raised from the dead, his Father raising him" (qtd. in Grant 57). Ignatius presents a Jesus who is definitely human (the emphasis on eating and drinking, as well as the witnesses who see him die), but who is also divine. This thinking would become the basis for the Apostles' Creed and church teaching.

JUST A MAN . . . : JESUS' HUMANITY

In their attempt to deal with Jesus' humanity, these five authors focus on several areas of his life. First, the books by Burgess, Mailer, and Saramago deal with his childhood and how ordinary it is. Almost all of these books show Jesus' relationships with women as examples of his humanity (Ricci's being the exception), though with differences: women as temptations or as more positive influences. The novels by Kazantzakis and Mailer show Jesus struggling with other temptations, such as his desire to live a normal life, his resistance to going to the cross, and even a desire for money. Ricci's book, however, takes a different approach. His assumes that Jesus is merely human and reinforces this idea by an inability to perform miracles, although people interpret what he does miraculously. All of these books bring Jesus down to a human level.

Man of Nazareth, however, downplays the humanity of Jesus more than do any of the gospels, as it focuses on Jesus' role as the Messiah. It follows the gospel accounts fairly closely, and, when it does expound on those stories, it is usually to expand the dialogue. However, one area in which the divinity of Jesus is downplayed is his childhood. Unlike the *Infancy Gospel of Thomas*, which makes Jesus out to be a super-child, this book depicts Jesus as a typical child, who performs no miracles, but he is fascinated by Egyptian magicians. However, when he later performs miracles, it is clear that he is channeling God's power, not using Egyptian magic.

Jesus also fights with other children, and he is quite successful, but that is due to his large stature, not to any supernatural help. He is described as "quick to take offence [sic] and hit out as his offender, even if the offender were much older and bigger" (70), an odd character trait for someone who will later preach love and forgiveness, even to those who strike one. Coale, in fact, says that this Jesus is "no ethereal esthete, no ephemeral saint. He's a strong muscular fellow, self-assured, unassailed by doubts . . ." (183). Also, Stinson writes, "Jesus is memorable for his powerful plain speaking and rugged athleticism. He comes across as a muscular, indiscreet, intellectual" (138). Burgess himself says of his Jesus, "I feared that the cinematic Jesus might be a weedy Dustin Hoffman. I wanted him to be massive, muscular, with the big-chested capacity for hyperoxidation that made Napoleon the man he was. The voice that delivered the Sermon on the Mount must have been immense" (305). Thus, even though Jesus' childhood shows him to be more like an ordinary child, his stature still clearly sets him apart.

The Gospel According to the Son includes other aspects of Jesus' childhood to suggest his humanity. When he is a child, he has a fever that is so traumatic that he forgets the story Joseph has told him of his birth. Before the fever, Jesus is puzzled by Joseph's telling him that he is the Son of God and comments, "After school, on days when we would scuffle with each other, I would lose such fights as often as I won. How, then, could I be the Son of the Lord?" (Mailer 19). One of the problems scholars have with the *Infancy Gospel of Thomas* is that it presents Jesus as a child who seems to be superhuman even then, raising friends from the dead. Mailer's Jesus, though, seems like a normal child who loses as many fights as he wins, which seems much more realistic to most readers.[1]

That presentation, coupled with the fever that Jesus experiences, which clearly shows that he is vulnerable to human ailments, reminds readers of just how human Jesus is.

Both Burgess' and Mailer's books also have Jesus following in Joseph's career path as a carpenter.[2] Throughout Burgess' novel, Jesus is referred to as Jesus Naggar, as naggar is Hebrew for "carpenter." In fact, he is so

---

[1] In *Lamb*, Christopher Moore presents an interesting combination of traits in Joshua's (Jesus') childhood. Jesus and his friend Biff pretend to be heroes of the Jewish faith, which is what one could easily imagine children doing, but Joshua always plays the heroes—David, Joshua, and Moses—while Biff plays the villains.

[2] As mentioned in the chapter on Joseph, some writers change Joseph and Jesus to a stonemason. Christopher Moore has Joseph remain a carpenter, but he has Joshua (Jesus) learn to be a stonemason from Biff's father. Moore doesn't develop this idea any farther, and he seems to have no real reason for doing so other than the fact that it enables Biff and Joshua to go to work together and, thus, give them opportunities for getting into trouble together.

accomplished by the age of fourteen that "he was as skillful in making ploughs as his foster-father (whom, of course, he called father)" (72). Jesus' being a carpenter does not come up in the novel again until the end of the book. Jesus talks to the carpenter who designed his cross, and he thinks the man's workmanship is shoddy. The old man thinks that no one notices, but Jesus reminds him that "God notices. God praises the good work, condemns the ill" (272). This scene does little to point out the human nature that Jesus may have embodied, as it shows a Jesus who believes that even the construction of a cross should be done to the glory of God. While this could very well be a human's reaction before being crucified, it sounds like someone who is not worried about the pain that is about to come.

In Mailer's case, Jesus serves as Joseph's apprentice for fourteen years, planning to become a carpenter himself one day. He seems to enjoy the work, at least when it goes well: "Still, there was wisdom to be found in doing good work. When the task went well, I was at peace. The scent of a well-made chest cheered me, and I could feel a fine spirit between the grain and my hand" (4). He even dreams of working on the Great Temple itself, but he is not skilled in gold and silver and wonders if a modest man should strive to such heights. Ultimately, at the age of twenty-seven, Jesus becomes a master carpenter, though he still works with Joseph. Mailer, like Burgess, does not develop the idea of Jesus as a carpenter; in fact, both seem to be checking off a trait of Jesus that they know they have to fulfill before they can move on to other issues.

The Gospel According to Jesus Christ focuses on the humanity of Jesus, omitting consideration of his divinity until over halfway through the book. Ruth Pavey comments that "in Saramago's characterisation, Jesus is neither wimp nor superman, just the thoughtful, tender-hearted son of a carpenter" (40). Ilan Stavans adds that Saramago's goal seems to be "to humanize the son of Joseph and Mary, to make His odyssey immediate, to shape Him as a perfect novelistic creature, one suitable to our *fin de siècle*" (676). This focus is not surprising, as Helena Kaufman reminds us: "What marks this novel with a Saramago stamp is the essential belief, shared in all his narratives, that the only possible story is the one that belongs to this imperfect world (*terra*). That is why his Jesus represents human struggle, and his story ends with death" (457–58). From Jesus' birth until the end of the book, in fact, Jesus is presented as a man who is later informed that he is the Son of God, though he thinks he can escape that fate. Jesus is born because Mary and Joseph have sex, as this book makes clear. In fact, the sex between Mary and Joseph is not even presented as particularly good sex; it simply meets Joseph's need, as he's the male in this patriarchal culture.

There is nothing special about Mary's pregnancy besides the beggar's appearance. She does not visit Elizabeth and make the baby in Elizabeth's womb leap, nor does an angel appear to Joseph, who is already married to Mary. There is no declaration at Jesus' circumcision by Simeon nor is there a visit by wise men. Even the shepherds who come to see Jesus do so to bring food to the family, who is living in a cave. As Jesus grows older, he performs no miracles, though he is blessed with an extraordinary memory, which enables him to do particularly well in school. He grows up with his brothers and sisters as an ordinary child.

When Jesus gets older, however, these authors shift the focus from what he did not do as a child, especially a lack of miracle-working, to how he relates to women. Both novels by Burgess and Saramago allow him a normal relationship with a woman. Burgess' novel allows Jesus humanity in his marriage to Sara. Jesus does not seem particularly tempted by women, and, in fact, his marriage seems to be a duty. He tells his mother that, in order to minister to all, he must "know the whole life of a man" (85). This novel describes Jesus nodding his head gravely when Mary asks him if he is set on marriage, "as if it were indeed a duty on which he had to embark and not a joyful entry into what can be the most joyous of states" (86). Concerning Jesus' marriage, Burgess comments, "That he *was* married, though briefly, entering on his mission a somewhat embittered widower, seemed to me to be very likely: a state of bachelorhood lasting into the late twenties would have been unusual in a tight Jewish community. If there was a marriage feast at Cana, it may well have been Jesus's own" (*YH* 306). Stinson feels that Burgess changes such scriptural stories, though, for good reason: "His departure from Scripture is intended mostly to provoke thought about, and to dramatize, the humanity of Jesus.

Thus, there is the surprise of the bridegroom of the wedding at Cana being none other than Jesus himself" (138). The marriage does not seem to be much of a surprise, as it is so perfunctory; if Jesus had taken some joy in the marriage, perhaps fallen madly in love with Sara, then it would come as a surprise and humanize Jesus somewhat.

Man of Nazareth skims over the five years of their marriage, except to point out that Sara had either two or three miscarriages (the book cites both figures). This illustrates that Jesus has sex while married. However, the novel never lets the reader know if Jesus is happy being married. The reader only knows that Sara is trampled to death by Syrian soldiers after the five years and that Jesus curses God after her death. It is here that God explains the idea of free will to Jesus. Again, Jesus seems not especially human, one who rages against God for years, bitter over what has happened to his wife. This is not surprising given the lack of love expressed in the novel. Instead, Jesus simply does not seek remarriage; he works hard in his shop until he decides it is time to pursue his ministry.

The main focus of Jesus as human in *The Gospel According to Jesus Christ* is in his relationship with Mary Magdalene. While other authors show Jesus tempted by Mary's sexuality, this book has Jesus having sex with her, then living with her as if she were his wife.[3] In fact, Saramago's novel presents Jesus and Mary's relationship not as a hindrance to his ministry, but as a support.[4] Mary can clearly see where Jesus is headed and stands with him in his decision to do so. Thus, rather than presenting Jesus as one who must not engage in the pleasures of this world, this novel seeks to show how those pleasures can make the life of someone, even of someone with such a high calling in life, much better.

---

[3]Margaret George's novel seems to present Mary and Jesus' relationship as a temptation when Jesus tells Mary, "[Satan's] bigger aim is to take that which is most natural and make it a stumbling block for us. . . . That is, the love of a man for a woman and a woman for a man" (438), and she argues in the afterword that it seems natural that at least one of Jesus' disciples would have had strong feelings for him: "I assume that Jesus was an attractive person, and it would be unusual if none of his female followers developed heightened feelings for him. This happens often between a mentor and a mentee, a teacher and pupil, a master and disciple" (629). This might be a temptation for Mary, but it never seems to be so for Jesus.

[4]Marianne Fredriksson, in *According to Mary Magdalene*, also makes clear that Jesus and Mary have sex. In her work, their sexual relationship teaches him that "there is so much joy in [his] body" (107), which he had never understood until then, and it also seems to benefit, not harm, his ministry.

Michéle Roberts' *The Wild Girl* goes even farther than Saramago's book does in its portrayal of Mary and Jesus' relationship. Not only is the physical aspect of their relationship portrayed positively, Jesus even tells Mary at one point, "I am the new Adam, Mary, and you are the new Eve. Together we bear witness to the continuation of creation. Between us, and inside each other, we bear witness to the fullness of God" (82). Drawing on the gnostic *Gospel of Mary*, Roberts depicts a Jesus seeing salvation in the reclamation of the Motherhood of God that has been lost with a focus on a patriarchal God. Thus, the physical union of man and woman, in addition to the spiritual reconciliation of the male and female within us, makes the kingdom of God manifest. *The Wild Girl*'s Jesus quotes from the *Gospel of Mary*, with a few slight changes to make this point: "I myself . . . shall lead Mary in order to make her male, so that she may become a living spirit resembling you males. For every woman who will make herself male shall enter the Kingdom of Heaven. And I shall lead you, Peter, in order to make you female, so that you may become a living spirit resembling these women. For every man who will make himself female will enter the Kingdom of Heaven" (59–60). Thus, a Mary is revealed whose physical relationship with Jesus is not just accepted, as in Saramago's book, but one that can help lead others to the recognition of the Kingdom of God.

The Da Vinci Code takes this progression one step further by actually depicting Mary Magdalene marrying Jesus. For Dan Brown, as with Burgess' novel, this makes much more sense than a bachelor Jesus: "Because Jesus was a Jew, . . . and the social decorum during that time virtually forbid a Jewish man to be unmarried. According to Jewish custom, celibacy was condemned, and the obligation for a Jewish father was to find a suitable wife for his son. If Jesus were not married, at least one of the Bible's gospels would have mentioned it and offered some explanation for His unnatural state of bachelorhood" (245). This also shows that there needs to be a physical union between man and woman in order to truly approach the divine, a view distorted by the church:

> Women, once celebrated as an essential half of spiritual
> enlightenment, had been banished from the temples of the

world. There were no female Orthodox rabbis, Catholic priests, nor Islamic clerics. The once hallowed act of Hieros Gamos—the natural sexual union between man and woman through which each became spiritually whole—had been recast as a shameful act. Holy men who had once required sexual union with their female counterparts to commune with God now feared their natural sexual urges as the work of the devil, collaborating with his favorite accomplice . . . woman. (125)

Thus, in Brown's novel, Christianity today has warped the original ideas about Jesus and about sex, and it is only by recognizing Mary and Jesus' relationship that the truth can begin to be known.

The novels of Kazantzakis and Mailer take the approach that Brown comments on, woman as temptress, to show Jesus' relationship with women in this way, not as leading to something to be enjoyed. *The Last Temptation of Christ* uses a variety of temptations to illustrate Jesus' humanity, with sexuality certainly a major contribution. Leavitt points out that "Jesus in the novel is consistently human, the desires and fears of his youth persisting to the end of his life: he is attractive to women and attracted by them; he is frightened to be alone in the desert and rejoices when he is again among men; he is tempted on the cross at the end of his mission as he is tempted in the desert at its beginning" (76). When Jesus travels to a monastery outside Jerusalem, he passes through Cana, knowing that he will remember how he almost married Mary Magdalene. The feeling is more than he expected, though: "He shuddered. Suddenly he saw her of the thousand secret kisses standing once more before him. Hidden in her bosom were the sun and the moon, one to the right, the other to the left; and day and night rose and fell behind the transparent bodice of her dress. . . . Lowering his eyes, he rushed by this trap of Satan's as fast as he could" (70). The temptation increases when he asks for Mary's forgiveness. She sees how he really feels, and she torments him by pointing out how badly he wants her, even though he is unable to admit it. Before he departs from her house, while she is pretending to be sleeping, he is tempted to touch her: "He wanted to leave, but at the same time he did not want to leave. Turning, he looked at the bed and took a hesitating step toward it. He leaned over—it still was not very bright inside the room—he leaned over as though he wanted to find the woman and touch her. . . . But as soon as he heard his own voice, he took fright. He reached the threshold with one bound, strode hurriedly across the courtyard and unbolted the door" (97). Because God will not allow Jesus to be with Mary, she becomes the forbidden fruit. Kazantzakis' novel, thus, follows the orthodox Christianity to render Jesus celibate, but tempted in every way, including sexually.

The Gospel According to the Son, in contrast, adopts the theory that Jesus may have been an Essene to present Jesus' childhood. The book builds on that to emphasize that Essenes were taught not to desire women or marriage: "It will be understood, then: I was taught not to pursue women or even to approach them. We were to live as warriors for the Lord. We were not to lie down with women when such acts could weaken our purpose. To live by this rule was law, even if the war would last for the length of one's life" (5). By making the source of Jesus' ideas on sex to be the Essene tradition, a minor religious sect, however, Mailer's book changes conventional Christian teaching of Jesus' own divine knowledge or his Jewish heritage. Thus, this approach does not eliminate the temptation for Jesus, but it raises the question of how orthodox that view is.

Mailer's book uses Mary Magdalene as temptress in the same way that Kazantzakis' book does. When the Pharisees first bring her before Jesus to ask him what should be done with her, caught in the act of adultery, he cannot bring himself to look at her. Even when he does, he tries not to make eye contact. When he does, he is reminded of the Song of Songs: "The joints of thy thighs are like jewels, the work of a master's hand . . . and thy navel is like a round goblet" (185). Jesus, however, does not give into this temptation; instead, he casts the demons out of Mary and forgives her of her sin, as in the gospel story in John of the woman, but not Mary Magdalene, taken in adultery. Perhaps it is the demons Mary carries that create this temptation and not the fact that Jesus is human, as well as divine.

In a similar way, Christopher Moore, in *Lamb*, uses women, in general, and Mary Magdalene (Maggie), specifically, as a temptation for Jesus. In keeping with the Essene background of Mailer's Jesus, Moore's Joshua is specifically told by an angel that he "may not know any woman" (83). However, since, like Burgess' Jesus, he feels he needs to know the entire life of a man in order to minister to men, he has Biff hire prostitutes, and he eavesdrops on their having sex. He tells Biff, "Just describe what's happening and what you're feeling. I have to understand sin" (113). Moore's Joshua is tempted by more than just having sex; he specifically wants to have sex with Maggie and be able to spend his life with her. A couple of days after Biff and Maggie have sex (Maggie thinks she's having sex with Joshua before they leave town), Joshua says to Biff, "The night you spent with Maggie I spent praying to my father to take away the thoughts of you two. He didn't answer me. It was like trying to sleep on a bed of thorns. Since we left I was beginning to forget, or at least leave it behind, but you keep throwing it in my face" (111). Unlike Burgess' book, in which Jesus has no desire for marriage or women, Moore's Jesus truly desires Mary Magdalene and the experience of carnal relations. This temptation is not fleeting, as in Mailer's book, but it stays with Jesus for years, making him someone readers can easily identify with.

In the same way, *The Last Temptation of Christ* considers more than the sexual temptation to show Jesus tempted by the idea of marriage and stability, the idea of simply being normal in his society.[5] His guardian angel (Satan in disguise) tells Jesus, "On our way, didn't you want to ask me the meaning of Paradise? Thousands of small joys, Jesus of Nazareth. To knock at a door, to have a woman open it for you, to sit down in front of the fire, to watch her lay the table for you; and when it is completely dark, to feel her take you in her arms. That is the way the Saviour comes: gradually—from embrace to embrace, son to son. That is the road" (Kazantzakis 459). The battle between the flesh and the spirit is one that Jesus has to overcome to

---

[5]In a similar approach, Marianne Fredriksson depicts Jesus not only tempted by Mary Magdalene but also tempted by his mother, in that he wants to be a good son: "How easy, so easy it would have been to be a good son, become a carpenter as the intention had been, and to please her, free her from her anxiety" (149).

fulfill his mission. Morton Leavitt writes, "Surely, Jesus favors the spirit, but he is drawn by his nature to demands of the flesh. He would overcome these if he could—and to some extent he does in the end—but the body, he knows, may truly be worthy, the earthly life at its best capable of beauty and a kind of immortality as well" (77). Kazantzakis' Jesus may recognize the benefits of the earthly life, but he knows they are clearly not for him.

However, the main temptation that Kazantzakis' Jesus faces is not sexual or even the desire to lead a normal life; it is the temptation not to admit that he is chosen by God and not to follow through with God's plan that he be crucified. This is present in the gospels occasionally. Kazantzakis' book draws on Jesus in the Garden of Gethsemane when he asks God to take away the burden he is called to bear. The Jesus of the gospels does not struggle with this idea long, unlike Kazantzakis' Jesus, who even builds crosses in an attempt to make God choose someone else, hoping that God would never use someone who has done such vile work. Before the crucifixion of the Zealot, he talks one night with a voice that only he can hear, presumably God's. It is obvious that God is trying to convince him of something, as Jesus keeps shaking his head, resisting God's advances, until he finally says, out loud, "I can't! I'm illiterate, an idler, afraid of everything. I love good food, wine, laughter. I want to marry, to have children. . . . Leave me alone!" (28). By the end of this conversation, he tells God plainly that he "shall make crosses all my life, so that the Messiahs you choose can be crucified!" (28). Here is a Jesus who is truly struggling with what God is calling him to.

The local Rabbi, Simeon, who has been promised that he will not die until he sees the Messiah, begins to wonder whether or not Jesus may be that Messiah. He recognizes that God is calling Jesus for some purpose and that Jesus is resisting. He finally asks, "Jesus, my child, how long are you going to resist him?" Jesus responds with a "savage shout: 'Until I die!'" (64). After this event, Jesus leaves home to go to the monastery outside of Jerusalem in an effort to escape God's call. He believes that if he dedicates his life to God in one way God will not require it of him in another. It is at the monastery that he finally begins to believe that he may be the Messiah.

This realization, though, does not mean that Jesus is willing to be crucified. Kazantzakis' novel, in the end, draws directly from the gospel accounts, and in the Garden of Gethsemane, Jesus asks God one last time for a different fate: "Father, . . . here I am fine: dust with dust. Leave me. Bitter, exceedingly bitter, is the cup you have given me to drink. I don't have the endurance. If it is possible, Father, remove it from my lips" (431). He even confesses his shortcomings to Judas when Judas asks if Jesus would be able to betray him if the situation were reversed; Jesus responds, "No, I do not think I would be able to. That is why God pitied me and gave me the easier task: to be crucified" (421).

Then, Jesus "stood his ground honorably to the very end; he . . . kept his word. Temptation had captured him for a split second and led him astray. The joys, marriages and children were lies; the decrepit, degraded old men who shouted coward, deserter, traitor at him were lies. All—all were illusions sent by the Devil. His disciples were alive and thriving. They had gone over sea and land and were proclaiming the Good News. Everything had turned out as it should, glory be to God!" (496). Instead of readily accepting his mission, two critics observe, "Jesus grapples with his spiritual formation, blending belief and unbelief into a unity, in order to emerge as Savior" (Middleton and Bien 2). Leavitt writes, "In this milieu Jesus of Nazareth is unmistakably a man and only partially a god; his divinity, in fact, may be no greater than that which all men are capable of attaining. But he perseveres, overcoming the many temptations that confront all mankind, above all, the temptation to live a normal human life, with all its sorrows and joys" (62). Kazantzakis' Jesus struggles more than do any of the other characterizations largely because of the multiple temptations that he has. In his humanity, he is tempted, but he struggles through it.

The Gospel According to the Son also shows Jesus suffering the temptation not to go through with the crucifixion. When Jesus prays on the night of his arrest, he asks that the cup will pass from him, but he ultimately says that God's will is more important than his will. This book develops this fear of crucifixion into an overall fear of death, which leads Jesus to the temptation to escape the crucifixion. Even before he has set out on his ministry, when he is still a carpenter, Jesus is afraid of Herod Antipas, but he does not know why: "When I would watch [Herod] pass in procession, I did not know why my blood raced like a steed and I was ready to bolt. My heart was speaking to me even if my mind was not; I had no sense of why I should feel such fear at the sight of King Herod Antipas taking his royal passage through the avenues of Sepphoris" (Mailer 20). Later, after John has been imprisoned by Herod, but before he has been put to death, Jesus hears a rumor that Herod is considering having him "stilled." It is then that he "decided that [he] would do well to look for a cave on the shores of the Sea of Galilee. For Yeshua of Nazareth would not seem the Son of God to the officers of Herod, only a poor Jew" (88). Jesus recognizes how others will view him and how that can easily lead to his death. Of course, this creates the irony that Jesus is put to death, at least in the gospels, by his claim to be the Son of God, not for any other reason.

After John's death, then, Jesus' fear of his own death becomes magnified. He sends his disciples out, nominally because he believes they need to go out and try to work miracles on their own and spread the gospel without him. The deeper reason he sends them away is so he can deal with his fears, especially the fear of what will happen to him. He knows that some people think that he is John the Baptist resurrected, and he is afraid of what that belief will lead people to do, especially Herod: "If Herod Antipas had slain John the Baptist once, he might not fail to kill him again. The way of John's death was a scourge to my sleep" (112). Mailer's Jesus does not overcome this fear even when he is on his way to Jerusalem. In fact, as Jesus approaches Jerusalem on the third day, the day he believes will be his last, his fears become so heightened that he can barely get up. He feels as if he is almost paralyzed with fear. This fear makes him doubt his ultimate calling and his true identity: "If prudence comes to us from God and cowardice from the Devil, the line between cannot always be discerned. Not by a man. On this morning I was no longer the Son of God but only a man. God's voice was weak in my ear; a low fear was in my heart" (204). The acknowledgment of Jesus as a man here underscores his humanity that this book is trying to suggest. It is not just that Jesus is afraid, which makes him human enough, but the idea that that fear might take him from being the Son of God to being simply a man.

It also serves as a reminder for the reader that fear helps to make us human and rising above that fear moves us closer to God. Oddly enough, though, it is not God that moves Jesus beyond his fear; it is compassion for Judas because knowledge of the betrayal that is coming gives him the strength to approach Jerusalem for the last time.

On Jesus' approach, his steps grow heavy again, so he stops in the Garden at Gethsemane. Here Jesus prays much the same prayer given in the gospel accounts, asking that the cup pass from him. On the cross, however, this temptation reaches its height. It is bad enough that Satan comes to tempt him one last time, offering to take him down from the cross, take revenge on the Romans, if only Jesus will worship him. Even before Satan arrives, Jesus cries out to God, "Will You allow not one miracle in this hour?" And after God responds, "Would you annul My judgment" and Jesus agrees, he still prays, "One miracle" (Mailer 238). This exchange echoes Jesus' cry on the cross that he has been forsaken, but this book intensifies that to show Jesus bargaining for his life. The Jesus of the gospels accepts his role in the Garden of Gethsemane and seems to willingly play out his role, but Mailer's Jesus asks to exchange God's judgment for one last miracle. However, he ultimately believes that God knows what is best, and he fulfills his calling.

One of the most interesting ways that this book reminds the reader of Jesus' humanity is when Jesus is being nailed to the cross. Jesus' fear of pain and death is certainly understandable, but an odd thought briefly crosses his mind. As the soldiers lay him on the cross, Jesus notices that "The wood was crude, and nailed together with slovenly blows of the hammer. It offended me that it had been built so poorly, but in any case they removed my robe and made me lie down upon the cross and stretch out my arms" (Mailer 234–35). In his moment of agony, Jesus, humanly, notices the mundane details of life that he knows best from his days of carpentry, like an electrician condemned to death who might notice the faulty wiring of an electric chair. It is in such a human action at a time of immense suffering that the reader can understand Jesus' humanity.

Mailer's book even provides Jesus with yet another temptation: greed. Despite his frequent outbursts against wealth and his unwavering support for the poor, near the end of his ministry he begins to understand the draw of plenty. When a woman anoints him with spikenard, he feels his loneliness subside, if only for a moment. Jesus knows he is still poor, but he says, "So for the first time, I knew how the rich feel, could understand their need for display. To them, a lavish presentation of their worth was as valuable as their own blood" (201). He does not ultimately succumb to this temptation, but his comment that his disciples will always have the poor with them causes him to lose Judas' loyalty, ultimately leading to Jesus' death.

This novel even shows Jesus struggling in theological discussions.[6] He does not have the difficult theological problems figured out; he questions whom he should associate with and whom he should not and why. In fact, he is often made to look foolish in debates and loses one outright.[7] In Nazareth, Jesus' hometown, where according to the gospels Jesus either does not or can not perform any miracles, he discusses healing on the Sabbath with a man in the synagogue. The man has ready answers for Jesus while Jesus falters throughout the debate. In the end, the man "laid his hand on [Jesus'] shoulder as if he were fatherly and [Jesus] was of lesser faith." Jesus is defeated: "He had shamed me. My powers left. Once again, and in my own synagogue, I was without strength" (Mailer 106). In the gospels, Jesus can not do any miracles in Nazareth because of the people's lack of faith; Mailer's book instead renders Jesus as more human than his neighbors.

Even near the end of his ministry, when he is in the Great Temple in Jerusalem, Jesus has a long discussion with a scribe about the law, Gentiles, and healing on the Sabbath. Although he ultimately says what he wants to say, he struggles throughout the argument: "I could hear more and more sounds of assent among those who listened. Some of my own people were muttering that he was right" (Mailer 169) and, later, "I was thinking that even a drunken

---

[6]Twice in Reynolds Price's short gospel, Jesus questions the goodness of God and the existence of evil: "if God was truly the Father of all and if so then who could watch the world of blood and hate and think God was loving?" (246). He seems to have come up with an answer by the end, though the answer seems unsatisfactory: "By the first day of Passover week Jesus thought he had answered his awful question—how could it matter if the Father loved his creatures? The Father was the only God; if Jesus was his Son then the question was meaningless—God's will was sovereign for joy or pain" (270).

[7]This description of Jesus is echoed in Jim Crace's *Quarantine* in which Jesus "was not so clear on any of the other, weightier and wingless issues of the day" (108) and he "had a simple view, a village view of god [sic], that was not scholarly" (109).

man would know what it was now politic to say. I was lacking in all knowledge of how to offer what would gain the most and offend the least" (170). This Jesus is not the all-knowing, all-powerful Jesus of the gospels. Here he often has a clever reply for those who would dispute with him but just as often does not. This is a Jesus who is witty and quick, but he does not seem to possess the divine knowledge that might be so useful in these debates.

Ricci takes a different approach than the other authors. *Testament*'s Jesus is far from divine; in fact, Wald-Hopkins notes Jesus is "the portrait of a difficult, alienated, but compassionate and charismatic, intellectual and religious rebel who is intensely human" (EE-01). In an interview, Ricci comments, "In my case I found the opposite. I found it [Jesus' divinity] completely uninteresting. The main thing that I wanted to do—that people like Mailer, Saramago, Kazantzakis, and all the rewriters of the Jesus story didn't in most cases do— is completely take away that divine element" (Starnino G1).

One of the main ways that Ricci's novel portrays Jesus as much more human than divine is through the miracles that Jesus works. Jesus seems to have learned some healing arts when he lived in Alexandria, though the reader never sees this education. Instead, a variety of narrators say that Jesus has lived in Alexandria and where he studied under teachers, but they do not say what he has learned. This background serves to provide a rational explanation for Jesus' healing. This novel makes evident that a superstitious culture was prevalent in ancient Israel, so that Jesus' healing arts can appear to the uneducated narrators as miracles.

There are numerous miracles that the novel takes pains to explain as Jesus working with the sick. Judas observes him treating a girl who is seemingly possessed by a demon: ". . . at the sight of Kephas [Peter], the girl, who despite her rantings had appeared relatively harmless until that moment, suddenly lunged at the poor man and began hitting him with her rag-covered fists. It took both Yaqob [Jacob] and Yohanan [John] to pull her off him" (Ricci 28). However, it turns out that she is pregnant. The seeming miracle is best understood when Jesus cleans off the girl's face: "From out of that demonic visage of grime and blood there emerged suddenly a child, an innocent" (29). Jesus is able to heal because he accepts something others do not accept, which shows that he is different from those around him. Obviously, no supernatural healing has taken place.

Even the most dramatic miracle, Jesus' resurrection of Lazarus (Elazar in Ricci's work), is given a physical explanation, though it is still quite dramatic for that. Elazar seems to already be dead when Jesus arrives, as Simon of Gergesa, the narrator of the final section, describes him as "stiff as a beam," and when a burning ember sparks from the fire onto his leg, he does not flinch (400–1). Jesus brings him back from the dead, though he does not call him forth from the grave. Instead, he "put his fingers right down inside the man's skull, right through the bone like that, and after he'd felt around in there for a bit, something gushed out from the fellow's head into Jesus's hands, dark and alive" (401). He tosses what he finds in Elazar's head into the fire, where it sizzles, and Elazar opens his eyes, alive again. Though Elazar's life is saved by Jesus, it is through natural means, the removal of whatever was in his head, and Ricci's Jesus certainly does not bring Elazar back after he's been dead for four days, as Jesus does in the gospel of John.[8]

Ricci's novel especially reminds the reader of Jesus' human limitations in the fact that Jesus is unable to heal everyone who asks him. Jesus hints to his followers that this lack of ability is because it is not God's plan to heal everyone, but he does not elaborate: "Yeshua's [Jesus'] answer to these charges was always that it was only by God's will that people were cured, not his own; and it was true that there were many who came to him for whom he could do nothing, though whether because of their own sinfulness and lack of faith, or because of God's greater plan, Yeshua wouldn't say" (146). And Mary Magdalene later says about the people whom Jesus could not heal, "But many others went away still baffled by the things he said or disappointed because they'd wished him to cure things only God could undo such as blindness or barrenness" (149). Ricci's point here is clear: Jesus can heal normal physical ailments, but he is unable to heal serious problems; that is God's territory.

---

[8]In a more complicated healing that raises the question of Jesus as either divine or human, Jim Crace shows Jesus merely saying to a dying man, "So, here, be well again" (26), a common benediction of the time. However, the next day, Musa is completely well. Jesus is not even aware that Musa has survived, and he certainly did not intend to heal him, yet it seems that he does so.

The novel leaves the question of Jesus' most dramatic miracle, the resurrection, for the reader. Only one of the four narrators follows Jesus all the way to the crucifixion, and it is clear that he, Simon of Gergesa, does not believe that Jesus rises from the dead. However, he repeats the rumors of Jesus' resurrection:

> Then there was the story that went around that the morning after Jesus was killed, Mary and Salome went to the grave and his body was gone. That might have had to do with the group who had come to the tomb for their relation, and somehow the story had got skewed, or maybe it had happened that the group had taken Jesus's body by mistake. But eventually it got told that he'd risen from the dead and walked out of the place, and there were people enough to come along then to say they'd met him on the road afterwards looking as fit as you or me. (453)

Jesus' limitations as a healer suggest that his resurrection is not physical, and in light of Ricci's interest in the findings of the Jesus Seminar, it makes more sense that Ricci is drawing on the idea of Jesus living on in his believers' minds. If Ricci's Jesus cannot raise others from the dead, there is no reason to believe that his resurrection is any different. For Ricci, there is always a scientific explanation for any supernatural-seeming event.

Thus, Ricci's novel, apart from the rest, grants Jesus no supernatural abilities at all. The other books emphasize the humanity of Jesus, lowering him to our level. Some of them do it by presenting him as a comparatively normal child; some present his relationships with women. All of them strive to create a human Jesus to whom readers can relate.

. . . Or More Than a Man?: Jesus' Divinity

All five of the books under consideration raise the question of Jesus' divinity and whether or not he is the Son of God. Most of the emphasis in their approaches seems to be whether Jesus can perform miracles or not.[9] If he can, then he must be divine; if not, then he must not be. However, they do not limit themselves to this approach exclusively. All but Ricci's novel show Jesus performing at least one miracle; however, the other four books also limit the miracles he can do. Either he can perform only the miracles God wants him to perform or he only has so much energy to expend on miracles. Burgess' novel also uses the fulfillment of prophecy to show how Jesus at least perceives himself to be the Son of God. All of the books, save for Ricci's, again, also show Jesus' struggle as to whether or not he is the Son of God. *Man of Nazareth*, for example, has him easily accepting it, while *The Last Temptation of Christ* and *The Gospel According to Jesus Christ* both show him resisting the idea.

Burgess' Jesus never seems to have any doubts that he is the Son of God and what his mission on Earth is; however, this book does downplay the miraculous aspects of Jesus' divinity and focuses on the teachings instead. Many of the miracles are included in the novel, such as the resurrection of Lazarus, the calming of the storm, various healings, and the casting out of demons, but many miracles are omitted, as well.

Before Jesus begins his ministry, he is married to Sara at Cana in *Man of Nazareth*. At the wedding feast, as in the gospel story, the hosts run out of wine. However, Jesus does not actually convert the water into wine here. Instead, he pretends to do so and makes a game out of it. However, legend changes what truly happened: "This so-called miracle has passed down into our annals, so that it appears that Jesus was establishing a precedent for the converting of other fluids to wine, but some remember the true tale and call water wine of Cana. I certainly believe that this feast ended soberly"

---

[9]Though Crace's Jesus may not work any miracles in the novel (it's unclear whether or not he healed Musa), his mere existence at the end of the work seems to be a miracle in itself. In the epigram to the book, Crace quotes from Ellis Winward and Michael Soule's book *The Limits of Mortality*: "An ordinary man of average weight and fitness embarking on a total fast—that is, a fast during which he refuses both his food and drink—could not expect to live for more than thirty days, nor to be conscious for more than twenty-five. For him, the forty days of fasting described in religious texts would not be achievable—except with divine help, of course. History, however, does not record an intervention of that kind, and medicine opposes it." By having his Jesus seemingly die, yet still walk out of the desert to begin his ministry, he creates an implied miracle that shows that Jesus has received divine help of some sort.

(Burgess 89). Even the miracles that are associated with the crucifixion are shown to be nothing more than coincidences or legends:

> The rain and the thunder and lightning were coming anyway, the end of a long drought was due, and it was only by a kind of dramatic fitness of which nature is only too capable that the death of a man and the flushing of the grateful earth were fused into an unworthy trinket of cause and effect. There were no earthquakes, no fallings of buildings, but there was certainly a rending of the veil in the Temple. An aged priest was struck dumb by, it was alleged, an angelic visitation, and in his inevitable faintness he took hold, for support, of the curtain that divided the assembly in the Temple from the Holy of Holies. He fell, and the veil was rent. (281)

Providing scientific explanation for what otherwise are seen as miraculous events does not entirely take away the association of the miraculous; it simply shifts the focus from miracles to Jesus' teachings.

Jesus even regularly reminds his disciples that the miracles have little to do with his mission. After he casts out a demon in Capernaum, people begin to flock to him for healing, but he tells his disciples that he does "not come merely to mend sick bodies" (141). Before he sends them out to preach on their own, he tells them, "Don't speak much of miracles, healings, giving sight to the blind. For miracles join all the acts of man's history in becoming matter for doubt to those who have not witnessed them. But the truth that is spoken remains truth for all eternity" (191). This approach is actually rather similar to what happens in the gospels when Jesus often tells the crowd not to look for a miraculous sign from him, and he refuses to perform upon command.

However, one miracle that Jesus (and, thus, *Man of Nazareth*) makes absolutely definite is the transubstantiation that occurs during the Eucharist. Jesus tells his disciples that "this sacrifice [his sacrifice] must be remembered, as the Passover is remembered, till the end of time. But it must be more than remembered—it must be renewed, it must be re-enacted daily, for the continuing redemption of mankind. . . . And now I teach you the mode of the daily renewal of the sacrifice—no mere remembrance, but a true re-enactment" (Burgess 242). Burgess' Roman Catholic education provides an understanding for him to make Jesus repeat the importance not only of the Last Supper, but how it is to be re-enacted throughout the centuries. Coale comments, "Chief among the beliefs from Burgess's Catholic heritage is his belief in the Eucharist, the Mass. For him 'this representation of a sacrificial death and the resurrection' remains a 'great source of inspiration, of refreshment.' It is 'the still center' of his faith, around which all else revolves" (5). The focus on this event in Burgess' novel makes it clear that Jesus accepts his role as Son of God and knows what his future role in the church will be.

Christopher Moore's Joshua (Jesus) is also aware of his role as the Son of God, though he doesn't know what he is supposed to do with that knowledge. This shows up early in his life through miracles he performs while he is still a child. When Biff first meets Joshua, in fact, Joshua's younger brother James is smashing a lizard with a rock; he then puts the dead lizard into Joshua's mouth, and it comes out alive again, all so James can smash the lizard again and repeat the process. He even tries to resurrect a dead woman when he is nine years old, but he is not quite capable of doing so at that point. What is interesting about this book having Joshua perform miracles when he is a child is that Moore says that, when doing research, he found many of the "gnostic Gospels [to be] either too fragmentary, or frankly, just plain creepy (the Infancy Gospel of Thomas describes Jesus, at age six, using his supernatural powers to murder a group of children because they tease him. Sort of *Carrie Goes to Nazareth*. Even I had to pass)" (441). While it's true that Moore's Joshua doesn't murder any children, his Joshua does perform a number of miracles as a child, and his attempts to resurrect people who simply end up wandering around like zombies until they completely drop dead certainly comes off as creepy in its own right. It is easy, though, to understand why authors such as Moore might want to have Jesus performing miracles in his childhood; Boulos Ayad writes, "It is difficult for a Christian to believe that Christ lived his life with-out evidence of miracles until he reached the age of thirty" (55). If one begins with the premise that Jesus knows he is the Son of God at an early age, it only makes sense that he would try out his powers to see what he can and cannot do. From a writer's perspective, it is little different from writing a story about Superman; the character must figure out when he realizes he is different from others, what he can do because of that, and how, then, he will use those powers.

As with Burgess' novel, *The Last Temptation of Christ* does not focus on Jesus' miraculous abilities, though it does relate them to the idea of Jesus as the Son of God. It is only after meeting John and after his time in the desert that Jesus truly begins to draw on the power of God, especially for healing. Jesus heals a Roman centurion's daughter, though he is not certain that he can do so. This event begins to convince the disciples that Jesus is the Messiah: "He had been frightened more than anyone else at the sight of the girl jumping out of her bed. The disciples, unable to constrain their joy, formed a circle and danced around him. . . . He was the real thing: he performed miracles" (Kazantzakis 324). Though Jesus does not emphasize this inference, those around him do, reminiscent of the disciples in the gospels. Those who follow Jesus, especially those beyond the twelve, want Jesus to perform miracles so that they too can know he is the one.

Mailer's Jesus, though, is not certain that he can perform miracles at all, despite the fact that he believes he is the Son of God. Thus, when he performs his first miracle, he does it quietly, hoping that no one will notice. When he turns water into wine at the wedding feast at Cana, he does so merely by eating a grape while contemplating the Spirit within. In the gospel accounts, Jesus' mother asks him to help out, while here she merely comments on the lack of wine. In the gospels, Jesus has men bring stone vessels filled with water, which he then changes to wine. In Mailer's work, Jesus notices the stone jars filled with water, but it is the eating of the grape, coupled with the contemplation of the spirit alone that brings about the miracle. He involves no one else, nor does anyone notice the miracle.

As Jesus gains confidence in his ability to perform supernatural acts, he becomes willing to perform them in public. He casts out a demon after preaching in a synagogue; he heals Peter's mother-in-law; he heals a man of leprosy. Only in the case of the healing of the leper does he tell the man not to tell anyone what he has done, and that is only because he believes the miracle is so great that it will draw too much attention to himself. However, unlike the Jesus of the gospels, in *The Gospel According to the Son*, Jesus has limited healing powers. In fact, his few healings take so much out of him that he has to withdraw from people in order to rest.[10] Later, as word spreads of his healing power, Jesus is inundated with people to heal. He does not feel that he can turn them away, but they take too much out of him: "Nonetheless, I could feel the desire of these people to touch me, and I gave way until they were too many and I lost the power to cure. Truth, their fingers so implored my flesh that I had to live with my own bruises when day was done" (89).

Later, Jesus even admits that there are people whom he can not cure, and these people frighten him. He thinks that he can see "darkness in their eyes, and that could make them seem like angels of Satan" (95). Even when Jesus does perform a miracle, such as the calming of the sea, he's not certain that he has anything to do with what has happened: "In truth, I do not know if I can say that this miracle was mine. Even on awakening I could sense that the end of the storm was near" (96). Later, when he raises a girl from the dead, he questions his involvement in that miracle, as well: "Nor did I know whether she had actually died and come back" (103). However, in *The Gospel According to the Son* Jesus still performs mighty miracles, such as the casting out of demons from the man in the Gadarenes and the resurrection of Lazarus. By depicting a Jesus with limits as to what he can do, this novel constantly reminds the reader that Jesus is very human, shifting the

---

[10]Reynolds Price also shows Jesus needing time to recover from healings: "He failed no one and was white with exhaustion when the last man, woman and child were gone and he could rest on Simon's packed floor" (250). Margaret George's Jesus, in *Mary Called Magdalene*, suffers from the same problem: "There are too many. . . . Too many. I cannot help all of them" (275). Jesus also cannot heal people who do not believe that he can heal them, which prevents him from healing Joel, Mary's husband: "But he is not a believer in my message. . . . I learned in Nazareth that if someone does not believe, I can work no healings there" (325).

emphasis away from divinity, even though it is clear that he remains the Son of God. This is yet another example of an author trying to craft a Jesus who is more in line with the modern worldview, one whom contemporary readers would be able to identify with.

This helps explain why this Jesus attacks the gospel writers for inflating their account of his miracles. He claims that he fed merely five hundred people, not five thousand, and he certainly didn't give them an entire meal. Instead, this miracle is transformed into a type of communion service:

> And I took those five loaves and divided them exceedingly small, until there were a hundred pieces of bread from each loaf. Then the two fish gave up more than twice two hundred small morsels. And, with five hundred bits of bread and five hundred of fish, I passed these morsels to each of the followers, doing it myself for all five hundred. I would lay one flake of fish and one bit of bread upon each tongue. Yet when each person had tasted these fragments, so do I believe that each morsel became enlarged within his thoughts . . . and so I knew that few among these hundreds would say that they had not been given sufficient fish and bread. (Mailer 120)[11]

Thus, Jesus argues that this presentation of the miracle is greater than the representation in the gospel accounts: "And this was a triumph of the Spirit rather than an enlargement of matter. Which for the Lord is but a small deed, considering that He made the heavens and the earth out of nothing, and could certainly have changed our five loaves into five hundred" (120). Paul Gray points out that "Mailer's Jesus takes pains to debunk or diminish most of the reports of his miracles in the Gospels. The story of the loaves and fishes was 'much exaggerated,' he confides" (75). Again, this is a constant

---

[11]Margaret George, in *Mary Called Magdalene*, approaches this miracle in much the same way. The disciples do not have enough food to feed the 5000, but Jesus tells them to give whatever they have to the people. When the people are grateful for the little they get, the disciples are surprised, but Jesus tells them, "The offering of the food means more than the food itself. . . . People are dying for lack of interest, and the spirit is hungrier than the body. A word can mean more than a loaf of bread" (419). However, George's Jesus can multiply food, as he does so for the disciples at their next meal. Thus, the fact that he did not do so for the 5000 was not because he could not do so, but because he wanted to teach the disciples to act on their own and not to depend on him.

reminder to the reader that Jesus is not the all-powerful deity that has been presented in the gospels, despite his clearly being divine. This novel presents him, instead, as a divinity with certain limits, which some would argue removes the capacity of divinity altogether.

Lest the reader of Mailer's book conclude that the miracles are all serious and that God has no sense of humor, as can easily be construed from the gospel accounts, this book includes a joyful portrayal of Jesus' ability to walk on the water. Jesus actually begins to swim to the boat, not attempt to walk toward it, but God surprises him: "Of a sudden, I was up and above the waters! I was walking! And I could even hear my Father's laughter at my pleasure in walking upon His water. Then came a second wave of His laughter. He was mocking me. For I had concluded too quickly that there was no extravagance in His miracles" (122). This is a reminder that miracles are exuberant and extravagant, more than anything else; they are not merely a way for Jesus to confirm his divinity or a pragmatic solution to terrible problems. This also continues the process of humanizing Jesus, showing him as someone who enjoys the power of God.

Oddly enough, the central miracle of Christianity, the resurrection of Jesus, gets little mention in Mailer's work. Jesus admits that he did rise from the dead, but his description of it is terribly plain: "For I know that I rose on the third day. And I also recall that I left the sepulchre to wander through the city and the countryside, and there came an hour when I appeared among my disciples" (245). However, Mailer's Jesus says little more than this.[12] He does not describe what happened while he was dead, as Lazarus does earlier in the work, nor does he describe the feeling of being reborn. It seems that the resurrection is an afterthought, not the central tenant of the faith.

---

[12]Christopher Moore approaches the resurrection much the same way. Since Biff, the narrator, dies before the resurrection, he cannot relate it to us. Instead, Maggie merely tells him, after he has finished writing his gospel, that "He [Joshua] came back." Biff merely replies, "I know, I read about it" (437). Nothing more is said about the resurrection. And, in fact, Moore's book sets the reader up for something completely different at the beginning of the book when Biff writes his opening sentences: "You think you know how this story is going to end, but you don't. Trust me, I was there. I know" (7). What this book really changes is how Jesus gets there, not where he ends up.

Given Jesus' relationship to God after his life on Earth, as this book presents it, this approach is not surprising. It seems as if God believes Jesus failed in his mission on Earth: "My Father, however, does not often speak to me. Nonetheless, I honor Him. Surely He sends forth as much love as He can offer, but His love is not without limit" (Mailer 247). Mailer's Jesus does imply that God may have a trick up his sleeve concerning the resurrection. Jesus later says, "Yet it is believed by most that God gained a great victory through me. And it may be that the Devil was not clever enough to comprehend the extent of my Father's wisdom" (247). While this statement makes it sound as if the novel is going to end with the orthodox position on the resurrection, Jesus adds just before the end of the book, "For my Father saw how to gain much from defeat by calling it victory. Now, in these days, many Christians believe that all has been won for them. They believe it was already won before they were born. They believe that this victory belongs to them because of my suffering on the cross. Thereby does my Father still find much purpose for me" (248). It is evident that Jesus does not believe that his crucifixion and resurrection were planned or even that they are a victory; instead, he must take comfort in the fact that God has been able to use them as if they are. This approach lessens the omniscience of God and certainly of Jesus, yet it still allows God predominance over Satan.

Saramago's Jesus can perform miracles, but he can only perform the miracles God wants him to perform so that God works through him. When he first has Simon and the other fishermen cast their nets back into the water, he does so more out of a sense of optimism than out of omniscience. He knows that his early miracles are nothing more than "magic tricks, clever, fascinating, with a few quick words of abracadabra, not unlike those performed with rather more style by Oriental fakirs, such as tossing a rope into midair and climbing it without any visible sign of support, no hooks, no hand of a mysterious genie" (293). However, Jesus doesn't seem to know how much he is capable of or even why the miracles happen: "To work these wonders, Jesus had only to will them, and if anyone had asked him why, he would have had no answer other than that he could hardly ignore the misery of fishermen with empty nets, the danger of that raging storm, or the mortifying lack of wine at that marriage feast, for truly the hour has not yet arrived for the Lord to speak through his lips" (293). Like the other books, *The Gospel According to Jesus Christ* shows a Jesus who clearly has powers because he is the Son of God, but he does not have the omniscience traditionally credited to him. Instead, like a human, he fumbles along, trying to figure out exactly what he is able to do.

After Jesus begins to see how much power he has, he believes that he is able to resurrect Lazarus, but Mary prevents him from doing so, telling him that no one has committed so much sin that they should be made to die twice. Jesus is also able to heal, but the people have to have faith in order to be healed: "Jesus cured one man who, being mute, was unable to plead, but he sent the others away because they did not have enough faith" (Saramago 351). This idea stems from what is in the gospels, but this book expands the idea. There is only one account in the gospels where Jesus could not heal people because of their lack of faith when Jesus returns to Nazareth, but it seems that people in Saramago's novel lack faith much more often.

Burgess' novel diverges from the others by focusing on Jesus' fulfillment of prophecy. In fact, Jesus seems to want to perform actions for no other reason than to make his actions conform with scriptural prophecy. The temptation in the wilderness, like the baptism by John, seem to be rites that Jesus must pass through but without any genuine meaning. After the resurrection, when Jesus is talking to his disciples, he says, "Totally fulfilled, everything. Even to the throwing of the dice for my garment. I liked that garment. . . . 'They parted my garments among them, and upon my vesture did they cast lots.' We no longer have anyone with us who can say: That, master, is in the twenty-second of the Psalms of David" (302–3). Jesus seems happy to have fulfilled the prophecies, and he does not seem bothered at all by Judas' absence, which he also would have attributed to fulfilling prophecies. Coale writes that Christ in *Man of Nazareth* is "little more than a wooden puppet, spouting his beliefs, marking time, until the political plots and his own crucifixion catch up with him" (183). Thus, though Jesus is presented as divine, as the Son of God, who preaches a loving, forgiving approach to life, in the end he is cold, merely doing what has to be done as a duty. There is little humanity to this Jesus, resulting in a lack of balance that leaves the reader wanting more.

Man of Nazareth does try to provide evidence that Jesus is the Son of God because of what he taught about love, which is still quite revolutionary, and not merely because of the miracles he may or may not have performed: "Christ's doctrine according to Burgess is more or less close to the mark. Christ preaches love ... Christ's message carries no political content but upholds the things within the spirit of love, as opposed to the things without, Caesar's trophies," writes Coale (182). Thus, this novel shifts the focus of attention from the miracles without denying their possibility and without taking away from the idea of Jesus as revolutionary, though the love that is the centerpiece of his teaching is seldom shown; it is usually simply described.

Concerning Ricci's religious beliefs, Paul Gessell writes, "Ricci still does not call himself a Christian. That's a term implying belief in the divinity of Jesus. And Ricci does not believe Jesus was divine" (F1). However, that does not prevent his portraying Jesus as divine, though much differently from the other writers. Typically, Jesus' divinity is portrayed in his miracles or his resurrection. *Testament*, however, shows a Jesus who can heal people through medicine, but not with supernatural power.

Jesus has empathy for everyone he meets, whether that person needs physical healing or merely acceptance.[13] Even the way he treats the people he heals illustrates the love he has for the people with whom he comes into contact. When he puts a splint on Jerubal's leg while on the way to Golgotha, the people are more amazed by his demeanor than by his ability to form a splint so easily and readily:

> The crowd had fallen quiet, watching Jesus work there in the
> rain. He hadn't done any miracle, maybe just what any doctor

---

[13]After Moore's Joshua (Jesus) realizes the full capacity of his healing powers (and after he has coffee for the first time, which would also explain his exuberance), he walks through a city healing people merely by bumping into them. Biff tries to get him to calm down, as he's drawing too much attention to them, but Jesus merely responds, "But I love these people" (128). He can't seem to stop himself from healing those who are hurting, no matter the consequences, because of that love.

would do, but still they could see there was something in him, that he wasn't what they'd expect in someone condemned. I saw his mother looking on, still at the back of the crowd, and how she watched him as if she was seeing him for the first time. Likely she hadn't known anything of him but the stories people told and so had been afraid he'd become a delinquent or worse. But now she saw him with Jerubal, not just the skill he had but the dignity. (442)

This presentation of Jesus shows that he is not just an ordinary man who happens to have healing powers; instead, he is someone who clearly stands out because of his love for others. Although this does not make him divine, it does set him apart from others.

Jesus also accepts those who are outcasts from his society. He accepts women and treats them differently from how any man of his time does; when Mary runs to greet him upon his return from a trip, she says, "But Yeshua [Jesus] embraced me openly, the first time any man had ever done such a thing" (128). His acceptance of women causes trouble, but he does not allow others' opinions on this subject to affect him, even those closest to him:

That Yeshua kept us women with him made him many enemies and caused much dissension even within our following. More than once it happened that some young man who had heard him preaching in the streets and been moved to attend one of our meetings instantly fled at the sight of Ribqah [Rebecca] and me; and even Shimon [Peter], at first, seemed on the verge of bolting at every minute, barely able to settle himself and sometimes rising to pace so that the meeting could hardly go on for the distraction he made. But Yeshua, though he listened patiently to every argument, didn't relent. (130–31)

Again, a love and acceptance that go beyond the normal social bounds show that Jesus has a wider view of love than do others in that culture. No one else comes close to the levels of love that he exemplifies, which

Ricci uses to set up the idea that he is clearly different from those who are around him.

Christopher Moore expands this idea of accepting everyone by having Joshua leave Israel and travel throughout the East. When he arrives in India, the first person he meets is an Untouchable. Jesus has already interacted with Simon (who is called Lazarus), whom Moore's novel turns into a leper, but this book never shows Joshua actually touch him. In India, Joshua moves "among them, healing their wounds, sicknesses, and insanities, without any of them suspecting what was happening." Showing a sense of humor, he also has "taken to poking one of them in the arm with his finger anytime anyone said the word 'Untouchable.' Later he told me that he just hated passing up the opportunity for palpable irony" (271). Although this scene is clearly meant to be humorous, it also shows Jesus willing to physically touch those whom society has labeled as outcasts. Moore's Joshua goes beyond merely healing people to touching them in ways that most people would not, magnifying a love that goes beyond most humans' understanding.

Testament's Jesus, like Jesus in the gospels, also accepts the poor and common, especially fishermen, from whom he draws most of his disciples. When Simon of Gergesa joins Jesus' group, he describes the disciples: "Working with them I saw they weren't so different from me in the end, like a crew of fishermen you'd meet at the Gergesa harbour" (Ricci 364). However, the group that Jesus accepts, which shows his ability to transcend mere human limits about acceptance, is the lepers.[14] He visits the leper colonies regularly, healing the ones he can and comforting those he cannot. Jesus takes Judas to a colony to teach him about acceptance:

> Yeshua [Jesus] was surely the first visitor from outside the
> camp whom many of these people had seen in months or

---

[14]Jesus in *Quarantine* also looks to the poor and the unclean as people who deserve God's love: "He'd even be prepared—and glad—to defile himself on those kept out of temples—lepers, menstruating women, prostitutes, the blind, even the uncircumcised—if they would listen to him, if it would cause discomfort to the priest. These were the ones, he thought, that god [*sic*] had created weak and blemished and imperfect by design. These were the chirping innocents that he should rescue from the devil's claw, for he himself was weak and blemished and imperfect by design. These people were his family" (150–51).

years. He told me they had shunned him when he'd first come, out of shame and their concern for his own purity. But now at his approach they came together quite openly, gathering on a little rock shelf that jutted out from the cliff face. It was an astounding sight, these dozens of lepers congregating there, men, women, and even some children, many of them so gnarled-limbed and deformed they were hardly recognizable as human. But what was surprising in lepers was that as putrid and corrupt as their outward form might be, their mental faculties were not affected in the least, so that you were suddenly astounded to hear from out of their mass of rotting flesh a perfect human voice. Thus it was that Yeshua did a most simple and amazing thing: he sat himself down amongst these lepers and conversed with them as if their affliction counted for nothing in his eyes. (58)

It is this ability of Jesus, the ability to treat everyone equally, no matter their gender, social status, or appearance, which illustrates his divinity. He does not condescend to these people or treat them any differently from how he treats others; instead, as Judas says of him, ". . . it was as though he had thus taken their affliction upon himself, to share the burden of it" (60), language that is reminiscent of the orthodox teaching of Jesus' crucifixion bearing the burden of humanity's sins.

Testament introduces a non-biblical character to highlight Jesus' divinity. Simon of Gergesa meets Jerubal when he is trying to catch up with Jesus, who has already begun the journey to Jerusalem. Jerubal has the ability to work wonders in his own way, as mere tricks, and he uses his abilities for his own ends. One of the first times Simon sees him do this is when Jerubal presents himself as a shaman to a village and supposedly casts demons out of the nearby forest. Simon is in the trees throwing out sticks covered with resin that seemingly explode, to convince the villagers that Jerubal is casting demons out of the forest. His reward for doing so is a feast with plenty of wine. In another instance, Jesus and his followers have some fish that goes bad, so they leave three baskets of it on the side of the road. Jerubal has Simon carry the fish to a nearby village, so he can sell it. Jerubal tells the village that Jesus told some fishermen to cast their net into the river, and it came up teeming with fish (an obvious reference to Simon Peter's first encounter with Jesus in the gospels). The villagers are encouraged to buy a fish and hang it over their doors for good luck, saving Jerubal and Simon from a horde of angry villagers a bit later.

By using Jerubal as a foil, this novel foregrounds how Jesus uses his abilities for the good of others, never for himself. The fact that the last person Jesus heals is Jerubal highlights this connection. Jerubal is motivated by fun more than greed because he usually gives away the money he gets, but Jesus is motivated by love for others, an *agape* love that exceeds social boundaries and almost every level of comfort.

No matter how others perceive him, what Jesus himself thinks about his role as the Son of God is important to his divine status. Jesus in *Man of Nazareth*, for example, never doubts who he is or what his mission is. When Jesus is talking with his mother, discussing the possibility of marriage, she reminds him of his birth and asks him if he believes what occurred. He does not doubt the miracle of his birth in the least; he merely thinks it is irrelevant to their discussion. And when Satan tempts him in the wilderness, Jesus tells Satan clearly that he is both flesh and spirit: "In both, he who was to come and has come and whose presence will be made manifest in the world. The Messiah" (Burgess 120). Jesus is "conscious of the fact that he is part of some preordained design, some 'necessary sacrifice,' if not entirely clear on exactly what it signifies" (183).

Jesus in *Man of Nazareth*, in fact, never questions who he is. He only reminds the disciples and those who would seek to follow him of what kind of Messiah he will be. He wants them to understand that he will not be an earthly king: "Earthly rule is but earthly rule, and who shall rule in the earthly dispensation is the smallest of man's concerns. You slay the tyrant, and you put a good man in his place, but the good man is very likely himself to turn into a tyrant. It is in the nature of earthly power for this to happen. It is not through change in the governing of men that men themselves are changed. For the change must come from within" (Burgess 186–87). It is clear that Burgess' Jesus recognizes that he is the Messiah, the Son of God, who has come to create a new kingdom, a new type of rule. Unlike Jesus in the other novels, here he never wavers, and he never questions either his status as divine or his role in God's plan.

Jesus in *The Gospel According to Jesus Christ* is also clearly the Son of God, as both the Devil and God tell him, but he is not what most people typically think of as the Son of God. He does not have any idea of God's plans, and he is certainly not God incarnate. Instead, he seems to be a man whom God has chosen to be the Son of God. Though Jesus tries to avoid this label, seeking to die as the King of the Jews, God announces to all at the crucifixion: "This is My beloved son, in whom I am well pleased" (Saramago 376).

Jesus' death, in fact, does not fulfill the orthodox role of redemptive sacrifice in Saramago's work. When Jesus is told by God that God wants him to be his martyr, it is so that God, "within the next six centuries or so, despite all the struggles and obstacles ahead of [them] . . . will pass from being God of the Jews to being God of those whom we will call Catholics, from the Greek" (311). This God is certainly not based on the gospels and may not have ultimate power himself, as Josipovici comments, "This God, it turns out, is a curious mixture of power and helplessness. He has grown tired of being worshipped by only a small group in a tiny corner of the world and has decided to extend his power over the whole earth. Yet he cannot do it by force or by some simple miracle, for the other gods, who rule over the Romans and many other nations, also have their rights" (31). This God is using Jesus to encourage more people to worship him and, possibly, to gain more power; thus, he and Jesus seem more concerned about themselves.

The different interpretation of Jesus' death is mirrored by the fact that this book conspicuously leaves out the resurrection. It does not indicate that the resurrection took place, nor does it have Jesus refer to it, for Jesus has no real idea what God's plan for him is. Jesus has not come to defeat death and to gain eternal life for all those who follow him (though they may receive that; God is not clear on this point, as he's talking more about what he will gain from the death than from what people will gain); thus, the resurrection is irrelevant. *The Gospel According to Jesus Christ*, then, presents a Son of God who is not truly God, nor is he the Savior of mankind. Instead, he is merely someone to spread God's name beyond the Jews so that God may have a wider realm of influence.

Jesus in *The Last Temptation of Christ* fights his divine calling through most of the book, despite early signs that he has been chosen by God. He is visited by shepherds and wise men, but only in a dream of Mary. Kazantzakis also includes other strange events surrounding Jesus' birth. Joseph is chosen as Mary's husband because his staff blossomed, showing that God has chosen him to be her husband. Mary and Joseph climb to the summit of Elijah to ask Elijah to intercede on their behalf and to have God bless them with a son that they will then dedicate to Elijah's service. While there, Joseph is struck by lightning, and he is paralyzed. Simeon certainly wonders about Jesus' calling in life, as he has witnessed some of the strange events of Jesus' childhood: "I've seen signs. Once when you were a boy you took some clay and fashioned a bird. While you caressed it and talked to it, it seemed to me that this bird of clay grew wings and flew out of your grasp" (153). This story comes from the *Infancy Gospel of Thomas* as an effort perhaps to show Jesus' burgeoning divinity.

Jesus, however, does not believe that he is the son of God; in fact, he doesn't want to be chosen by God at all. He asks Andrew about John the Baptist, about why Andrew leaves him, and Andrew says that he wanted to find the Messiah. He assures Jesus that John is not the Messiah, so Jesus asks Andrew if he has found the Messiah now. Andrew answers that he has, but he answers so quietly that Jesus does not hear him. Jesus is seeking out information from others to tell him who he might be, as he does not know, and he is afraid that he might be the Son of God as others think him to be.

But it is Judas who encourages Jesus to turn to John the Baptist to discover whether or not he, Jesus, is, in fact, the Messiah. When Jesus is baptized, the crowd sees a miracle that seems more pagan than Christian: "The flow of the Jordan had abruptly ceased. Schools of multicolored fish floated up from every direction, circled Jesus and began to dance, folding and unfolding their fins and shaking their tails, and a shaggy elf in the form of a simple old man entwined with seaweed rose up from the bottom of the river, leaned against the reeds, and with mouth agape and eyes popping from fear and joy, stared at all that was going on in front of him" (Kazantzakis 239). The book also includes the image of the descending dove from the gospels, but no one hears what it says to Jesus. It is apparent that Jesus is the Son of God, but the very pagan presentation of the scene raises questions about the kind of Messiah he might be. Oddly enough, the book does not develop this theme; it simply stands as one pagan influence in a novel that is otherwise largely influenced by Christian legends, the gospel, and Kazantzakis' imagination.

Despite this scene, John is not sure of Jesus' role in God's plan. He knows that Jesus might be the Messiah, but he is bothered by Jesus' insistence on love; he believes there needs to be fire, as well. He advises Jesus, but he makes it clear that he is still not certain whether or not Jesus is the Messiah: "If you are the One I've been waiting for, hear my last instructions, for I think I shall never see you again on this earth, never again" (Kazantzakis 243).

Just before the resurrection of Lazarus, Jesus finally seems to have accepted his role as the son of God, as equal with God. Simeon hears him speaking poorly of the Temple, and he cautions Jesus about being boastful; Jesus responds, "When I say 'I,' . . . I do not speak of this body—which is dust; I do not speak of the son of Mary—he too is dust, with just a tiny, tiny spark of fire. 'I' from my mouth, Rabbi, means God" (Kazantzakis 365). When the Rabbi accuses him of blasphemy, Jesus refers to himself as "Saint Blasphemer" and laughs, but he has clearly and finally begun to think of himself as God (366). This knowledge enables him to reach outside of the orthodox interpretation of the Messiah and speak what others considers blasphemy. In fact, observes Morton Leavitt, Jesus "is not the same hope that Simeon, Joachim, and Judas have long awaited; even his followers are slow to realize that he might be the Messiah. In his parables, in his travels through Samaria, in accepting the publican Matthew among his disciples, he is rebelling against the formalistic Old Law of the Jews" (70). He can come to this point, however, only after he accepts his role as the Son of God.

The event that causes Jesus to truly understand his role as the son of God is a vision in which God presents him with a text from Isaiah: "He has borne our faults; he was wounded for our transgressions; our iniquities bruised him. He was afflicted, yet he opened not his mouth. Despised and rejected by all, he went forward without resisting, like a lamb that is led to the slaughter" (386). From then on, he understands that the role of the son of God is to be crucified, not to rule over the Romans, and he accepts his fate, even through the temptation on the cross, where he dies by saying, "It is accomplished! And it was as though he had said: Everything has begun" (496).[15] It is this acceptance that convinces Jesus that he is the Messiah, but not the Son of God that Judas and the others expect.

Just as the early church struggled with Jesus' divinity and humanity, so, too, do the authors who re-tell his story. Not surprisingly, in a much more secular era, they focus on Jesus as a human much more so than on Jesus as divine. They try to create a Jesus readers can identify with, not one who is larger than life. A character without faults or at least some sort of conflict is uninteresting; thus, they create a Jesus who struggles, who is clearly tempted, and who sometimes even fails.

---

[15]In *Quarantine*, Jim Crace only presents Jesus in his time in the wilderness, but even he presents Jesus and the idea of his sacrifice. When he crawls out from his cave near the end of the book, he remembers a passage from the scriptures: "Make sacrifices to god [*sic*], and then prepare yourself for the winds of judgment." Crace then comments about Jesus, "He was prepared.He was the sacrifice" (192).

Telling the Story, Redux

E ach of these authors has his own reasoning for trying to tell a story yet again that most people already know yet. Nino Ricci seems to tell it to struggle with his own religious past, while Anthony Burgess seems to use his novel to confirm what he believes. Jose Saramago appears captivated by the story, yet he is without any religious belief to speak of. Norman Mailer, with characteristic arrogance, seems to believe that he can identify with Jesus and can tell the story better than it has already been told. Nikos Kazantzakis tells the story, it seems, because he believes it and because he wants others to believe it. He may be unconventional in his beliefs, but his belief in Jesus is sincere.

Authors continue to come back to the story of Jesus, perhaps the most compelling story ever, for manifold reasons. They can be counted on to skew their views of Jesus through their religious, historical, and the biblical backgrounds, creating new interpretations of God, new motivations for Judas, and new temptations for Jesus. Their attempts to tell the story serve to force readers to see the story in fresh ways, which is nearly always beneficial.

There will always be those who are offended or angered by attempts to change the gospel story, but these novels should not be seen as undertaking that. They are admittedly fiction, and, while fiction can often tell the truth straighter than nonfiction, none of these books attempts to present a portrayal of Jesus as anything more than imaginative. This approach does not limit the power of these stories. Kazantzakis' portrayal of Jesus striding through the crowd to protect Mary Magdalene from being stoned still affects me more than any image in the gospels. It does not matter to me that it did not necessarily happen in that way or even that it might have; given what I know about Jesus, I could easily see it happening. It rings true in a way that no other description does.

It is this benefit from allowing those who have so immersed themselves in the gospels to see Jesus, his times, and his followers in new ways that should be the focus in examining these novels. Whether or not one agrees with the portrayals, one is forced to rethink his or her view of Jesus, which leads to new ideas, a result all novelists must be satisfied with.

Thus, as readers, we should come back to these novels to have our preconceived views of Jesus shaken again and again, going back and forth between them and the gospels to see if we might find a truth we have missed along the way. For that reason alone, writers should continue to tell again and again The Greatest Story Ever Told.

References

Aggeler, Geoffrey. *Anthony Burgess: The Artist as Novelist*. Tuscaloosa, AL: University of Alabama Press, 1979.

American Atheists. "The Bible and Jesus Myth." 11 May 2004. http://www.atheists. org/church/myth.html.

Antonakes, Michael. "Nikos Kazantzakis and Christ as a Hero." *Journal of Modern Greek Studies* 22:1 (May 2004): 95–105.

Axton, Richard. "Interpretations of Judas in Middle English Literature." *Religion in the Poetry and Drama of the Late Middle Ages in England*. Eds. Piero Boitani and Anna Torti. Cambridge: D.S. Brewer, 1900. 179–97.

Ayad, Boulos Ayad. "From the Christian Apocrypha: The Miracles of Christ During His Childhood and the Childhood of John the Baptist." *Coptic Church Review* 22:2 (Summer 2001): 55–63.

Barclay, William. *The Master's Men*. New York: Abingdon Press, 1959.

Begieling, Robert. "Twelfth Round." *Conversations with Norman Mailer*. Jackson, MS: University of Mississippi Press, 1988.

Bellan-Boyer, Lisa. "Conspicuous in Their Absence: Women in Early Christianity." Cross Currents 53:1 (Spring 2003): 48–63.

The Bible. NIV Version. Grand Rapids, MI: Zondervan, 1986.

Blair, E.P. "Joseph Husband of Mary." *Interpreter's Dictionary of the Bible*. 1962 ed.

———. "Judas." Interpreter's Dictionary of the Bible. 1962 ed.

———. "Mary." Interpreter's Dictionary of the Bible. 1962 ed.

Bloom, Harold. "'The One With the Beard is God, the Other is the Devil.'" *Portuguese Literary and Cultural Studies* 6 (Spring 2001): 155–166.

Brandon, S.G.F. *The Trial of Jesus of Nazareth*. New York: Stein and Day, 1979.

Brown, Dan. *The Da Vinci Code*. New York: Doubleday, 2003.

Burgess, Anthony. *Man of Nazareth*. 1979. Toronto: Bantam, 1982.

———. *Little Wilson and Big God*. New York: Weidenfeld and Nicolson, 1986.

———. *You've Had Your Time: The Second Part of the Confessions*. New York: G. Weidenfeld, 1991.

Casey, Paul F. "Blurring Genre Boundaries: Judas and His Role in Early Modern German Drama." *Infinite Boundaries: Order, Disorder, and Reorder in Early Modern German Culture*. Ed. Max Reinhart. Kirksville, MO: Thomas Jefferson University Press, 1998. 101–120.

Chilton, Bruce. "John the Baptist: His Immersion and Death." *Dimensions of Baptism: Biblical and Theological Studies*. Eds. Stanley E. Porter and Anthony R. Cross. London: Sheffield Academic Press, 2002. 25–44.

203

Coale, Samuel. *Anthony Burgess.* New York: F. Ungar Publishing Co., 1981.

Crace, Jim. *Quarantine.* New York: Picador, 1998.

Cunneen, Sally. *In Search of Mary: the Woman and the Symbol.* New York: Ballantine Books, 1996.

D'Angelo, Mary Rose. "Restructuring 'Real' Women From Gospel Literature." *Women and Christian Origins.* Eds. Ross Shepard Kraemer and Mary Rose D'Angelo. New York: Oxford University Press, 1999. 105–128.

Farmer, W.R. "John the Baptist." *Interpreter's Dictionary of the Bible.* 1962 ed.

Filas, Francis. Joseph: *The Man Closest to Jesus: The Complete Life, Theology, and Devotional History of St. Joseph.* Boston: St. Paul Editions, 1962.

Filson, F. V. "Peter." *Interpreter's Dictionary of the Bible.* 1962 ed.

Fredriksson, Marianne. *According to Mary Magdalene.* Trans. by Joan Tate. Charlottesville, VA: Hampton Roads, 1999.

Galeotti, Gary. "Satan's Identity Reconsidered." *Faith and Mission* 15:2 (Spring 1998): 72–86.

George, Margaret. *Mary Called Magdalene.* New York: Viking, 2002.

Gessell, Paul. "'Jesus, Son of Man.'" *Ottawa Citizen* 2 May 2002: F1.

Glenday, Michael. *Norman Mailer.* New York: St. Martin's, 1995.

"The Gospel According to Mailer." *All Things Considered.* National Public Radio. 23 April 1997.

Grant, Robert. *Jesus After the Gospel: The Christ of the Second Century.* Louisville, KY: Westminster/John Knox Press, 1990.

Gray, Paul. "The Gospel According to the Son." *Time* 28 April 1997: 75.

Hand, Elizabeth. "The Word Made Flesh." *The Washington Post* 1 June 2003: T6.

Haskins, Susan. *Mary Magdalene: Myth and Metaphor.* New York: Harcourt, 1993.

Jansen, Katherine. *The Making of the Magdalen: Preaching and Popular Devotion in the Later Middle Ages.* Princeton, NJ: Princeton UP, 2000.

Josipovici, Gabriel. "Son of God Tries to Outwit His Mad Father." *The Independent* 11 September 1993: 31.

Kaufman, Helena. "Evangelical Truths: Jose Saramago on the Life of Christ." *Revista Hispánica Moderna* 47:2 (December 1994): 449–458.

Kazantzakis, Helen. *Nikos Kazantzakis: A Biography Based on His Letters.* New York: Simon and Schuster, 1968.

Kazantzakis, Nikos. *The Last Temptation of Christ.* Trans. P.A. Bien. New York: Simon and Schuster, 1960.

King, Karen L. *The Gospel of Mary of Magdala: Jesus and the First Woman Apostle.* Santa Rosa, CA: Polebridge Press, 2003.

Klassen, William. *Judas: Betrayer or Friend of Jesus.* Minneapolis: Fortress Press, 1996.

Knox, John. *The Humanity and Divinity of Christ, a Study of Pattern in Christology.* Cambridge: University Press, 1967.

Knutson, Galen C. "The Feast of Saint Mary Magdalene." *Worship* 71:3 (May 1997): 205–20.

Leavitt, Morton P. *The Cretan Glance: The World and Art of Nikos Kazantzakis.* Columbus, OH: Ohio State UP, 1980.

Légasse, Simon. *The Trial of Jesus.* London: SCM Press, 1997.

Lienhard, Joseph T. "John the Baptist in Augustine's Exegesis." *Augustine: Biblical Exegete.* New York: Peter Lang, 2001. 197–213.

———. *St. Joseph in Early Christianity.* Philadelphia: St. Joseph's University Press, 1999.

Mailer, Norman. *The Gospel According to the Son.* New York: Ballantine Books, 1997.

Maisch, Ingrid. *Mary Magdalene: The Image of a Woman Through the Centuries.* Collegeville, MN: Liturgical Press, 1998.

McGing, Brian C. "Pontius Pilate and the Sources." *Catholic Biblical Quarterly* 53.3 (July 1991): 416–438.

McKendrick, Jamie. "Father, Son and Much Free Spirit: The Gospel According to Jesus Christ." *The Independent* 12 September 1993: 31.

Middleton, Darren J.N. and Peter Bien. "Introduction: Spiritual Levendía: Kazantzakis's Theology of Struggle." *God's Struggle: Religion in the Writings of Nikos Kazantzakis.* Eds. Darren J.N. Middleton and Peter Bien. Macon, GA: Mercer University Press, 1996.

Moore, Christopher. *Lamb: The Gospel According to Biff, Christ's Childhood Pal.* New York: HarperCollins, 2002.

Nash, Elizabeth. "Saramago the Atheist, an Outsider in His Own Land." *The Independent* 9 October 1998: 17.

Pagels, Elaine. *The Gnostic Gospels.* 1979. New York: Vintage Books, 1989.

Pavey, Ruth. "Jealous God." *New Statesman and Society* 6:267 (August 27, 1993): 40.

Perkins, Pheme. *Peter: Apostle for the Whole Church.* Columbia, SC: University of South Carolina Press, 1994.

Poirier, Richard. *Norman Mailer.* New York: Viking Press, 1972.

Preto-Rodas, Richard A. "A review of O Evangelho segundo Jesus Cristo." *World Literature Today* 66:4 (Autumn 1992): 697.

Pyper, Hugh. "Modern Gospels of Judas: Canon and Betrayal." *Literature and Theology* 15:2 (June 2001): 111–122.

Ricci, Nino. *Testament.* Boston: Houghton Mifflin, 2003.

Roberts, Michèle. *The Wild Girl.* London: Minerva, 1984.

Sandmel, S. "Caiaphas." *Interpreter's Dictionary of the Bible.* 1962 ed.

———. "Herod." *Interpreter's Dictionary of the Bible.* 1962 ed.

———. "Pilate, Pontius." *Interpreter's Dictionary of the Bible.* 1962 ed.

Saramago, Jose. *The Gospel According to Jesus Christ.* Trans. Giovanni Pontiero. San Diego, Harcourt, 1991.

Schaberg, Jane. "Fast Forwarding to the Magdalene." *Semeia* 74 (1996): 33–45.

Southern Baptist Convention. *The Baptist Faith and Message.* 11 May 2004. http://www.sbc.net/bfm/bfm2000.asp#i.

Starnino, Carmine. "The Catholic Connection: In a Novel About Jesus, Nino Ricci is Still Preoccupied with Roots." *The Gazette* 18 May 2002: G1.

Stavans, Ilan. "A Fisher of Men." *The Nation* 258:19 (May 16, 1994): 675–76.

Stinson, John J. *Anthony Burgess Revisited.* Boston: Twayne, 1991.

Stoffman, Judy. "The Next Temptation of Nino Ricci." *Toronto Star* 11 May 2002: J15.

Thimmes, Pamela. "Memory and Re-Vision: Mary Magdalene Research Since 1975." *Currents in Research: Biblical Studies* 6 (1998): 193–226.

Van Biema, David. "Mary Magdalene: Saint or Sinner?" *Time* 162:6 (11 August 2003): 52–. Expanded Academic ASAP. Tennessee Electronic Library. Squires Library, Cleveland, TN. 28 January 2005.

Wald-Hopkins, Christine. "Retelling the Story of Jesus: Fictionalized Account Presents Complex Hero." *The Denver Post* 6 July 2003: EE–01.

Wernick, Robert. "Who the Devil is the Devil?" *Smithsonian* 30:7 (October 1999): 112–123. Online. EBSCOhost.

Winkett, Lucy. "Go Tell! Thinking About Mary Magdalene." *Feminist Theology: The Journal of the Britain and Ireland School of Feminist Theology* 29 (2002): 19–31.

Wood, James. "The Gospel According to the Son." *The New Republic* 12 May 1997: 30–36.

Ziolkowski, Theodore. *Fictional Transfigurations of Jesus.* Princeton, NJ: Princeton University Press, 1972.

INDEX

CPSIA information can be obtained at www.ICGtesting.com
Printed in the USA
LVOW03s2349300114

371694LV00005B/81/P

9 781933 483153